Black Male Outsider

Black Male Outsider
Teaching as a Pro-Feminist Man

A MEMOIR

Gary L. Lemons

State University of New York Press

Published by
State University of New York Press, Albany

For information, contact State University of New York Press, Albany, NY
www.sunypress.edu

Production by Diane Ganeles
Marketing by Anne Valentine

Library of Congress Cataloging-in-Publication Data

Lemons, Gary L.
    Black male outsider : teaching as a pro-feminist man / Gary L. Lemons.
        p. cm.
    Includes bibliographical references and index.
    ISBN 978-0-7914-7301-6 (hardcover : alk. paper)
    ISBN 978-0-7914-7302-3 (pbk : alk. paper)
1. Women's studies—United States.   2. Feminist theory—United States.
3. Male feminists—United States.   4. African American feminists.   I. Title.

HQ1181.U5L46 2008
305.32089'96073—dc22

                                                                2007010148

                    10 9 8 7 6 5 4 3 2 1

*For Fanni (my life partner), Gabriel, Danyealah, and Elmore (our children),
and all the students whom I have taught over the years
who believe in the transforming power of black feminist thought—
you gave me the time, space, and encouragement
to write with candor about my determination
to become a pro-woman(ist) "professor,"
committed to gender justice.*

CONTENTS

PART 3: FROM THEORY TO PRACTICE:
CLASSROOM CASE STUDIES

ACKNOWLEDGMENTS

I begin with a special thanks to all the students cited in this book. Without their permission to include autobiographical writing from classes they completed with me, I could not have illustrated the efficacy of black feminist thought as a transformative pedagogical strategy. The work of the students represented in this text only represents a very small portion of the amazing body of memoir writing produced in my classes at a small liberal arts college in New York City where I taught between 1991 and 2004.

I owe much gratitude to a select group of individuals on the faculty and in the administration at the college during the time I taught there. They offered unwavering collegial support for the development of my pedagogy. Among them were Jacqui Alexander, Amit Rai, Minelle Mahtani, Jerma Jackson, Kai Jackson, Jan Clausen, Sara Ruddick, Sekou Sundiata, Barrie Karp, Toni Oliviero, Michael Vanoy Adams, and Jane Lazarre. I am especially grateful to have known Jane as a beloved colleague. Our work together toward increasing racial diversity at the college was a continual source of personal inspiration for me as a black professor of antiracist studies. I came to understand the real meaning of collegial support in our relationship. Her memoir *Beyond the Whiteness of Whiteness* has remained on my course syllabi over the years. I also want to thank Professor Linda Rohrer Paige, another beloved colleague and "best" friend (of nearly thirty years since we were students ourselves), who teaches at Georgia Southern University. Over the years, the many invitations and generous hospitality she has extended to me as a guest speaker on her campus speaks to the long-standing commitment to progressive gender and racial politics she has maintained.

I will always be indebted to bell hooks, who coadvised my dissertation on the pro-woman(ist) writings of Frederick Douglass and W. E. B. Du Bois. Since then her writings on black masculinity, feminist memoir writing, and progressive education have immeasurably contributed to the foundation of the feminist antiracism I practice in the classroom. I am also continually grateful to a particular group of black women feminists who have immensely enabled my growth as a gender-progressive black male scholar: Jacqui Alexander, Aaronette White, Beverly Guy-Sheftall, Michele Wallace, and Johnnetta Betsch Cole. I want to thank Aaronette (my "feminist sister") especially for her faith in my work and helping me to get this book in the right publisher's hands.

There is a select group of pro-feminist men whose gender-progressive ideas on masculinity have also influenced my thinking tremendously. Their presence in different periods of my scholarly life has left an indelible imprint. Collectively, their scholarship on feminist masculinity has been important for critically grounding my work as well as literally providing public venues for its engagement. These include Calvin Hernton, John Stoltenberg, Thandabantu Iverson, Tom Digby, Steven Schacht, and Keith Pringle. While a graduate student at New York University, I had the distinct pleasure of meeting the novelist John A. Williams. The memory of my work for him as a teaching assistant during my last semester at NYU has remained with me over the years.

During the two years it took me to write this book, one individual's involvement in the process was indispensable. A former student of mine while I taught at the college took on the job of editing the manuscript. Jennie Jeddry's commitment to the editing process was unwavering from beginning to end. I needed critical input from someone who had directly experienced my pedagogical practice. Each chapter that I delivered to her was returned to me filled with incisive comments and questions. They pushed me to explore areas in my thinking that needed further exploration and clarity. I thank other former students beginning with Louisa Solomon and Taneka Williams for their contributions in reading early versions of the manuscript.

I will always be grateful to Donna Millhollon for her research years ago in search of sources that led to my first published essay on predagogy. One particular student from the past stands out from all the rest—Joseph Thompson. His ongoing presence in my life over the years has been a continual source of intellectual and spiritual support. From his first graduate class with me years ago (through his doctoral work and beyond as a colleague in African American studies), he has remained one of my closest pro-woman(ist) allies. His critical insight into the politics of black male gender progressive thinking challenges me in ways that deeply enrich my comprehension of its complexity.

Few individuals shared in my day-to-day writing and revision process, however. Those who did represented a small group of family and intimate circle of pro-woman(ist) mentors. Among them were the folk who lived with me everyday, who tolerated my unexplained mood shifts, after I'd spent endless hours at the computer in the subterranean, small office space in the basement of my house. My partner, Fanni, relieved me of many of the daily household duties, insisting that my writing time should be uninterrupted. When I asked her to read chapters from the manuscript, she did so with keen critical insight, producing page after page of critical marginalia (sometimes to my chagrin). Our children, who found themselves written into the narrative fabric of the text, graciously consented to my request for their inclusion. My mother, Thelma Lemons, and brother, Gregory, generously contributed support in reading and discussing with me narratives in the book about our family history. As well, I express gratitude to Sue Hairston, my cousin, for providing historical documentation that assisted me in completing chapter 4.

In conceptualizing feminism as a mode of self-recovery for men consciously resisting internalized wounds of patriarchy, I acknowledge the direct impact on the confessional strength of this book of my participation as a facilitator in addiction recovery programming. In particular, I thank Joann Chambers Oliver, a leading specialist in the field, for being my mentor. Working with her for two years toward establishing a site for recovering addicts in our local community, I challenged men in our weekly recovery meetings to participate in gender-progressive critiques of black masculinity that were particularly related to our daily interactions with women and children.

For me personally, writing this book was a journey of spiritual recovery. I have Rev. James E. Howard to thank for that. Over the course of a year, this revered minister and counselor (who turned eighty years old during the year) guided me to the spiritual value of writing a memoir about teaching for gender justice in the college classroom. As we engaged in the hard work of revisiting my past, I realized more than ever the necessity of breaking silence about the effects of internalized patriarchal violence and white supremacist thinking on black males. I came to experience the joy of inner healing—of laying bare wounds from childhood. During times when I could not speak about the trauma of my past, Rev. Howard compelled me to break through years of silence, rooted in shame and embarrassment as a survivor of childhood domestic violence. The realization of this book is a testament to the power of recovery work for black male *self*-liberation.

I would like to thank the following students in the fall 1994 session of a course I taught called "The Novel of Passing" for their commitment to the seminar and for permission to reproduce in chapter 2 excerpts from some of their final exams: Peggy Bennett, Megan Chase, Tara Crichlow, Carolyn Egazarian, Ann Fuller, Wubnesh Hylton, Elaine Mejia, Hannah Miller, Carla Montoya, Rachel Weiss, and Brooke Wilmes.

Samples of student writing that appears in chapter 6 are taken from several classes I have taught over the years to confront white supremacy.

Without their work, I could not illustrate the varying complex ways race intervened in their lives across differences of gender, class, and sexuality. I am a better teacher because of their willingness to put their lives on the line in the memoir-writing process, and I want to thank each of those whose writing is reproduced here: Louisa Solomon, Andrea Barrow, Renequa Johnson, Jennie Jeddry, Emily Carris, Laila Olisa Lake, Andrew Daul, Tobe Bott-Lyons, Matthew King, and Eli Oberman. You taught me that the struggle *to become* whole never ends.

Quotations from class writing assignments that appear in chapter 7 have come with permission from the following students, whose commitment to black feminist pedagogy not only required them to confront the history of institutionalized, multiple oppressions faced by black women, but also rigorously, emotionally, and spiritually challenged them to lay bare their own internalized issues of race, gender, class, and sexual domination. Their willingness to write "from the head to the heart" lies at the core of my belief in the transforming power of black feminist thought. Thus, I extend a heartfelt thanks to Andrew Daul, Kate Englund, Matthew Hamilton, Anna Keye, Seamus Leary, Amy Mack, Nat Meysenburg, Bianca Nejathaim, Jennifer Pincus, Darragh Sheehan, Tyler St. Jean, Mona Weiner, Eleanor Whitney, and Sharon Zetter. Through your own passionate "words of fire," I have come to hold on a bit tighter to my conviction that antiracist feminist education is liberatory for all humankind.

For many of the insights expressed in chapter 9, I give thanks to the women students in my Redefining Womanhood course. I recite their names here to thank them once again for participating in an amazing teaching and learning experience for me personally: Leah Albrecht, Stacy Bowers, Isabelle Elisha, Ann Fuller, Andrea Laramie, Claire Mysko, Shoshana Oxman, Karen Ruiz-Cordell, Rachel Weiss, and Noelle Williams. Again, I would like to thank Jacqui Alexander, whose critical perspective on Audre Lorde's notions of the erotic continues to affirm and deepen my own thinking regarding its transformative power. Finally, my gratitude extends to several people: Pam Jackson for excepts from her memoir that appear in the Pro-Wo(man)ist Postscript, Leah F. Cassorla for completing the index superbly, and Kim Vaz for her unyielding support of my work in Women's Studies.

Those at the State University of New York Press I wish to thank begin with acquisitions editor, Larin McLaughlin, who first recognized the value of this book and its potential contribution to studies in feminist pedagogy. I thank Wyatt Benner for his meticulously careful reading of the text during its production phase, and Diane Ganeles for judiciously overseeing its completion.

⇒ ◀

In chapter 2, excerpts appear from the following sources: (1) Bonnie Tu Smith and Maureen T. Reddy, eds. *Race in the College Classroom: Pedagogy and Politics*, pp. 277–85. Copyright © 2002 by Rutgers, the State University. First published by Rutgers University Press. Reprinted with permission. (2) Maureen T. Reddy, ed. *Everyday Acts Against Racism: Raising Children in a Multiracial World*, pp. 162–63. Copyright © 1996 by Seal Press. Reprinted with permission.

Chapter 7 originally appeared under a different title in *Identifying Race and Transforming Whiteness in the Classroom*, pp. 213–33. Virginia Lea and Judy Helfand, eds. Copyright © 2004 by Peter Lang. Reprinted with permission.

In chapter 9, an excerpt appears from *Teaching What You're Not: Identity Politics in Higher Education*, pp. 259–84. Katherine J. Mayberry, ed. Copyright © 1996 by New York University Press. Reprinted with permission.

PREFACE

WRITING IN THE DARK, WRITING FROM THE INSIDE OUT

In 1968, when I was fifteen years old—during my first year attending the newly integrated, majority-white high school in Hot Springs, Arkansas—I discovered that teaching would be my life's calling. My first teaching job was in my hometown, at the former high school where Bill Clinton graduated years before. My father, as he once told me without bitterness, not only could not attend this school, but was once spat upon by white students there for walking on the sidewalk in front of it. In my very first year of elementary school, at the all-black Catholic school in our town, my parents were told I had to leave at the end of the school year because I needed "special" education it could not supply. I was slow. Neither my white woman teacher nor the mother superior who headed the school had any idea that my slowness was not due to my inability to learn (as fast as the other kids), it had to do with my undiagnosed severely poor eyesight. Once an eye doctor examined me and prescribed glasses, I could finally see. Before then, I had been a child totally unaware that my vision was so badly impaired. Though I would be severely harassed by kids all the way through elementary, junior high, and high school for wearing glasses with lens the thickness of the bottom of a Coke bottle, I held on to a passionate love for the idea of schooling and the classroom.

When thinking about why I became a college professor, having spent over twenty-five years teaching in one form or another in "institutions of higher learning"—I think back to my childhood days of having had to overcome the stigma associated with learning disability, in those days synonymous with notions of "special" education. As a black male pro-feminist professor, I have come to think of my approach to college teaching as a strategic form of *special* (as in "extraordinary") education grounded in resistance struggle against domination and social injustice.

Over the course of thirteen years teaching at a small, private college in New York City's historic Greenwich Village, I developed an antiracist pedagogy founded upon black feminist thought. As an African Americanist with a literary background in narratives of racial passing by black writers in the United States, I came to the college with a tenacious zeal for teaching feminist autobiographical writing by women. With its interdisciplinary curricular structure, small classes, and seminar style of teaching, the college represented an amazing intellectual environment for pedagogical experimentation. It would become the testing ground for my curricular exploration as I conceptualized pedagogy that simultaneously confronts ideologies of white supremacy, sexism, and patriarchal masculinity. Teaching black feminist memoir writing over the years, I developed a critical location to ground my ideas on the efficacy of feminist antiracism. In my work in the college classroom, teaching memoir writing against racism and sexism functions as a pivotal tool toward the realization of its practice.

In writing in this book about my struggle to teach black feminist antiracism in a college in which the majority of students were white females, I rely on the confessional mode to render its complexity. Sharing publicly the intimate details of how I became a male *feminist professor* represents a strategic moment for me to reveal the intimate details of my journey toward an emancipatory vision of black manhood. Thus, *Black Male Outsider* functions as a pedagogical autobiography of black male liberation. With unbridled candor, it lays bare my yearning to be free from years of internalized wounds of white supremacist thinking and patriarchal masculinity. At risk of sounding overly dramatic, I am no longer afraid to admit that embracing black feminist thought was a life-saving action for me. Its transforming power continues to fuel my passion for teaching students autobiographical writing designed to promote social justice. In my pedagogical practice in the college classroom, students studying black feminist autobiographical writing come to know the critical place social activism holds in its discursive power. Across race, gender, class, and sexual difference, students engaging it find the power within themselves to confront inner wounds of domination. In the process, they learn to write from the *personal to the political* as an act of social agency toward inner healing and self-determination.

A former student of mine once characterized my approach to teaching memoir writing as requiring students to "write from the inside out."

In writing this autobiography of black feminist pedagogy, I struggled to find the courage to do precisely what I asked students to do in my memoir-writing courses. It would be the beginning of my undoing, leaving me vulnerable open to attack. Disclosing soul-wounding aspects of my past as a black boy outsider wrought in me a fear I had never experienced. As daunting as the task appeared, writing from the inside out in this book constituted an act of patriarchal "self" *un*doing. It necessitated a fundamental self-makeover of my identity as a black man in a culture of patriarchy and white supremacy, where for many years I had not fully realized the internal injury each had simultaneously wrought against the welfare of my selfhood.

Several years ago, when the idea for a book about my approach to teaching black feminist thought occurred to me, I had no intention of writing about the conundrum of being black, male, and feminist. With no intention of revealing much detail about the transformation of my gender and racial consciousness, suffice it to say, I felt completely justified in "objectively" representing the challenges of teaching gender-progressive antiracism in a majority-white college. What more was necessary to illustrate its educational value outside of documented classroom case studies? I had to admit that the fear of writing about teaching feminism from an autobiographical standpoint (both mine and the writers' work I teach) produced a form of mental and emotional paralysis. After all, what right did I have to speak in feminist terms as a black man—in an academic environment in which the majority of students were white females who identified themselves as feminists?

When I began writing the book, it quickly became painfully aware to me that I could not write it as objective documentation of my work in the classroom. To be truthful to the self-transforming impact of black feminist thinking in my personal life, I had to rethink my autobiographical and pedagogical standpoint in the entire project. I could not honestly write about the "self-transforming" power of black feminist thought without autobiographical *self*-engagement. Heeding an inner voice calling me to confess openly about the process of my becoming a feminist professor, I had to begin writing from the inside out. Two years before I began the memoir, Professor Minelle Mahtani (a beloved feminist colleague of mine at the college) invited me to speak in her class. She had assigned her students to read an essay I wrote some years ago about teaching the "novel of (racial) passing" from a black-male-feminist standpoint. I remember vividly one of her students asking me how I became a feminist. Without any autobiographical reference, I responded quickly with a rather convoluted, theoretical statement on my belief in female equality and women's rights. I revealed nothing about my personal background. On a deeply visceral level, shame filled me. I could not tell her my story.

When I began writing seriously about my journey toward becoming a feminist professor, I soon discovered it called for me to delve into nooks and crannies of my past. A place of silence and secrets. What price would I pay for exposing them? I had never planned to look there. Yet narrating my professional concerns increasingly demanded that I expose myself—that I be vulnerable in ways that I had not been taught to be. But writing from the inside out required me to open myself up to public scrutiny. In the script of black machismo, a pro-feminist black man is a contradiction in terms. But it is precisely the contradiction of black feminist manhood this memoir confronts. Devon W. Carbado asserts in *Black Men on Race, Gender and Sexuality* that "[a] fundamental goal of male feminism should be to facilitate the process of men unbecoming men, the process of men unlearning the patriarchal ways in which they have learned to become men. . . . Manhood is a performance. A script" (1999a, 425). John Stoltenberg had convincingly argued the same position earlier in *The End Manhood* (1994). Writing about my rejection of the script of patriarchal manhood necessarily means writing about being "othered" as a black boy outsider in my childhood. Revealing the process of my becoming a feminist black man requires me to disclose the fact that I failed the heteronormative masculinity test. Growing up, I did not conform to the script that codified it. Writing this book, as an adult man having embraced black feminist thinking as a radical form of male recovery, I have learned that it is better to love justice than to love manhood. Laying bare my recovery process, I can let go the long repressed pain of boyhood outsiderness. No longer internalizing white supremacist ideology, I can recollect painful feelings of being too dark-skinned in classrooms full of white students in high school and college. Now, no longer fearful of the patriarchal father, I can remember the traumatic feelings of being a childhood survivor of domestic violence without inflicting violence upon women or the mother of my children. No longer searching for a father's acceptance, I can recall feelings of being emotionally abandoned by my father as a child—without shutting out my own children. No longer intimidated by black males, I can call to mind the feelings of outsiderness prompted by the vicious taunts of mean-spirited black boys in junior high school—without hating all black men. No longer afraid that my sexuality will be called into question as a feminist-identified man, but knowing it invariably will be in a culture of heteromanhood thinking, I can recollect feelings sexual self-loathing engendered by the moral dogma of my conservative religious upbringing—

without letting go of my faith. With unbridled candor I summon up deeply hurtful gender and racial feelings from my past to narrate them without bitterness. Recalling the path I took toward becoming a professor of feminism, I teach in solidarity with *all* gender-progressive persons (respective of the complexities inherent in identity politics).

In retrospect, reflecting upon my "objective" answer to the student's question in my colleague's class, I now know that it was far from sufficient. There was neither time (in spite of my shame) nor a simple way to express the intricate complexities of my self-proclamation. In actuality, an adequate response to the student's question literally required writing this book. *Black Male Outsider* not only serves as a defense for my profession of feminism, but also argues for the efficacy of black feminist thinking as a self-recovery site for all who have been wounded by patriarchy and white supremacy. Scaling away layers of internalized patriarchal and white supremacist thinking in this memoir, I experienced the act of writing it as a process of soul cleaning. The more I scraped through the thickly layered, crusted-over pain of past boyhood hurts and heteronormative notions of masculinity attached to feelings of racial inferiority, the clearer I began to see the work in this memoir as spiritually grounded. It was about cleansing myself of the toxic waste of inhumanity. Like the recovery work substance-abuse addicts must do to "stay clean," in a culture of domination pro-feminist black men must continually struggle to be self-reflexive, proactive, radical agents of human concern and social justice.

Pro-feminist black men helping each other and other men to recover from the ill effects of male supremacist ideology, heterosexism, and homophobia (inside and outside black communities) is vital to the integrity of the gender-progressive professions we make. In this way, we promote the belief that all men should be in a perpetual process of soul work toward the rejection of white supremacist patriarchy. Writing into the dark places within, I have reclaimed the label of gender and racial outsider once attached to my body, searing to my mind, and piercing my spirit as a young black boy. In writing this memoir, I discovered that being on the outside of heteronormative ideas of masculinity can be a strategic site of empowerment for a black male professor of feminism. On the margin of masculinity, teaching black feminist thought, I have come to love myself as a black man outside the bounds of patriarchy. Writing into the darkness of my soul, I reclaimed my wounded past as a strategic location to teach education as the practice of inner healing. Writing into the darkness of my soul enabled me to speak from the heart about becoming a feminist professor. It is the grist from which this book emerged—where the spirit resides.

Black Feminist Thinking at the Heart of
Black *Male* Liberation

Indisputably, contemporary black men opposing (hetero)sexism, male supremacy, and homophobic notions of black masculinity have created a notable body of pro-feminist writings. The institutional influence black studies has had in higher education is undeniable. It began almost forty years ago when black students and academics across the United States called for curricula specifically focused on the history and culture of the African diaspora. At the same time, the advent of women's studies and the second wave of feminism in the 1960s also had a profound effect on the transformation of college and university curricula across the nation. Concurrently, in the studies devoted to the lives of black women, we witnessed a black feminist renaissance in writing, scholarship, and activism.

Since the 1960s and the movement for black power and the rise of the women's liberation movement, black feminism has remained a controversial subject in black communities. In the decades that followed, the meteoric rise of such black women novelists as Alice Walker, Toni Morrison, and Terri McMillan, among others, has kept the debate on black sexism alive in popular culture as well as in college and university classrooms across the nation. More often than not, women's studies (not black studies) has been a critical location for the study of black women's historical struggle to represent themselves in their own voices. In courses about black women's struggle for equality in education, politics, economics, religion, art, literary expression, and of course gender, black women feminists in the academy have seriously and strategically engaged the fact that black women simultaneously confront issues of sexism, classism, and homophobia while they must battle racism in their daily lives.

Through our studies of black feminist thought, I compelled students in my classes at the college to consider a critique of black women's oppression in the context of their own daily experience—to see it around them, to know it beyond textual exploration. Rooted in black women's lived experience, black feminist thought posits the notion that racism cannot be understood without an examination of its interrelationship to gender, class, and sexual oppression. In the last thirty years, black feminism has become a formidable intellectual/activist force against the oppression of black women within and outside black communities. Following in the tradition of Maria Stewart, Sojourner Truth, and Anna Julia Cooper, whose writings on gender equality in the nineteenth century, established them as the "foremothers" of black feminism, today black feminism has emerged as a critical location for the study of black women's history. In the history of black feminism in the United States, black male participation has played an important role. The increasing amount of pro-feminist scholarship and activism by black men not only owes its credibility to the work of contemporary black-women-feminist scholar/activists but also to a number of pro-women's rights black men from the past—chief among them Frederick Douglass and W. E. B. Du Bois, the "forefathers" of contemporary feminist profession by black men.

My search for gender progressive-black males led me to the woman-suffrage writings of Frederick Douglass and W. E. B. Du Bois. As a graduate student at NYU during the late 1980s who was just beginning to contemplate a dissertation topic, I had never read the work of two black men more dedicated to the cause of women's rights. I was inspired by the pro-woman activist lives they led and had a particular interest in each man's autobiographical representation. I also found the feminist ideas they espoused ripe for analysis. Douglass and Du Bois became the primary subjects of my doctoral thesis on the impact of feminist thinking in the lives of black men. I call Douglass and Du Bois my "feminist forefathers." In the political memoirs of these men, in which they spoke eloquently about their belief in women's equality, I discovered that I could be *black*, *male*, and *pro-feminist/womanist*.

The contemporary relevance of Douglass and Du Bois's writings on the equality of women may be viewed in relation to a historic, black-gender-progressive conference held at Morehouse College in 1996 (a year after the Million Man March). "To Be Black, Male, and Womanist/Feminist," organized by Black Men for the Eradication of Sexism (BMES), a small group of male students from Morehouse supported by women students from Spelman College, called for black males to support womanist/feminist resistance to sexism. Publicly denouncing sex oppression, BMES declared, "We believe that although we are oppressed because of our color, we are privileged because of our sex and must therefore take responsibility for ending that privilege" ([1994] 2001, 201). Acknowledging the interconnection between racism and sexism, these words echo the feminist commitment Douglass and Du Bois espoused. Members of BMES attribute its founding to their course work, a year before the conference, with noted black feminist and Spelman professor Gloria Wade-Gayles. Mark Anthony Neal maintains that "[m]any black men who consider themselves feminists, were initially impacted by black women feminists. . . . But what was just as crucial to my own development as a feminist, was the identification of other black men who embraced feminist politics" (2003, 1). In praise of the pro-woman(ist) contributions W. E. B. Du Bois made to the movement for woman suffrage, I have said elsewhere: "Profeminist-identified Black men have begun to set the stage for a womanist men's counter movement against sexism. Reclaiming the feminist politics of [Frederick Douglass and W. E. B.] Du Bois opens up the possibility for progressive dialogue between Black men and women about the necessity of a new vision of black liberation—one infused with the spirit of womanist feminism" (Lemons 2001b, 67).

In *Scenes of Instruction: A Memoir* (1999), Michael Awkward was one of the first contemporary gender-progressive black men to write extensively about his profession of feminism. Like Frederick Douglass and W. E. B. Du Bois, Awkward writes with painstaking candor on the subject of becoming a pro-feminist man. Though never having met Michael Awkward, after reading his memoir I feel a deep bond with his struggle as a feminist-identified man. Over the years, it has been often a lonely struggle to profess my beliefs inside and outside the classroom—there are feelings of loneliness, isolation, and self-doubt that have made me question the credibility of black male feminism, especially as a black male professor in all-white or majority-white classrooms. I have drawn on the legacy of Douglass and Du Bois's activist commitment to female equality and women's rights to validate my work in the classroom. Their lifetime devotion to the fight for woman suffrage has continually remained a source of personal inspiration for me.

Introduction

When the Teacher Moves from Silence to Voice

"Talking Back" to Patriarchy and White Supremacy

[A] real challenge exists for black male feminists in consciously policing their own patriarchal privilege even as they challenge the conventions of patriarchy, particularly when doing so in the name of black women . . . the real value of feminism to black men comes from its ability to literally transform our worldview, particularly in response to our acceptance of very rigid versions of black masculinity.

—Mark Anthony Neal

Moving from silence into speech is for the oppressed, the colonized, the exploited, and those who stand and struggle side by side, a gesture of defiance that heals, that makes new life and new growth possible. It is that act of speech, of "talking back," that is no mere gesture of empty words, that is the expression of our movement from object to subject— the liberated voice.

—bell hooks

Black Male Outsider is a work about "the transformation of silence into language and action," in the words of Audre Lorde. In *Sister Outsider,* Lorde speaks poignantly about the transforming power of breaking silence and its potential for bringing people together across differences: "The fact

1

that we are here . . . is an attempt to break . . . silence and bridge some of [the] differences between us, for it is not difference which immobilizes us, but silence. And there are so many silences to be broken" (1984, 44). Above my desk at home, in a simple black frame, I have reproduced these words as an epigraph to continually remind me that transforming silence into language is a powerful tool in self-recovery practice. As the preface states, this is a book about my personal journey toward self-recovery outside the boundaries of male supremacist and white supremacist thinking. At the same time, it is an autobiography of pedagogical transformation, an attempt to break silence of my childhood past as a "black boy outsider." I am no longer ashamed for being a traitor to patriarchy. Silent about years of internalized patriarchal wounds of being a black male outside the script of heteromasculinist notions of manhood, two years ago I determined to begin writing about my life as a black male professor of black feminist thought. Free from the laws of patriarchy and white supremacy, in the college classroom I confront sexism and racism, as well as heterosexist and homophobic ideas of gender related to them. In sum, I teach black feminist antiracist studies to promote social justice.

At the heart of the memoir's narrative impulse is the story of my journey from patriarchal object of male marginalization to pro-feminist subject of my own telling. Metaphorically, it represents a movement from silence to voice, from the margin to the center of my reason for being a pro-feminist man. The memoir focuses on my work at a small, private, liberal arts college in the New York City for more than a decade (from 1991 to 2004). Organized into three parts, it speaks candidly about my personal decision two decades ago to embrace black feminist thought as a strategy for male self-transformation. It represents my struggle toward self-healing against patriarchy and white supremacy. Part 1 formulates a theory of antiracist pedagogy based on black feminist thinking. Part 2 functions as a narrative backdrop for my journey of self-recovery: from 'black boy outsider on the margin of masculinity to pro-feminist professor.' Part 3 examines my pedagogical practice in the form of a series of classroom case studies.

I was drawn to the work of bell hooks, Audre Lorde, and Alice Walker (among other black feminists who *re*shaped my vision of black manhood), and over time I conceptualized a pro-woman(ist) memoir-writing pedagogy that contests the boundaries of gender, race, and sexuality, while at the same time combating sexism, heterosexism, and homophobia. Together, parts 1, 2, and 3 chart the evolution of black feminist thinking in the theory and practice of my teaching. The memoir makes a case for education as the practice of social justice and the efficacy of black feminist thinking in memoir-writing pedagogy.

In the process of writing a memoir about teaching, I came to realize that I did not fully comprehend the problematics of teaching black feminism as a black male at a college predominated by white female students, many of whom identified with white feminists. Before enrolling in my courses, many of those white female students had never studied black feminist thought. Considering the history of racism in the white-female-dominated feminist movement in the United States, *race*, more than gender difference, became "the" issue in the classroom. My approach to teaching feminism focused on black women. It concentrated on antiracism primarily because the overwhelming majority of the students I taught were white who had little knowledge of the history of black struggle against white supremacy or black feminist resistance to racism. Rather than gender, class, and sexuality, it was *racial difference* that fueled classroom dynamics in dramatic ways. In the thirteen years I taught at the college, I often wondered whether black feminist thinking could be a viable strategy for teaching white students and students of color antiracism.

Speaking Truth to Power: Writing and Teaching from the Margin

> Black feminist pedagogy as a philosophy of liberation for humankind, is designed to enable students, through the social, economic, cultural, moral and religious history of Third World people, to reexamine and see the world through a perspective that would instill a revolutionary, conscious, liberating ideology.
>
> Gloria Joseph

Writing about the necessity of men embracing feminism is one thing. Writing a memoir about growing up as a "black boy outsider" who becomes a feminist professor as a black man is another. A black man teaching black feminist thinking in an all-white classroom to confront white supremacy is no joke. I have done it long enough to understand the racial, gender, and sexual pitfalls associated with it—for students as well as myself. But writing a memoir about my experience teaching black feminist antiracism was personally a much more daunting task. As I reveal in the chapters that follow, it meant confronting racist, sexist, and heterosexist demons within me and the shame, secrecy, and self-silencing fears they produced in me for most of my life. Writing about them dredged up deep inner feelings (rarely shared publicly) about who I am, what I teach, and my approach to it. It meant summoning up painful memories of boyhood outsiderness that had long ago been locked away.

Not only was teaching black feminist thinking at the college self-empowering for me, but it also allowed all students the opportunity to engage a complex representation of *blackness*. It opened up transformative space for the possibility of radical engagement in black subjectivity for students of color and for white students. Black feminist thought in the classroom is about teaching that rejects the reduction of black identity to a set of specious racist myths and stereotypes. Teaching memoir writing against race and gender oppression challenges students to interrogate ways racism and sexism may function in their own experiences. I tell them that a purely analytical response to oppression, an approach solely through the intellect and exempt of emotional investment in human devaluation, is void of humanity, spiritually bankrupt, and ultimately not *self*-sustaining. Students acknowledging inner wounds of race and sex oppression begin a journey of self-transformation—from silence to voice.

Coming to know the history of black women's struggle against racism *and* sexism completely changed my thinking about their place in black antiracist struggle. It not only exposed the myth of black liberation as the recovery of black manhood, but also gave me the critical tools to analyze gender oppression, both in its general effects on all women and its particular effects on black women. Having grown up in a home where domestic violence was a feature of my early childhood and midteenage years, I witnessed firsthand the subjugation and abuse of the woman closest to me during those times. My mother is a survivor of domestic violence, which means that my brother and I are survivors as well. Terms like "domestic violence," "sexism," and "patriarchy" were not terms I had even heard of as a child.

Over time, studying feminist black women's struggle against racism and sexism has allowed me to understand that the politics of liberation that inform them are not diametrically opposed, as sometimes represented. While "black" studies historically have represented a male-centered ethos in which liberatory thinking about the freedom of black people was about male liberation, feminist studies created by black women taught me that the sexist (and sexual) oppression of women and girls in black communities is as deadly as racism is for all people of color *and* for white people. Black feminist thought places the study of black liberation in an entirely different light. As such, it as the driving force for antiracist pedagogy (in a majority-white college classroom), has offered me the pedagogical tools for teaching writing that touches the heart and soul—that compels students to examine critically the impact of whiteness and white supremacy on gender, class, and sexual oppression. To continue this work in life beyond the classroom with family, friends, and, most importantly, within oneself is critical. Teaching writing from the inside out is not a theoretical approach to liberation pedagogy; it is about education that seeks to examine critically the day-to-day lived practices of students and professors engaged in it.

Teaching black feminist thinking at the college became a way for me to unlearn whiteness. As I will discuss in greater detail as the memoir unfolds, most white students who took my classes over the years possessed little academic or personal experience of talking about race, much less engaging the topic of whiteness and its relation to white supremacy. In contrast, most students of color (of African descent, Latino/a, indigenous, or Asian) enrolling in classes I teach came with at least some degree of critical sophistication in discourses on race. Among them, the experience of being racially "othered" in majority-white spaces was a common point of connection. At the same time, the experience of gender, class, and sexual differences among them complicated racial politics within the "student of color" label. Like white students, they too possessed their own problematic relationship to talking about race with one another. However, unlike white students at the college, they were always being made aware that race talk was happening in a white-dominated context. There were students (white and of color) who made an indelible imprint on my pedagogy. They gave me the courage to write this book. In the groundbreaking essay "Black Feminist Pedagogy and Schooling in Capitalist White America," Gloria Joseph maintains that "[e]ducation has always been central in antiracist struggle. . . . Black feminist pedagogy embodies a philosophy . . . of liberation" (1995, 463–65). The history of U.S. black feminism shows that black women have long advocated the classroom as a strategic location for teaching antidomination political ideologies. (See the education studies by bell hooks, Lisa Delpit, and Beverly Daniel Tatum.)

Teaching in resistance to white supremacy and male supremacy is, according to bell hooks, "a gesture of defiance that heals, that makes new life and new growth possible." My work in the classroom is about possibility, renewal, and self-transformation for the collective liberation of voice, mind, body, and spirit. Students learn quickly that studying black feminist thought is not about intellectual investigation alone. After teaching in a majority-white college for over a decade, certain things became apparent to me, among them

- that pedagogy founded upon black feminist thought about race and gender poses a liberatory challenge to the ideology of white supremacy for white students *and* students of color;
- that black feminist pedagogy as a specific response to racism and sexism offers a more complex critique of white supremacy than a race-only approach (which may or may not address the institutional and systemic nature of racism predicated upon the myth of white racial superiority);

- that many black students and other students of color in a majority white institution bear an enormous racial burden as "minorities," particularly with regard to their white counterparts, white faculty, and white administrators;
- that these same students, often in crisis about their "minority" status (and inevitably facing racism) in the institution, may retaliate against black faculty and other faculty of color whose pedagogy raises issues relating to the interconnections between race, racism, and white supremacy; and
- that for progressive black faculty committed to social justice who challenge the institutional politics of majority-white colleges and universities, the day-to-day experiences in these institutions can be toxic to the progressive faculty's pedagogical aims.

Black feminist pedagogy integrates the head and the heart, promoting healing for the mind, body, and spirit. While its critical lens focuses on the experiences of black women, its vision of liberation—as Alice Walker has said—is "committed to the survival and wholeness of entire people, male *and* female" (1983, ix). Black feminist commitment *to the survival and wholeness of entire people, male and female* is precisely what Gloria Joseph speaks about in her straightforward definition of black feminist pedagogy, and it is precisely what bell hooks articulates in her call for profeminist male comrades to make public our allegiance to feminist movement for the eradication of sexism.

In 1996, I published an essay about teaching entitled "Young Man, Tell the Stories of How We Made It Over: Beyond the Politics of Identity," inspired by Audre Lorde. Defending my aims for teaching a course called "Redefining Womanhood, Rewriting the Black Female Self," on which the essay is based, I state: "Teaching students how to interrogate and critically oppose the [oppression] of women as a black/male/feminist is not about 'teaching what I'm not,' *but about teaching what I am*—an advocate of a feminist movement in which women *and men* united across race, class, and [sexuality] struggle to end [sexist] oppression" (1996b, 259–60). As a public declaration, "teaching what I am" emerges from a long personal struggle to break silence with the traumatic experience of domestic violence growing up on the margins of masculinity. "Teaching what I am" represents a critical means to denounce the myth of black male antifeminism, while reconceptualizing black masculinity in feminist terms. In this way, my liberatory vision of the college classroom obtains credibility. The classroom becomes a site of personal and pedagogical healing and instruction for critical self-consciousness. Strategically, such a vantage point infuses my teaching with a passion for social justice.

White students came to my courses on black feminism with high anxiety and fear that I would force them to disclose "racial" secrets—particularly regarding their "personal" relationship to experiences of whiteness, white privilege, and white supremacy. Female and male students of color also came with their own anxieties and fears, but their uneasiness was about taking a course on black feminist thought focused on memoir writing. How students of color felt in a majority-white classroom was always on my mind. Despite the fact that whiteness was always mediating our interactions, their presence in the classroom provided me the comfort of feeling in solidarity with them. There were times when I felt my dark skin powerfully and viscerally connected to the skin colors of students of African descent. In these moments, when color entered the classroom (on rare occasions in the form of two, sometimes three students of color, at the most), my will to voice— to "talk back" to whiteness—was strong, urgent, forceful. Those same moments also revealed the often painful, frustrating, and exasperating experience of students of color studying black feminist antiracism in an overwhelmingly white education setting.

Writing about teaching black feminist thought at a majority-white college, also brought home the reality that as much as I desired the presence of students of color in my classes, I am always having to strategize how not to alienate white students as well

- about being white while studying black feminist thought and having that reveal itself in a number of ways—but mainly in what they say (*or do not say*);
- about being white and having to confront notions of whiteness, white privilege, and white supremacy in class;
- about being white and having to read/study/engage black feminist texts that not only pose a challenge to sexism but also to racism, heterosexism, classism, and homophobia simultaneously;
- about being white and having to dialogue about it with each other;
- about being white and having to discuss openly in class its meaning(s) with a student or students of color and with me; and
- and having to write about being white autobiographically in the form of a *memoir of race.*

I maintain that a pedagogy of black antiracism focused only on a critique of white supremacy is dangerous for white students and students of color. Black antiracism formulated in the belief that white supremacy is the sole problem facing people of color today is inherently flawed, for it fails to recognize that racism cannot be studied as a discrete form of domination, disconnected from other forms of oppression. Progressive black antiracists have never believed this. As one of the most committed black male pro-feminists of the past, W. E. B. Du Bois well understood the interconnection between sexism and racism. In 1920, writing in *Dark-water: Voices from within the Veil*, he proclaimed: "The uplift of women is, next to the problem of the color line and the peace movement, our greatest modern cause. When, now, two of these movements—woman and color—combine in one, the combination has deep meaning" ([1920] 1999, 165). Years ago, before reading the pro-feminist writings of Du Bois, Frederick Douglass, and a number of other black men from the past, I had no idea how deeply black feminist movement against sexism and racism would later touch me. In one of my early pedagogical essays, I state: "Resisting my own intense feelings of pessimism when reflecting upon the present state of race relations in the United States, I imagine Frederick Douglass and W. E. B. Du Bois waging war against both racism and sexism. Remembering their struggle as antiracist feminists reaffirms my vision of the classroom as a site for social transformation" (Lemons 1996a, 169). Contemporary black men advancing the cause of feminist antiracism in the classroom constitutes a radical gesture in the historical tradition of black male pro-feminist thinking.

✷ PART 1 ✷

Formulating a Pedagogy of Black Feminist Antiracism

Whiteness looms over my past like a spectral presence, pressed into my consciousness like the image of an ancient fossil figured in stone. I must come face to face with it, see it for what it is . . . Confront it to live—in a different way, free from its history of torture and terrorizing . . . it is (in)visible all around me . . . (Within and outside me)—It rages against me; I war against it with wild abandon. Yet (within and outside of me) I rage against another foe. It is the misplaced mantle of patriarchal manhood. Like the ever-present phantasm of white supremacy terrorizing, it lures me into the phallic fallacy of the indestructibility of Superman. He was the manliest white man I ever saw as a little black boy— "Faster than a speeding bullet; leaping tall buildings in a single bound." But he was still a white man. I will rid myself of the race and gender demons that hunt/haunt/ hurt me. I will tell—how they wounded me . . . to recover, to heal, and to teach for wholeness. Never more silence. "Silence=death," Marlon (Riggs) said.

❯ 1 ❮

Toward a *Profession* of Feminism

Men who actively struggle against sexism have a place in feminist movement. . . . [M]en have a tremendous contribution to make to feminist struggle in the area of exposing, confronting, opposing, and transforming the sexism of their male peers. When men show a willingness to assume equal responsibility in feminist struggle, performing whatever tasks are necessary, women should affirm their revolutionary work by acknowledging them as comrades in struggle.

—bell hooks

[M]ost profeminist Black men have to prove themselves to feminists and nonfeminists alike. That is, many people in our society are not used to the radical definitions of manhood that profeminist men are choosing to explore; nor are they used to the racial notion that men, particularly Black men, can be feminists. However, scholars have meticulously documented that men have supported each historical wave of feminism, including Black men.

—Aaronette White

Just as Sojourner Truth argued that she, too, was a woman, I argue that Black men also can be feminists, even though they bring different experiences to the table. . . . [T]he question as to whether men can be feminists arises among feminists and nonfeminists alike. I have come to believe that some men can appropriately be called feminists. As an African American feminist woman, I argue the case for men in general who wish to state boldly their advocacy for feminist beliefs and actions. . . . Accordingly, my view is that anyone who believes in the eradication of institutionalized sexism should be welcomed as a feminist in various feminist struggles. I believe this is especially the case if that person recognizes that institutionalized sexism is equally reinforced by institutionalized racism, economic injustice, and homophobia.

—Aaronette White

11

As the memoir's theoretical underpinning, this chapter engages the complex relationship between race and gender within the feminist thought of black women and men, particularly related to my classroom practice. I employ both the terms "womanist" and "black feminist" to reference it and to identify my standpoint in this book. Beginning with a discussion of these highly distinctive terms, I do not assume that they are interchangeable. Related to black women's critique of sexism, each term has its own distinct history and epistemology. Narrating the development of my feminist consciousness, I find both terms strategically enabling.

To Be a Womanist and/or Black Feminist Man?

Many years ago, as a graduate student studying black feminism at NYU, I read in the opening pages of *In Search of Our Mothers' Gardens* Alice Walker's definition of a *black feminist* with intense personal interest. For me, when Walker conceived the term "womanist" to distinguish a black/feminist of color, she opened up a strategic space full of possibility for *black male* profeminists. With its emphasis on the humanity of all people—across gender difference—I found in womanist thinking an ideological and political space to identify myself as a black man supporting feminism. Moreover, while not explicitly stated, its visionary gender-inclusive politics appears expansive enough to embrace "transgender" identity. As Patricia Hill Collins critically delineates in the insightful essay "Womanism and Black Feminism," even as Walker names a standpoint of female autonomy particularized to black women, she "aspires to a universal meaning of *womanist* that transcends particular histories, including that of African-American women" (Hill Collins 2001, 35).

However, Walker's pronouncement in the early 1980s has provoked much debate particularly with regard to sexuality among gender-progressive black women as a signifying difference between "womanism" and "black feminism." Some heterosexual womanists have ignored Walker's view of sexuality as something that transcends the boundary of heterosexuality (as in "womanist": a woman who also "loves other women, sexually and/or nonsexually" (Walker 1983, xi). With forthrightness, Hill Collins directly addresses the issue related to three major concerns of black women having to do with religion, race, and black male gender allegiance. "The relative silence of womanists on this dimension of womanism speaks to many African-American women's continued ambivalence in dealing with the links between race, gender, and sexuality, in this case, the 'taboo' sexuality of lesbianism. . . . [T]he visibility of White lesbians within North American feminism overall directly conflicts with many Black women's article of faith that homosexuality is a sin. . . . Many African-Americans define Black feminism as being exclusively for Black women and as rejecting Black men" (Hill Collins 2001, 37, 39, 40). In closing, Hill Collins asserts that antiseparatist arguments made by noted womanists Shirley Williams and Geneva Smitherman are, indeed, valid. They assert that a separatist agenda for black feminists is counterproductive to the welfare of black communities. They are silent on the controversy surrounding sexuality. Understanding the sexual politics that separate womanists from black feminists, I hold to the integrity of Walker's standpoint against heterosexism. Homophobic nationalism was clearly *not* her intention in conceptualizing a personal and political standpoint for black female autonomy.

Progressive black feminists focused on men and feminism—like bell hooks, Alice Walker, and Aaronette White, among others—have boldly spoken out for gender inclusiveness in the struggle to end sexism and the oppression of all women. They gave me the courage to pursue a radical antiheterosexist relationship to feminism. I have embraced the *pro-black* thinking found in both womanist and black feminist thinking. As is the foundation of my pro-woman(ist) professorship, I am committed to a politics of gender inclusiveness in feminism—with respect to differences—as the framework for progressive feminist movement across boundaries of race, class, and sexuality. A longtime ally to women and men in struggle against patriarchy, I reject any tie to race, religious, and/or gender loyalty supporting women's liberation invested in heterosexism and homophobia.

In 1998, I published an essay entitled "To Be Black, Male, and Feminist: Making Womanist Space for Black Men on the Eve of the New Millennium." My aim in writing this piece was to situate contemporary black male advocacy of feminism within the historical context of black women *and* men's pro-womanist struggle against gender and racial oppression:

> We [must] resist the power of patriarchy that would have us believe we are more powerful because we can exercise power over women. Such male supremacist thinking is particularly dangerous for black men precisely because our history in the United States has been about the racist obliteration of our manhood. Is our attainment of patriarchal power through the oppression of women any less insidious than racist white people's perpetuation of a system of racial oppression to dehumanize us? Many of us have become so obsessed with fighting racism as a battle for the right to be patriarchal men that we have been willing to deploy the same strategies to disempower black women as white supremacists have employed to institutionalize racism. (Lemons 1998b, 45)

Black men embracing womanism/feminism, however, is not simply a matter of gender and racial solidarity enjoined at the discursive level alone. Whether we refer to ourselves as *pro*-womanist or *pro*-feminist, black male feminism must continually define itself in relation to the activist history of black women and men against (hetero)sexism and racism. In "Ain't I a Feminist?" Aaronette White poses a critical question: "[W]hy would a Black man advocate for change that would deny him his patriarchal piece of the pie?" (2001/2002, 29). It is a question with personal and political resonance for every black man in a culture of male supremacy, where *all* men (in spite of race, ethnicity, and/or class) benefit from being a "man." With this question in mind, in this chapter I seriously ponder the question not only to flesh out the social self-transforming benefits I have experienced teaching against male supremacy, sexism, and heterosexism as a pro-feminist professor, but also to pinpoint its effects as an agent of personal self-healing in my life. Crafting pro-feminist pedagogy of antiracism in the college classroom, most specifically, I contextualize its complexities within historical and contemporary interpretation. Historicizing black men as professors of feminism enables me to correct the myth that "among men [it] is the cultural property of White middle-class men . . . probably due to the fact that feminist White men are formally organized . . . and have greater access to various print media sources than do feminist men of color" (White 2001/2002, 28). Without the benefits of formal organization, networks, and publishing resources, black men advocating feminism in and outside academia have begun to make our voices heard.

While all men stand to benefit from feminist self-transformation, for black men the struggle against the history of white supremacy necessarily "colors" the way we view feminism. Racism in the past and present makes a profound difference in how we must reconceptualize feminism as an ideology of healing in our lives. "Black" in the phrase "black, male, and pro-womanist/feminist" is not simply an adjective of racial distinction— it embodies a constellation of differences. What shifts, moves, and transmits across distance and time in the difference that race signifies in black men's advocacy of feminism cannot be reduced to a trendy expression of gender consciousness; so much more than this is at stake for we committed black male gender progressives who call ourselves "womanists" and/or "black feminists."

Action Speaks Louder than Words (or Feminist Labels)

Whether a black man should be allowed to call himself a feminist is a bone of contention for many black women feminists and for black male detractors of feminism, but for differing reasons. Joy James, for example, in *Transcending the Talented Tenth* (1997), sounds a cautionary note about the efficacy of black male pro-feminism when she complicates the women's rights activism of W. E. B. Du Bois as he characterizes it his autobiographical writings. James points to "nonspecificity and erasure in Du Bois's profeminism" in the representation of black women's political agency (James 1997, 53). She says, however, that "we can strategize for a gender progressivism that unpacks this legacy to transcend the limits of Du Bois's profeminism. Doing so requires addressing the profeminist politics in the writings of present-day progressive intellectuals. *Given the racial and sexual biases that inform our concepts of political, intellectual, and moral ability, it is unsurprising that black male intellectuals intentionally or inadvertently reproduce sexist thought*" (56; emphasis added).

James praises Manning Marable's essay "Grounding with My Sisters," a pro-feminist rereading of the black liberation struggle: "Although increasingly we find similar writings by black male profeminists, Marable's 1983 text was one of the earliest statements of such politics" (James 1997, 58). A germinal chapter in his book *How Capitalism Undeveloped Black America* (1983), "Grounding with My Sisters: Patriarchy and the Exploitation of Black Women" is, indeed, an exemplary text in which a black male historian critiques sexism in the history of gender politics in the black liberation struggle. James offers an instructive note for black men's conceptual rendering of male feminism (no matter how well intended), particularly regarding black women's intellectual, political, and activist histories. Representations of black women that substitute the history of political agency they achieved for a portrait of "black female victimization offer problematic profeminist politics" (James 1997, 59). James's historical and contemporary critical perspective on black male pro-feminism is well founded and invaluable for understanding its pitfalls. Even as gender progressives, we black men professing feminism must be continually self-critical of our own gender, intellectual, and political motives as allies of black women— not only in word, but in deed. At the same time, we must be willing to place our pro-feminist professions on the line, justifying what we *say* and *do* to advance feminist movement *when and where* black women are concerned. Moreover, we must speak to its opponents (male *and* female) inside (and outside) black communities.

Promoting the viability of feminism in black communities, Marable calls for an ideological shift away from the historically masculinist agenda of black male liberationists and toward a liberatory vision of freedom reconceived in the feminist "wisdom" of black women: "Black male liberationists must relearn their own history, by grounding themselves in the wisdom of their sisters. . . . The underdevelopment of Black America will end only when Black men begin to seriously challenge and uproot the patriarchal assumptions and institutions which still dominate Black civil and political society" ([1983] 2001, 120, 146). Not only was Marable one of the first contemporary, gender-progressive black men to document sexism in the history of black liberation struggle, he was also among the first to speak against black male opposition to feminism. He cites the black sociologist Robert Staples as one of the leading *anti*feminist black male voices of the 1970s: "[F]ew Black sociologists writing about the Black woman have been more consistently wrong than he has" (138). While Staples was not the only black male (or female) voice heard during the time, his fervent opposition spawned the "black sexism debate" based on an acerbic article he published in the *Black Scholar* (March/April 1979). Entitled "A Response to Angry Black Feminists," it was nothing less than a diatribe against the feminist writings of Michele Wallace and Ntozake Shange. Revisiting the debate on black sexism in light of the ongoing resistance to feminism in black communities today, I wrote my own critique of black male sexism in "A New Response to 'Angry Black (Anti)Feminists'" (Lemons 1998a, 274).

Considering the long-standing accusations of black males against feminist black women, what are some of the accusations pro-feminist black men might incur from antifeminist black males (and from some black women feminists)? Based on some of the attacks incurred by black feminist women, we are generally *guilty* not only of the same crimes against race and gender, but of sexuality as well. To begin with, to its detractors a *black* man speaking and acting in feminist ways is a betrayal of racial loyalty. Secondly, a *black man*'s speaking and acting in feminist ways constitutes gender heresy. To add fuel to the fire, the traitorous attitudes and behaviors of a pro-feminist black man go against the heteronorms of black masculinity. Thus, as stated, any black male who embraces feminism is not a man. If not a man, then what is he? To the *anti*feminist black male, he is a *wo*man. In this gender-reductive equation—neither a gay, nor a straight, nor a bisexual man professing feminism can be a man, in the heteronormative, *anti*male-feminist definition of it. In vulgar sexist and misogynist terminology, he is a "bitch."

Occupying the same ideological position as Stephen Heath, in terms of some black women's gender-separatist politics, a pro-feminist black man is an *impossibility*. It is, as noted, a contradiction in terms bound up in racist and sexist ideas of black manhood. Quite legitimately, some of the same questions confronting a white man's profession of feminism should be applied to the motives of a black man, or of any other man of color. Is black male feminism simply another form of male appropriation? As women and men from different race and gender backgrounds have questioned (and continue to question) men's motives for feminist allegiance, black men's feminist profession must continue to be interrogated—but not simply dismissed or negated because we possess no racial privilege. Aaronette White has noted, "Most profeminist Black men have to prove themselves to feminists and nonfeminists alike" (2001, 5). In a culture of racism and sexism, white men who profess pro-feminist sensibility have achieved a level of credibility that gender-progressive black males have not. This phenomenon exists because public outlets, media, and publishing resources for black men's feminist voices have only recently opened up. Is there any wonder, as White suggests, that "[m]any people in our society are [still] not used to the radical definitions of manhood that pro-feminist men are choosing to explore, nor are they used to the racial notion that men, *particularly Black men, can be feminists*" (5; emphasis added). In defense of male feminism, she astutely points to the record of male participation in "each historical wave of feminism, *including Black men*" (5; emphasis added).[1] White male scholars have recorded the history of white and black men's involvement in the feminist movement, especially during the rise of the movement for woman suffrage in the nineteenth century. According to Devon Carbado, "[F]eminist discourse about men and feminism is, by and large, a discourse about white men and white feminism" (1999a, 418). Similarly, as the history of black feminism has documented, female participation in the feminist movement has been focused on white women.

In truth, until the late 1980s, on the heels of a black male, antifeminist backlash against the feminist writings of Ntozake Shange and Michele Wallace, few contemporary black men publicly supported feminism. Not since the nineteenth-century gender/race debates about woman suffrage and Negro suffrage had so much controversy arisen about black people and feminism. Maintaining the defensibility of feminist black men in "Ain't I a Feminist?" Aaronette White argues "that Black men also can be feminists, even though they bring different experiences to the table. . . ." (2001/2002, 28). For White, the critical test of identification resides in the assertion of a belief "in the eradication of institutionalized sexism" (28). Anyone who espouses this belief "should be welcomed as a feminist in various feminist struggles" (28). In the tradition of black feminist women's historical critique of multiple oppression, her qualifying statement about the interrelationality of domination reaffirms the idea of feminism as a gender-inclusive and racially inclusive politics of struggle. White asserts, "I believe this is especially the case if that person recognizes that institutionalized sexism is equally reinforced by institutionalized racism, economic injustice, and homophobia" (28). It is the radical assertion of gender and racial inclusiveness in black feminist thinking that opens the door for "anyone" to embrace feminism, whether or not he or she chooses "feminist" as a self-identifying label.

In the introduction to *Feminism Is for Everybody: Passionate Politics* (2000), bell hooks (addressing the need for making feminist thought accessible to the masses) invites us to "come closer" to feminism: "Come closer. See how feminism can touch and change your life and all our lives. Come closer and know firsthand what feminist movement is all about. Come closer and you will see: feminism is for everybody" (2000, x). As part of the foundation for my defense of black male feminism, in the spirit of the universal appeal of Alice Walker's concept of black feminism I advocate the necessity of womanist education to end domination for all people. The possibility of womanist thinking in the lives of black men is enormous. One such example can be found in Rudolph Byrd's womanist adaptation in *Traps: African American Men on Gender and Sexuality* (2001). As an imaginative reconceptualization of her vision in male terms, he looks to the iconic figure of Zora Neale Hurston's "High John De Conquer."

New Voices, New Direction

> In the tradition of John: A mode of masculinity for Black men who are committed to the abolition of emasculating forms of masculinity; *a mode of masculinity for Black men who are committed to the abolition of racism, sexism, homophobia, and other ideological traps.* (Emphasis added)
>
> —Rudolph Byrd

In the prologue to *Traps*, Rudolph Byrd, one of its coeditors, poses a germinal question toward articulating the liberatory possibilities of black male pro-feminism: "What would it mean for Black men to be in the tradition of John? If we chose to reclaim this tradition, and adapt it to meet our very modern circumstances, how might our lives, the lives of others, and the communities we share with others be transformed?" (2001a, 5). Rather than debate whether men can be feminist, I position this question as a pivotal point of departure in my black-male-feminist defense. First, it means openly affirming any black male espousing a gender-progressive view of masculinity linked to feminist self-transformation. Secondly, it means support for any black male advocating feminist education for the eradication of all forms of domination. Black men embracing feminism, publicly claiming its liberatory benefits in their lives, are rewriting the script of heterosexist black masculinity mired in homophobic machismo.

Books, edited collections, and articles on the subject of pro-feminist black men began to appear more frequently in the mid-1990s, and they contested black male analyses of racism void of its relation to sexism, heterosexual male privilege, and homophobia. These works have opened up pro-womanist/feminist space for black men to dialogue about feminist possibilities in their lives, creating a radical discourse of black male recovery. Rejecting the pre(script)ions of heteronormativity and homophobic notions of masculinity that would have us believe that feminism is a racist strategy aimed to emasculate all black men, we are free to reimagine ourselves as allies of all women in feminist movement. In the process, we end the hold of patriarchy over our lives. We end the grip of heteromasculinist thinking about what it means to be a man. In particular, several recent edited collections have signaled the increased appearance of gender-progressive voices of black males establishing a foundation for pro-feminist discourse by black males on gender, race, and sexuality. The new works include *Representing Black Men* (ed. Marcellus Blount and George P. Cunningham, 1996), *Black Men on Race, Gender, and Sexuality* (ed. Devon W. Carbado, 1999), and *Traps: African American Men on Gender and Sexuality* (ed. Rudolph Byrd and Beverly Guy-Sheftall, 2001). *Representing Black Men* was one of the first contemporary edited volumes by black men on black men in "dialogue with feminism(s)" focusing on gender and sexuality. It includes Michael Awkward's widely anthologized, groundbreaking essay on black-male-feminist identity: "A Black Man's Place in Black Feminist Criticism."

Black Men on Race, Gender, and Sexuality continues to define the project of black male progressive thinking by black males on the relationship between "engendered contemporary racial discourse" and sexuality. About the book's agenda Carbado declares, "My hope is that this volume will inspire Black men to take up anti-patriarchal and anti-heterosexist positions as they engage in antiracist politics. This volume is dedicated to black community building across differences" (1999a, 12). Carbado's gender analysis of race and sexuality related to feminism provides an incisive framework to introduce and conclude the impressive list of his contributors. In the introduction, he rightly credits black feminists for having transformed black antiracist discourse through their critical insight on gender and sexual oppression. He notes black heterosexual men's silence on these subjects as the primary purpose for his conception for a collection of essays about them. Citing what he perceives as the key reasons for the silence of heterosexual black males on gender and sexuality in antiracist discourse, Carbado builds a convincing case for the necessity of black men's pro-feminist profession. He attributes four reasons for black antiracist silence on gender and sexuality: "1) the gendered construction of Black racial victimhood, [a by-product of] *intentional and functional sexism* [*sic*]; 2) the heterosexist construction of

Black victimhood; 3) the antiracist normalization of hetero-male identity; and 4) the linguistic limitations of identity terminology—that is, the extent to which race, gender, and sexuality operate as distinct identity signifiers; each linguistically submerges the others" (3).

Arguing against the "compartmentalization" of struggle, Carbado decries its formulation as rooted in a separatist ideology that contributed to a failure of political mobilization: "Black civil rights efforts often are not connected to women's civil rights efforts, which often are not connected to gay and lesbian civil rights efforts" (3). While Carbado does not claim that the essays in this volume constitute a feminist text (though many of the contributors do identify themselves as feminist or write from that perspective necessarily), he clearly couches them within an extended argument around the issues that would shape its contents. In "Straight Out of the Closet: Men, Feminism, and Male Heterosexual Privilege" (the epilogue), focusing mainly on what he conceives as the project of the black-male-feminist critic, he acknowledges Michael Awkward and Luke Harris's theoretical work on black-male-feminist criticism. Noting the critical import of self-reflexivity in any black male profession of feminism, Carbado points to it as the thematic center of Awkward's essay, in which Awkward "suggest[s] that Black male feminist acts must begin by interrogating what it means to be a Black man in a gendered and racialized social context. That is, Black men should be self-referential, examining and being critical of the ways in which they benefit from androcentric norms" (Carbado 1999b, 359).

As much as he is concerned about theorizing the aims of feminist criticism articulated by black men, Carbado is even more concerned about the privileges inherent in the social construction of (male) heterosexuality. In several key sections of the epilogue, Carbado (drawing on the antiracist/antisexist work of Peggy McIntosh) defines and identifies male and heterosexual privilege through lists he creates. It is, however, the forty-one-point list he formulates on heterosexual privilege (440–42) that provides an insightful experiential base for identifying heteronormative behavior. Carbado moves beyond just identifying male and heterosexual privileges and challenges the reader to act against them: "My purpose in constructing the 'identity privilege' lists is to suggest that identity privilege should be self-referentially contested. We have to remake ourselves if we are to remake our institutions. We cannot hope to institutionalize our political commitments unless we localize our politics" (442–43). Just as Michael Awkward's germinal essay "A Black Men's Place in Feminist Criticism" should be required reading on the problematic of black male feminism, for anyone (black males in particular) investigating the racialized politics of gender and sexuality in the context of heterosexual privilege Devon Carbado's essay is indisputably necessary reading.

While they were not linked directly to a pro-feminist/womanist agenda, new gender-progressive works on black masculinity by black men emerged in the 1990s. The complex interrogation of black masculinity significantly enlarges the critical range of studies related to black men, particularly as they seek to demystify the myth of black machismo and the monolithic image of black manhood. There is a glaring absence of the subject in the history of U.S.-dominant cultural readings of masculinity (as related to white male identity), and these new works embody the work of black male gender progressivism. They include *Are We Not Men? Masculine Anxiety and the Problem of African-American Identity* (1996) by Philip Brian Harper, Maurice O. Wallace's *Constructing the Black Masculine: Identity and Ideality in African American Men's Literature and Culture, 1775–1995* (2002), and *Manning the Race: Reforming Black Men in the Jim Crow Era* (2004) by Marlon B. Ross.

According to its coeditors, Rudoph Byrd and Beverly Guy-Sheftall, *Traps: African American Men on Gender and Sexuality* "is the first anthology that historicizes the writings by African American men who have examined the meanings of the overlapping categories of race, gender, and sexuality . . ." (Byrd and Guy-Sheftall 2001, xiii). While calling into question the racial grounds of *Men in Feminism* (one of the earliest critiques of pro-feminist male identity), Byrd and Guy-Sheftall maintain that "[t]he first imperative [of *Traps*] is to contest and dispel the notion that African American men have not supported nor have had any engagement with feminism" (xiv). They correct the erroneous claim that white men were the only long-standing male advocates of women's rights. What makes *Traps* so powerful as a self-proclaimed, feminist-identified text relies upon two things: (1) Beverly Guy-Sheftall's coeditorship as a black woman feminist (considering her record of publications and commitment to black gender-progressive politics) and (2) Rudolph Byrd's concept for a model of radical black masculinity based upon a mythic figure in African American folklore—"High John the Conqueror." As stated earlier, Byrd begins *Traps* with a prologue that defines "a mode of masculinity" in "the tradition of John." Enumerating the attributes of the tradition, he articulates seven characteristics to delineate it. Many of its qualities directly echo those Alice Walker conceives as typical of a feminist of color.

The tradition of John promotes "a mode of masculinity for Black men who are committed to the liberation and survival whole of black people." It is characteristic of a "mannish[ness]"—"[o]ften referring to bodacious, defiant, willful, and risky behavior, as in 'He's smell himself' or 'You trying to be grown.'" Similar to the sexual politics that defines the vision of a womanist, in this mode of masculinity there is an acknowledged affinity for the "Spirit." Love is a key element in men's relationship to other men "sexually and/or nonsexually." There exists a love of women "sexually and/or nonsexually." A man in the tradition of John "loves children, ancestors, and difference [itself]." Moreover, he is a lover of "creativity, song, and dance." He is "free, as in 'I ain't worried about that' . . . [c]ommitted to coalitions, but capable of independent action. Nonviolent, but capable of self-defense." The mode of masculinity "John" represents is anchored in an impressive list of personal and social values, including "tenderness," "justice," "freedom," and "peace." The thing that most defines the radical nature of the tradition of John is its standpoint on the experience of multiple oppression (Byrd 2001a, 1–2). What ties Byrd's imaginative and visionary rewriting of the black masculinity script to the projects of *Representing Black Men* and *Black Men on Race, Gender, and Sexuality* is that all the editors would generally agree that the tradition of John offers a revolutionary "mode of masculinity for Black men who are committed to the abolition of racism, sexism, homophobia, and other ideological traps" (Byrd 2001a, 2)—traps that have kept us bound to the falsehood of black machismo, I would add. Convincingly, Rudolph Byrd imaginatively envisions a "mode of masculinity" embodied in the tradition of John that not only is the masculine complement to the womanist vision of Walker, but also offers black men a discursive space to reimagine themselves—beyond the bounds of their past.

Transgressing the Religious Boundaries of My Past

Telling students I was a preacher, an ordained "elder" in a black Pentecostal church, was critical for the success of the pedagogy I practiced. I revealed it not simply as a point of interest but as way of allowing students to come to an understanding of the impact of religious conservativism in my struggle to embrace progressive notions of gender and sexuality. Some students would refer jokingly to my "preaching style" in the classroom. For many years, I struggled to make the antiracist pedagogy of black feminists emotionally and spiritually relevant to students in my classes. It did not represent a veiled attempt to proselytize but rather a strategic opportunity to stretch the boundaries of intellectual inquiry—particularly for students interested in education for self-recovery. Aaronette White's concept of feminism enabled me to understand that in black feminist vision of holistic teaching, the secular and sacred are rooted in the inherent value of the whole being, in being well. According to White, "Feminism is a spiritual response to how one should treat women, other men, and children."[2]

Embracing feminism (conceived by black women) as a spiritual response to domination ran counter to my religious upbringing. I grew up serving and teaching in black Pentecostal churches most of my life. I did not grow up learning about feminism. Conceptualizing feminism as a spiritual response dismantles the myth that spiritual power is patriarchal, ordained as the province of males only. Yet, the simple but deeply moving definition of feminism Aaronette White offers above implicitly embodies principles of human conduct I learned as a child in church. Even in the midst of church teaching rooted in patriarchy, I learned the meaning of love, faith, and compassion. Today, I practice feminist thinking founded upon these ideals—not those predicated upon male supremacy.

I situate my profession as a pro-feminist educator in the tradition of feminist black women and men (including Frederick Douglass and Alexander Crummell) who fashioned themselves as "preachers" of human rights. Maria Miller Stewart, Sojourner Truth, Harriet Tubman, Julia A. Foote, and Nannie Burroughs—all professed a providential calling in support of black people's humanity, rights for black women, and rights for women of all races and classes. According to Beverly Guy-Sheftall, these black women represent "important foremothers for a cadre of contemporary womanist theologians" (Guy-Sheftall 1995, 51). Moreover, having long ago established an ideological link between feminist political struggle and spiritual vocation in the service of human rights, they secured a historical foundation for the academic and spiritual *callings* I have answered.

In my struggle to teach black feminist antiracist studies, I promote (1) a love for education as the practice of social justice; (2) faith that pedagogy founded upon it will transform students' social consciousness; and (3) compassion for students' self-recovery process, for many of them confront internalized wounds of racism and (hetero)sexism. The prime goal of the memoir-writing classes I teach is to show that education can be liberatory for the mind, body, *and* spirit. bell hooks's belief in holistic learning for self-actualization has deeply influenced my vision of antiracism in the classroom. Writing about students' desire for holistic education, hooks writes in *Teaching to Transgress*: "There are times when I walk into classrooms overflowing with students who feel terribly wounded in their psyches (many of them see therapists), yet I do not think that want therapy from me. They want an education that is healing to the uninformed, unknowing spirit. They do want knowledge that is meaningful. They rightfully expect that my colleagues and I will not offer them information without addressing the connection between what they are learning and their overall life experiences" (1994, 19). As early as I can remember, even as conservative as my religious upbringing was, the church was a place of personal affirmation, a sanctuary, a haven. As I grew older, it became a place of emotional refuge from experiences of racism and the mean-spirited black boys who tormented me in junior high school. In church, I received awards for being different from boys like them. There, most adults (particularly older ones) praised my quietness, politeness, intelligence, and God-fearing obedience. For all of the ways being a "church boy" contributed to my outsider gender status at school, the black churches I grew up in provided me with a spiritual foundation rooted in gender and racial compassion. As far back as I can remember, at the church I attended from age six to sixteen, my grandmother and other "mothers" of the church told me that I would grow up to be a "preacher." In the Gaines Street Church of God (that many years later my father would pastor), I served as a Sunday school teacher and superintendent, choir member, and performer of any other duty bestowed upon me. In the eyes of the small congregation, my service was all about preparation for the day I would preach the gospel. Suffice it to say, the "saints" adored me—in spite of my vocal (but always polite) resistance to the prophetic calling they had lovingly imposed upon me. The older I got, the more the church became a refuge from black boy culture in junior high school *and* the reality of domestic violence at home.

At the all-black elementary and junior high schools I attended—it was still years before education became integrated in my hometown—life was torturous most of the time. Much of what being a part of that culture represented was considered sinful in church: the church prescribed no participation in "worldly" activities (movies, games, any socially questionable outings) and no relationship with girls that could possibly compromise its religious values. As a church kid, I stayed to myself. However, being a "church boy" at school was a major negative in black boy school culture. I tried to survive in it, but it took a devastating toll on my gender self-esteem. I was not a normal boy; I did not do things other boys did—play ball (of any sort), swear, "feel" up girls. So these were the origins of the "black boy outsider identity" imposed upon me. Yet being a boy outsider had as much to do with the experience of violence at home as did my failing the test of hetero-boy-masculinity at school. Over the course of a decade (from the time I was six to the time I was sixteen), my younger brother and I witnessed my father's violent abuse of our mother. In the mind of defenseless children, living with his abuse of her was like taking the eye-blackening, nose-bloodying, hard-knuckled punches ourselves.

To counteract the psychic blows of witnessing the violence my father inflicted upon our mother I withdrew into the world of happy white families on television—*Ozzie and Harriet, My Three Sons, Father Knows Best*, and *The Brady Bunch*. In the all-white world, the *good* white father represented in these sitcoms never resorted to physical abuse at home. TV land also became another place of escape from boy culture. For the most part, until I left home for college at seventeen, home was a self-imposed prison. Outside of school and church-related activities, I had little social interaction with boys my age—black or white. Growing up in a home of family violence further excluded me from experiences of "normal" boyhood. As the older of two sons, I witnessed the abuse in ways my brother did not. I lived in paralyzing fear that any one of the violent episodes would lead to our mother's death. I had no time to be a boy; I had to be a witness. Even when having become physically strong enough as a teenager to combat my father's abusive behavior, I was so afraid of his power as a man that no physical force of my own could intervene against his violent temper. All I could do was witness—silently. I could have told someone but never did. I never told anyone—it was our family's shameful secret. When not in school or at church, I was at home. I had to be. I had to be at home when it happened—when he killed her.

Growing up, I remember there being few boys my age in church before I started going to White Lily, the Pentecostal church my mother joined when I was sixteen. The kids I grew up with before this time were girl cousins—a slew of them. Until we were preteens, our gender difference was not an issue with them or with me. Until junior high school, we did not think much about girl/boy dichotomies. We simply loved being with each other, doing a lot of dumb kid stuff. In church we were just a big clan of kid cousins, brothers, and sisters—singing, performing plays for Christmas, reciting poems and passages from the Bible for Easter. At sixteen, my brother and I left the Church of God to go with our mother, who had gotten "saved" (given her life to Christ) at White Lily (across town).

Away from my girl cousins for the first time in my life, I began to retreat further into a TV world of white sitcoms (where nothing really bad ever happened to white people) and the world of a new black Pentecostal church, which featured shouting, speaking in unknown tongues, and fiery preaching from the pulpit. With it came also a community where dogmatic prescription was everything—particularly about outer appearance. Females could not wear pants, lipstick, nail polish, or short dresses or skirts. There was to be absolutely no liquor drinking or cigarette smoking, and no attendance at movie theaters. More noes than yesses. The dress code for males was not as rigidly policed as the one for females, but the same legalism applied to both sexes when it came to moral conduct. While in small ways I protested this new hyperreligious experience, church continued to be a place of hiding from the life of black males my age. At White Lily, there were also very few black males my age. It did not matter. The church on Gaines Street had been a haven from the punitive imposition of black masculine culture in my life, and what counted most was that the new Pentecostal church also functioned as a sanctuary for a male outsider like me.

Apart from its rigid dress and moral codes, in the Pentecostal church there were few explicitly heteromasculinist rules to follow—which was ironic, considering it was steeped in patriarchal dicta. As long as it was kept in the closet (and the church unaware of it), any man could be a "nonpracticing" homosexual. In fact, there exists a "Don't ask, don't tell" policy on homosexuality in many black Pentecostal churches. From the congregation, to the choir, to the pulpit—one's sexuality only becomes an issue if you choose to make it one. I grew up having internalized, oppressive religious beliefs on sexuality rooted in belief in the evils of sex (outside marriage) and homosexuality. These were not healthy attitudes toward sexuality, and I look back on the formative years in church (before the age of eighteen) as the most harmful period of religious indoctrination in my entire life. I learned that too much education would lead one away from the church, that sexual desire was evil, that women were inferior to men, and that homosexuals and lesbians were damned. I was a "church boy" growing up in a black religious, sexually repressive environment. But upon the advent of school integration, I was bused to a high school that was mostly white, and as a "black" student experiencing the subtle (and overt) racial inculcation of white supremacy, I adapted. I was a black boy forced to fit into both cultures. Having grown up in an all-black heteromasculinist culture until age fifteen, ill equipped to pass the black male test, I rejected black masculinity as a punitive form of gender identity. By the age of eighteen, I was also a black boy who had experienced ten years of domestic violence. Like the black male protagonist of Ralph Ellison's celebrated novel, I had come to see myself as an "invisible man." While I quickly learned *to pass as a smart white student* in high school (as a black student desperately trying to rise above the racist stigma of blackness), no one *really* knew or saw me for who I was— a deeply wounded black boy.

Aaronette White's concept of feminism as a spiritual response to a culture of male supremacist ideas of manhood embodies much potential for also formulating a model of black male self-recovery linked to inner healing. Being committed to a liberatory vision of black male spiritual recovery, a commitment integrally connected to my work as a professor of black feminism in the classroom, has enlarged its pedagogical scope and social imperative. The viability of black male feminism resides in its proactive engagement in revolutionary, antisexist principles of social change for all peoples. From this standpoint, gender-progressive black men's commitment to feminism grounds itself in a politics of social agency that defies the myth of black machismo. Thinking about feminism as "a spiritual response to how one should treat women, other men, and children" allowed me to integrate the seemingly irreconcilable differences between the feminist pedagogy I practice and the Pentecostal background that challenges it.

Worlds apart—one white, the other black. One secular, the other religious. One purportedly progressive, the other unabashedly conservative. For years, I traversed these two dramatically different worlds. One was symbolized by my status as a black professor in a private, majority-white college in Greenwich Village, New York City, known for its history of sexual liberation. The other world was represented by my experience as a minister and cofacilitator of an addiction recovery program in a black Pentecostal church located in the majority-black-and-Latino Tenth Ward of Newark, New Jersey, where I served for six years. Every Wednesday after teaching classes in one of Manhattan's most celebrated neighborhoods, I traveled by train and a bus to get to the recovery meeting at the church in (what was at one time) one of Newark's poorest neighborhoods. Over time, as a leader and member of the recovery group, I came to understand that the soul-searching work we did in our sessions was very similar to the work I required students to do in memoir-writing classes I taught at school. In both environments, through the discourse of self-critical autobiographical reflection, individuals were learning how to "deal, feel, and heal" (a common phrase in twelve-step recovery-based programs) from inner wounds of race, gender, class, and sexuality.

Race and class differences represented stark contrasts between the mostly economically privileged, young, majority-white college students I taught in Greenwich Village and the older, mostly poor, underclass black women and men in the recovery group in Newark. Yet memoir writing united both groups. Teaching memoir writing and being a participant/leader in writing for self-inventory in my recovery group, I confronted years of silence about being a race and gender outsider. Working in a self-recovery program with low-income women and men over the last few years, I have become increasingly conscious of the striking racial and class inequalities of the white and black worlds I inhabit. One thing I am clear about is that writing for self-transformation is healing for individuals in both settings, regardless of our differences. As asserted in the introduction, I maintain that autobiographical writing at the center of pedagogy conceptualized to confront racism and (hetero)sexism can be a powerful tool for self-liberation in the college classroom.

Twenty years ago, before I began seriously studying black feminist thought, I could not have imagined that I would become a feminist professor. I think of my work in the college classroom as a life's *calling*—beyond my academic training. As such, my commitment to teaching for social justice is at once personal, political, and spiritual. It continuously calls me to

- challenge my religious upbringing: to reject a patriarchal worldview, to stand against the belief that women (as the "weaker sex") should be governed by the dictates of men, and to oppose all forms of heteronormative masculinity and manhood, whether or not grounded in religious dogma, black masculinist cultural, or social ideology that promotes the subjugation of women;
- defy the idea that black men should not embrace feminist ideas of masculinity and manhood in fear of effeminization; and
- resist the notion that the academic, secular classroom is not a place for self-recovery practice associated with emotional and spiritual healing, in part by asserting its value in intellectual inquiry, particularly in my approach to teaching memoir writing.

On the grounds stated above, I defend the practice of black male feminist professorship. Based upon them, the next chapter functions as a pedagogical overview to reveal the personal and political themes of self-recovery that run through the autobiographical narratives of part 2 and the classroom case studies that comprise part 3.

❧ 2 ❧

A *Calling* of the Heart and Spirit

Becoming a Feminist Professor;
The Proof Is in the Pedagogy

When professors bring narratives of their experiences into classroom discussions it eliminates the possibility that we can function as all-knowing, silent interrogators. *It is often productive if professors take the first risk, linking confessional narratives to academic discussions so as to show how experience can illuminate and enhance our understanding of academic material. But most professors must practice being vulnerable in the classroom, being wholly present in mind, body, and spirit.* (Emphasis added)

—bell hooks

Despite the historic public "professions" black male feminists have made in the last ten years in amazing articles and books, there exists no extensive discourse specifically about the work many of us do as black male "professors" of feminism in the classroom. While Lisa Delpit and Beverly Daniel Tatum have written in a masterly way on the subject of the black pedagogue, bell hooks, herself a noted black feminist educator, has asserted that while perspectives in pedagogical studies have become more diverse, there remains a noticeably small number of progressive educators of color writing about teaching. I speak in solidarity with black, male, gender-progressive educators actively opposing racism, (hetero)sexism, and homophobia outside heteronormative notions of black masculinity. Being black men who profess feminism as a strategic site for becoming less manly in traditional patriarchal ways, toward becoming more radically self-possessed, necessitates our talking about how feminism works in our lives. What constitutes the feminist work we do? Where does it happen? Many of us are teachers—professors in some of the nation's most elite colleges and universities. What do we do as pro-feminist, black male professors in the classrooms in which we teach? How do we promote feminism in these spaces?

This chapter is about the *calling* that led me to become a "professor" of feminism and how I practice it in the classroom. As the introduction clarifies, teaching black feminist thinking that confronts white supremacy—primarily linked to a critique of sexism and heterosexism—enabled me to conceptualize memoir writing as a strategy for self-recovery in the classroom. In this vision, it becomes a site of *personal* and *political* transformation through autobiographical writing where students learn to interrogate the institutionalization of white supremacist ideology and patriarchal thinking in their own life experiences. Memoir-writing pedagogy formulated in black feminist thinking can be a powerful tool for en(gendering) critical race consciousness for students *and* teachers in the classroom—across differences of gender, race, sexuality, and class. As an African Americanist primarily focused on literary studies, and calling into question racism rooted in white superiority, I developed my approach to antiracist pedagogy employing a genre in black fiction known as the "novel of passing" and the discourse of autobiography by black feminists (both female and male).

This chapter not only serves as a pedagogical overview for the "classroom case studies" that comprise part 3 but also serves to represent the theoretical influence African American narratives of racial passing have had on enlarging my vision for the transforming power of "trans"identity politics. A transidentity politic defies boundaries, borders of separation, and simplistic either/or categorization. Destabilizing ideas of white superiority, the idea (and reality) of "black" people crossing the color line (*passing* as white) underscores the performativity of identity. Passing across lines of race, gender, and sexuality opens up radical space for a discussion for something we may begin to theorize as border-crossing masculinity—masculinity that defies heteronormative male identity, while transgressing the boundaries of patriarchal thinking. Many semesters, over the years of teaching the Novel of (Racial) Passing as a course at the college, I came to learn from transgender students that critical connections could be made between racial and gender identities across the boundaries of genetic and social construction. I found that the problematics of "trans"racial identity explored in the fiction were in many ways similar (although not identical) to those encountered in the experiences of transgender students. The idea of crossing race, gender, and boundaries of sexuality in the classroom as an oppositional standpoint proved a provocative approach to feminist antiracism through the politics of "black" identity. Formulating a radical approach to teaching antiracism that was not only about "thinking black" but also about "thinking feminist" came with my introduction to the memoir-writing style of bell hooks, as the pedagogical narratives to follow in this chapter will demonstrate.

As a black feminist theorist, critic, and teacher, bell hooks has been the single most important influence in my development as a professor of feminism. Her memoir-writing style was the catalyst for my vision of teaching autobiographical composition as a strategy for self-recovery. Her work in *Feminist Theory: From Margin to Center* compelled my rejection of patriarchal thinking. As she has in much of her own autobiographical writings, in this chapter I weave together "professional" concerns with confessional narratives to reveal the challenges of being a feminist professor who is a black man. The task requires, as I have said, that I break silence about my ongoing personal struggle for self-liberation. Letting go years of internalized patriarchal thinking rooted in religious dogma, I embrace a higher *calling* that promotes education as the practice of social justice.

Feminist Theory and Black Male Confessions

It was in 1986 that I read a feminist text for the first time. It was *Feminist Theory: From Margin to Center*. It changed my ideas about the relevance of feminism for black men. Like shelter from a violent storm, it covered me, providing me a place of safe haven from the body-bruising torrents of gender and racial oppression that had nearly drowned me in their fury. *Feminist Theory* gave me a place to stand, a place *to become* a different form of man.

Before reading *Feminist Theory*, I was a black man full of internalized racial and gender rage, without a way to get at the root cause of the anger that possessed me; I had no way to analyze how the years of being a black boy outsider had wounded me. The invitation *Feminist Theory* offered men initiated a transformative process of self-recovery from which much of the memoir writing in this book emerged. bell hooks's idea that men could be "comrades" of feminism led me on an internal journey of self-examination, not only of being a black man in a culture of white supremacy but also of being a black male subsumed in a (hetero)sexist and misogynist culture. "Could men actually become feminists?" was a question I had often asked myself in the early days of my search for black men who advocated feminism. *Feminist Theory* makes a powerful call for men's participation in feminist struggle to end sexism. hooks strategically underscores the political necessity of white people's involvement in antiracist struggle.

> After hundreds of years of anti-racist struggle, more than ever
> before non-white people are currently calling attention to the

primary role white people must play in anti-racist struggle. *The same is true of the struggle to eradicate sexism—men have a primary role to play. This does not mean that they are better equipped to lead feminist movement; it does mean that they should share equally in resistance struggle. In particular, men have a tremendous contribution to make to feminist struggle in the area of exposing, confronting, opposing, and transforming the sexism of their male peers.* (hooks 1984, 81; emphasis added)

Not only does hooks reaffirm my belief in the possibility of men as "comrades in [feminist] struggle" (67), she reminds me of the crucial necessity of nonwhite people "calling attention to the primary role white people must play in anti-racist struggle." She has consistently called for strategic alliance in antiracist and feminist struggles. In *Feminist Theory*, hooks showed me that being black and being feminist were not ideological opposites. As this book seeks to reveal, black feminist thinking offers gender-progressive, black male professors a radical mode of being for challenging patriarchy and white supremacy in our classroom professions. The stories of our work as pro-feminist "brothers" in the college classroom has yet to be told.

Black Feminist Theory in Practice

The first memoir-writing course I taught at the college in 1993 was based on bell hooks's book *Talking Back: Thinking Feminist, Thinking Black* (1989). It served as the primary text for the class. Designed for first-year students, it was called "Writing from Margin to Center: bell hooks and the Political Essay." In hooks's slender volume of personal essays about the politics of feminism and race in her life, I discovered a form of memoir writing that connected feminist thinking with antiracist politics, and I also discovered that it represented an amazing tool for teaching writing for social justice. The formulation "thinking feminist, thinking black" enabled me to politicize my pedagogy focused on the relationship between gender and race. In a class of fifteen students eleven of the students were white females. The effectiveness of the memoir-writing strategy had to do with students' willingness to "talk back" to racism related to white supremacy, sexism, and homophobia. It was this class that first ignited my passion for teaching black feminist antiracism. I found in *Talking Back* a well of pedagogical possibility. After teaching it as a model for memoir writing in 1993, I incorporated it as a composition strategy in all my courses. Insisting that white students and students of color talk and write about dehumanizing effects of racialization in class discussions and in their memoir writing relied on two things: (1) the willingness of students to disclose (most often) intensely painful experiences, and (2) the critical maturity of students to interpret them critically and to share their analysis of them publicly in class.

Black feminist focus on the interrelation of domination serves as the foundation for the pedagogy I practice—precisely because it links a critique of patriarchy not only to female oppression, but also to the experience of heterosexism and homophobia in the lives of gay, lesbian, and transgender persons. Black feminist opposition to separatist projects to end women's oppression represents a visionary opportunity for *all* men to become gender-progressive allies in antidomination struggle. One of the principles of contemporary black feminist thought is cited in the founding statement (1974) of the Combahee River Collective (the Boston contingent of the National Black Feminist Organization, started in 1973). Radical in conception and visionary in focus, the statement's opposition to lesbian separatist politics and biological determinism promotes an inclusive politics for uniting (black) people struggling against race, gender, class, or sexual forms of domination. With stunning clarity, it argues the critical necessity of having black women and men together oppose sexism:

> Although we are feminists and Lesbians, we feel solidarity with progressive Black men and do not advocate the fractionalization that white women who are separatists demand. Our situation as Black people necessitates that we have solidarity around the fact of race, which white women of course do not need to have with white men, unless it is their negative solidarity as racial oppressors. We struggle together with Black men against racism, while we also struggle with Black men about sexism. We realize that the liberation of all oppressed peoples necessitates the destruction of the political-economic systems of capitalism and imperialism as well as patriarchy. (Combahee River Collective [1974] 1983, 275–76)

Black women and black men working together to oppose all forms of domination in and outside our communities—across our gender and sexual differences—undermines a masculinist vision of black liberation as the struggle against racism alone. In solidarity, black people opposing all forms of oppression ensures that our fight for self-determination is not trapped in sexist and homophobic dogma.

The statement above speaks to the visionary power of black feminist thinking. Voicing it in an all-white classroom, I wondered how much of its liberatory power resonated with the students hearing it. What stake did they imagine themselves having in the liberation of black people, especially when my critique of white supremacy implicated them as white people? Of what self-transformative value was it to them? Was its position of political inclusiveness lost on them? Many white students felt threatened by my emphasis on a critique of white privilege and insistence on the recognition of race in progressive feminist analysis of gender and sexual domination. While many felt that feminist focus on race, racism, and white privilege made the classroom an unsafe space for intellectual inquiry, there were those white students (and students of color) I taught who realized that black feminist, antiracist pedagogy was, indeed, liberatory also for them. In a classroom where white supremacy and heteronormative notions of gender and sexual identity were continually being called into question, no one was safe from critical interrogation—not even me. As the classroom case studies illustrate, many students viewed it as a critical site for the development of race consciousness, as well as a strategic location for resisting domination with and without white identity. Black feminist thinking could be a place for white students to free themselves from the myth of white superiority and the burden of being unable to live up to heteropatriarchal ideas of white identity.

From the time I began teaching at the college in 1991, white students (more often than not) enrolled in my classes not only with little or no insight into the history of black resistance to white supremacy, but also with no knowledge of its connection to black women's opposition to sexism and heterosexism inside and outside their own communities. I raise the issue here, early in the book, because it remained an issue during the entire time I taught at the college. I do not subscribe to the belief that one must experience oppression or domination to "truly" understand it. Many white students studying with me critically and emotionally connected to the history of black antiracist movement in the United States. But what was the impact of my pedagogy on students of color? Students of color—and black female students, in particular—enrolling in classes I taught usually possessed sophisticated knowledge of black feminist politics. I was especially interested in their views on sexism, heterosexism, misogyny, and homophobia in black communities.

I would not be totally truthful, however, about my experience teaching black feminist thought in a majority-white college without expressing feelings of disappointment and loss each time I walked into a classroom (at the beginning of a semester) to face a room of all white faces. Yet, my unwavering belief in the transforming value of black feminist thinking in a white classroom kept me coming back to it. I had to believe my pedagogy was making a difference to both students of color and white students. My faith in black feminist radical vision of political inclusion never waned.

(En)Gendering a Critique of Race, Unlearning Whiteness

Against a history of black machismo fixed in homophobic notions of masculinity, we black men professing feminist beliefs have begun to speak for ourselves, defying the long-standing masculinist, nationalist rhetoric that black liberation would only come when we regained our manhood. Profeminist black men have refused to fix the dreams of male liberation on the misguided notion that racism is the most salient problem facing blacks today. Rather, as we have learned from black women feminists (many who have actually taught and mentored us in college and universities across the country or who are our blood relations or life partners), sexism, heterosexism, and homophobia are among the most pressing problems in black communities all over the nation. Black women feminists have challenged us black men of conscience to speak in our own voices in defense of rights for *all* females to live free from gender, class, sexist, misogynist, physical, emotional, mental, and sexual exploitation and violation. This book is a case in point. Black men educating others for the eradication of sexism, while confronting whiteness and heterosexism, contests all forms of black masculinity that support a politics of domination that attaches our manhood to a homophobic view of the world.

Considering the fact that white females often predominate or are the sole constituents of classes I teach on black feminism, issues of gender bound up in race are always controversial. Since most of the white female students in my classes are feminist-identified, and many do not identify as heterosexual, on the surface a white-female-feminist classroom would seem conducive to a feminist approach to memoir writing. However, it is precisely the racial component of my pedagogy that is a continual source of tension. A black feminist approach to gender oppression inherently deals with the subject of race. In this context, my body is the signifier of race. It stands in a multitude of complex and shifting ways that complicates the classroom dynamic. As a racially conscious black male professor, my feminist thinking on gender is largely colored by race. Thus, in a majority-white (or all-white-female) college classroom, my approach to teaching memoir writing for "unlearning whiteness" is full of tension at every turn, especially when it requires students to examine whiteness from a confessional standpoint.

While teaching black literature at the University of Delaware some years ago, I had my students read Langston Hughes's collection of short stories entitled *The Ways of White Folk* (1933). To my surprise, one of the black women students in the class shared with the class and me that taking the book to her place of employment was not a good idea. One of her coworkers accused of her of being racist because of the book's title. Why is it that when black people speak about "white folk" in the company of people who are white, they accuse us of being racist? On the surface, it would not seem likely that a black-authored book about white people's "ways" would provoke such a response. Yet in a culture where white people do not routinely recognize themselves as *white*, any mention of the term as a racial inscription (by blacks or any other person of color) would normally create tension (in whites). Why is this? In a culture of white supremacy, whiteness performs as the ultimate sign of neutrality, fairness, equality, justice, the "American Way."

For some years, I have noted that white students and students of color have become more defensive in my "race classes" when the discussion of race shifts to *whiteness* (related to "the ways of white folk") and white supremacy. White students, particularly white males (who typically drop my class after the first week or so), object to talking about whiteness and white supremacy on the grounds that these are terms associated with racists and the Ku Klux Klan. Few students come to my classes at the beginning of a semester understanding the systemic nature of white supremacist thinking, in which we are all implicated. Even students of color have accused me of targeting white people by unfairly picking on them in the critiques of racism and white privilege I advance. Even in a majority-white liberal college, many white students (and sometimes students of color) who take my classes are terrified even to talk about race at all. Teaching that interrogates ways of *being white* related to "white skin privilege" can sometimes feel that way for students unaccustomed to thinking about whiteness as a racial signifier. Actually, the same is true for those students who spend a lot of time thinking about it. They are more willing to talk openly about their racial fears. Considering the fact that antiracism is not widely taught as a course of study in higher education, one would be hard put to find many college students adept in the subject. As white people learn their entire lives how to be racist through white supremacist thinking, they (as well as people of color) must unlearn it.

The reality is that in a culture of white supremacy, colonized people of color—just like racially unconscious white people—are central to its existence. Students of color and white students unlearning whiteness discover ways that colonization makes us all complicit in the perpetuation of white supremacist idea(l)s. None can claim immunity. Many students of color have rejected my approach to antiracism, claiming that I pander to white students. As the voices of white students included in this text will prove, however, white students must bear their share of the burden of race—as they too confront internalized wounds of whiteness. I cannot deny that unlearning whiteness begins a painful process of decolonization for white students and students of color who enroll in the courses I teach. No student is exempt from the primary assignment the process requires. Few of my white students or students of color desire to remember painful wounds of racism, particularly in the context of a pedagogy that compels them to write from the inside out about its relation to wounds of sexism, heterosexism, classism, and homophobia. But this is precisely what memoir writing about race calls for in black feminist pedagogy.

Why Can't We All *Just* Get Along?
Would That It Were So Simple

Critically interrogating whiteness in a majority-white classroom compounds the experience for students of color—and not only racially. Discussions of gender, class, and sexuality are particularly challenging for students of color in a space dominated by white students. Teaching students of color in such an environment is risky. Some students of color courageously express their discomfort in class. Others share with me in conference how dispiriting a majority-white classroom can be—particularly when white students avoid talking candidly about race as a gesture of "political correctness."

For some white students in a liberal-white education environment, there exists a pervasive attitude that even to discuss *race* is racist. As a black male who has spent most of his education in majority-white schools on the margins of whiteness and heteronormative ideas of masculinity, I relate strongly to the feelings of marginalization and isolation students of color express. Often how they represent those feelings is largely determined by their perception of their white peers and of me (black, male, pro-feminist in a majority-white-female context).

My relationship with students of color in a majority-white classroom over the years has represented a complex and complicated negotiation of intraracial, gender, class, and cultural arrangements. In most instances, whiteness as an institutional power continually worked to undermine our relationships, instilling in students of color a grave mistrust for faculty of color. Students of color were often frustrated in my classes, and would say to me outside them, "We can never be who we really are in a majority-white classroom." I understood, more than I let on. As faculty and students of color in many majority-white colleges and universities, we must continually negotiate the boundaries of our "colored" identities among the white, intellectual ruling class in the "ivory tower."

I know that the life of the mind for many students of color in the white classroom is about much more than the course she or he signed up for; it is about survival in a classroom space where she or he may well be the only person of color. I can identify on another level. Even though I came to the college as a black professor with sixteen years of education in majority-white institutions (including three years of high school), I continued to feel ill at ease in a white classroom. That feeling has never left me. In fact, I always feel ill at ease in all white spaces. I cannot simply tell students of color to "get over it." What I do say to them (and to white students, too) is that teaching antiracism from a black feminist stand-point has enabled me to confront the personal demons of racism and sexism that haunt me. Students of color want to know how and why I remain in white institutions of higher learning. They want to know whether I really understand the nature of their plight as the "minority" in white-majority schools.

One of the most strident critiques of my pedagogy from students of color, and the one I most resist, is that it benefits white students the most. In a college where there are so few students of color, and even fewer in my classes, I cannot deny that it would seem that white students—as the overwhelming majority in my classes over the years—are indeed the main beneficiaries of my work in the classroom. However, in defense of black feminist pedagogy—as I have conceived it in a majority-white or all-white classroom—unlearning whiteness is not just for white people. Perhaps, this is what makes students of color who reject my approach to it so resistant to the notion that white supremacy is a system of ideas in which we— whites and nonwhites—are implicated. Some suggest that by situating antiracist pedagogy around a critique of whiteness and white supremacy, I place white students at its center.

In part, the criticism has merit. However, no matter how pedagog-ically skillful I have been in positioning myself in relation to race in the classroom (it is beyond my power to alter its racial makeup), the space has remained almost always dominated by the presence of white students. Many do not represent themselves as *white* students. En-abling them to experience critical opposition to whiteness as a signi-fier of self-empowerment is difficult. For many white students (who do not consider themselves racist) owning up to whiteness via white iden-tity while resisting/rejecting the privilege(s) associated with it (as a sig-nifier of racial superiority) is tantamount to admitting one's racism. Helping white students *and* students of color to understand how diffi-cult unlearning whiteness can be was always more challenging than I imagined.

It's All About Style: Writing to Provoke Progressive Critical Race Thinking

One of the most provocative writing assignments students engage in the memoir-writing courses I teach based upon bell hooks's writing style happens at the beginning of the semester. It entails their having to recollect in writing the earliest memory of being racialized. Drawing on this narrative in various ways during the term, they explore hooks's "autocritographical" method through a series of writing workshops (three or four, each in cycles of two-week/four-class-session periods) linked to the production of "style analysis" papers. The style analysis paper explores the various subjects hooks takes up. For example, she addresses such topics as the interrelation of race to her undergraduate education at Stanford and as a professor at Yale, white supremacy and the politics of drag for gay men of color, sexism and violence in intimate relationships, and homophobia in black communities. I structure each workshop around a subject taken from one or more of the style analysis papers. In the process of each two-week reading/writing cycle, students write their own auto(race)critography on the prescribed topic having emerged from that of the style analysis paper. It acts as an analytical reservoir to help students think critically about the social implications of the narratives they write.

As one of the three or four cycles we undertake, for example, a workshop might examine the issue of race and its relation to education. Thinking about the subject from hooks's feminist standpoint (illustrated in the style analysis paper), students render a personal narrative forged in critical resistance to the interrelated ways racialization in U.S. education practice perpetuates gender, class, and sexual oppression simultaneously. At the end of the first week of a writing workshop students will have produced at least two to three short style analysis papers and a memoir of race based on them. During the second week of the workshop, each student reads her or his memoir in class. Collaboratively, with assistance from a writing fellow assigned to the course, I establish writing groups (of three students each) in which students read and systematically critique one another's work outside and inside class. We begin a revision process leading to one or more drafts of the memoir (as needed). The revision stage is a critical step in students' understanding of the craft of composition—the rhetoric of its mechanics. Of the three to four autobiographies produced, students select one to develop into a longer or "extended" version as the culminating writing assignment in the course. The final draft of the memoir requires that its critical overlay be interfaced with other secondary sources to broaden the range of the students' analysis.

In memoir-writing classes, from first-year to advanced, students keep a "race journal." A critical/personal resource for composing the memoir of race, students' journal entries on race are the stuff from which the memoir emerges. As a preliminary requirement in the memoir-writing process, in theory, the journal would contain student accounts of racial experiences. Through the race journal, students begin to see, hear, feel, taste, and touch the ever-pervasive specter of race. I tell them this is a good thing, believing that a critical knowledge of the mechanics of racism is necessary to possess the power to dismantle it.

Through organized writing workshops inside and outside class, students work through the very difficult issues of disclosure, style, and form in crafting a racial memoir. Besides providing custom-made handouts and exercises to bring students into a critical understanding of the relationship between content, form, and craft, staff from the college writing center led sessions with us in our classroom space and scheduled group workshops with us in the writing center, each time providing a forum where students could talk candidly about issues they were encountering in the process. Among them, disclosure (to reveal or not, and to what depth) was paramount. Having white students and students of color talk about racial "secrets" was never easy. For some students, the fear of talking and writing personally about race never waned. If asked, these students would most likely say that *black* feminism is *not* for everyone.

Teaching the "Novel of (Racial) Passing" for the First Time

One of the first black literature courses I taught at the college was Female Representation in the Harlem Renaissance and the Novel of (Racial) Passing. I designed it as an introductory class for first-year students. It explored gender relations in novels by Nella Larsen, Jessie Fauset, and Wallace Thurman related to the theme of racial passing and the politics of skin color. In the class of fifteen, all the students were white and female except for two black females. While none of the students actually questioned my ability as a male professor to teach a course about female identity, the white female students called into question my emphasis on race in the texts we read. I remember clearly one class session well into the semester when several of them strongly took issue with a feminist critique of gender that focused "too much" on race. They told me that feminism was about gender, not race. Moreover, they challenged ways I "personalized" the readings by having them think about the implications of gender *and* race in their daily lives. The class was about literature, they informed me, not about their having to examine the novels and relate them to their personal lives. Caught off guard, I said very little in response, shifting the discussion back to the assigned reading. The class ended without further dialogue about the issue they raised.

At the beginning of the next class session, white female students confronted me, letting me know they had met as a group after the previous class to share their concerns about the way I had been teaching the course. They accused me of making the class unnecessarily difficult, and said that their lives outside of class had nothing to do with discussions of literary texts in class and that they found it altogether too emotionally frustrating and stressful. Whether or not the two black female students agreed with the charges, they remained silent. I did not question them to avoid the suggestion they had to side with me because of our shared racial identity. In summary, my response to the class was a reiteration of my objective stated in the syllabus: "to examine the race, gender, class, and sexual politics of the novels under consideration."

On another occasion in class, a discussion about Madam C. J. Walker's invention of the straightening comb turned into a heated debate. It began with my asking the two black women students their thoughts about "processed" hair as a standard of beauty for black females. Neither felt straightened hair was about adherence to a standard; it was a matter of personal taste, they said, and added that it was easier to manage. When I further pressed them to interrogate notions of individual taste and beauty norms associated with the dominant culture, class dynamics intensified. They showed discomfort in their voices, and I sensed they felt targeted. At this moment, white women students began to defend them, agreeing that straightened hair was, indeed, more manageable (based on their experience). Despite my further attempt to complicate our discussion, neither black nor white students agreed that female hair treatment has anything to do with race or cultural difference.

No one in class seemed to appreciate the fact that in white supremacist culture, Madam Walker could become a millionaire simply by inventing a "hot comb" to *de*naturalize black female hair. Would my argument have received better reception had I been female? Had the females in this class bonded across racial lines to spite me because of my gender, my race? As for the representation of race in the novels, had the students really believed that it made little difference in the lives of the interracial female characters they had studied all term? Did the students not understand the racist ideology at work in the decision these white-skinned/"black" females made to pass as white in the novels? Did they understand the myth of the "tragic mulatta" has as much to do with race as gender? Could they understand the link I made between black female oppression, whiteness, and white supremacy? After the semester had long ended, however, a campus rumor emerged from that course, a rumor I have been unable to squelch to this day—that my "race classes make white girls cry."

From that one class, I learned much about teaching African American literature in all-white or majority-white-female classrooms. One lesson I learned in particular guided me through all the classes on race I have taught at the college since then. It is that whiteness and white privilege operate together as a formidable force in a majority-white or all-white classroom. Based upon students' prior experience and/or a racist mythology about black males, when the professor is black and male, whiteness and white privilege determine whether his *race* and *gender* will materialize as a threat in the white female imagination. When female students of color have told me that my self-proclaimed feminist label makes my blackness and maleness less threatening to white females and my antiracist pedagogy more palatable to white students' taste, sometimes I agree. Over the years, white female students and female students of color have both demonized and defended me as a feminist. From the few white male and black male students who have taken my classes over time, I have received a similar response. Critical race pedagogy focused on whiteness makes most students I have taught feel threatened. The way female and male students of color respond to my pedagogy is similar to that of white students, but it poses a different set of challenges.

Looking back to the contentions that informed my first teaching experience at the college, I did not fully realize at the time how well black feminist pedagogy would serve the needs of the students taking my classes. Racism and sexism would not be the only sources of tension in them. On the one hand, its progressive curriculum and seminar-based pedagogy offers an educational sanctuary for white students and students of color seeking a more open and nontraditional college experience. On the other, its exclusiveness has much to do with the high cost of attending a private school. My "race classes" were often hotbeds of controversy. However, many students in them discovered a voice to speak to the complex and often contradictory nature of the identity politics they embodied. Because black feminist pedagogy is rooted in the notion of education as the practice of liberation, white students and students of color find black women's struggle against multiple oppression inspiring and self-transforming. Yet, at the same time, it silences many white female and male students.

White silence in the classroom speaks volumes about many white students' racial fears. It also reveals much about the racial blindness, naïveté, and sometimes willful ignorance they exhibit in relation to these fears. Examining students' reactions, I posted on the inside of my office door this statement (printed on a small black sticker with bold white letters): "The first rule of white club is not to speak about whiteness" (a play on a line in the movie *Fight Club*). For students of color and white students courageous enough to break out of "white club," confronting white silence in the classroom can be emotionally draining. Many white students having to speak or write about race fear being shut down by other white students or students of color—who in turn often feel they unfairly bear the burden of race talk. Rooted in complicated racial issues sometimes related to me or the antiracist nature of my pedagogy, white silence has even silenced me on occasion during a class. At times when it seemed to take the form of white student resistance to me, I have reaffirmed myself in the writings of the black feminists I teach. Whiteness does not disappear from the classroom simply because white students *and* students of color choose to ignore its presence. As stated earlier, my task in the classroom is to enable students to deconstruct it. In this way, black feminist pedagogy is a project of reconstruction. Counter to popular media representation, race is not an exploitable "card" to be pulled out as in a game of spades.

White students and students of color confronting white silence— breaking through the fear and anxiety that stand as a major obstacle to open dialogue about whiteness, its interrelation to white supremacy, and the ill effects of it on people of color *and* white people—is a dynamic process mutually beneficial to students and teacher. I have learned from working with some of my bravest students who write and talk back to whiteness; they have empowered my own struggle to break silence about the strongholds of internalized racism and (hetero)sexism in my own life.

("Trans")Racial Blues and the "Whiteness of Blackness"

"Brothers and sisters, my text this morning is the 'Blackness of Blackness.'"
"That blackness is most black, brother, most black . . ."
". . . black is . . ."; ". . . an' black ain't . . ."

—Ralph Ellison, *Invisible Man*

Another black literature text I used when I began teaching at the college was the prologue of Ralph Ellison's *Invisible Man*. It marked a pedagogical turning point for me, who had been educated or had taught in majority-white schools for over thirty years. Before teaching *Invisible Man*, I had not fully understood the power of African American literature as a tool against racism. It was from the novel's title character that I learned the signifying relationship between *blackness* and *whiteness*. The signifying trope of racial invisibility in a culture of white supremacy, the "invisible man" represents a *body* of contradictory (intersecting) racial signs—he is *black*, but at the same time he is *invisible*. He moves, speaks, and lives as a racial oxymoron—a slippage, a gap, a rupture on the fault line of color. The invisibility of his blackness is a disadvantage and an advantage simultaneously. It renders him faceless and nonexistent to whites, on the one hand. On the other, it allows him to "pass" over the color line.

To my mind, a "seen-but-not-seen" racial identity (enabling a "black" person to pass as white in the stereotypical, black/white paradigm of race in the United States) becomes a provocative location to theorize about racial passing and its potential as a launch site for writing against racism that promotes a pedagogy of racial healing. Several important questions arise in this consideration. Could whiteness exist without blackness, when it depends so much upon the Other for racial superiority? If blacks could (invisibly) pass for white, who would be black, the signifier of racial inferiority? Who could really, without a "shadow" of doubt, claim to be white? These questions from Ellison's tropical novel on the "blackness of blackness" would chiefly inform my conceptual thinking for the course I teach called The Whiteness of Blackness, the Blackness of Whiteness. It explores racial contradictions found in (bi)racial identity to expose the myth of white superiority, while calling out stereotypical falsehoods associated with blackness. The course does not purport or suggest that race mixing is the solution to racism. Rather, by focusing on the problematic of black/white, white/black racial dynamics in the formation of (bi)racial identity in the novel of passing it determines to get under the skin of racism—to the bone of the ideas that give it form.

In the service of antiracist teaching, the novel of passing becomes a power tool for critical race consciousness. I maintain that in the "novel of (racial) passing" (a well-known genre in African American fiction), it is always the biracial (black?) body (capable of passing as white) that contests the color line, that undermines notions of racial purity associated with whiteness. A pedagogy of antiracism grounded in a critique of whiteness (in a white or majority-white classroom) is risk-taking

> for the teacher and student. Despite its transformative possibilities for progressive antiracist education, teaching narratives of racial oppression often requires that we (black teachers in particular) bear the burden of the emotional fall-out such pedagogical strategizing causes in the classroom. Even white students claim-

ing to be antiracist exhibit anger, fear, guilt and resentment toward us and students of color when having to read stories of black people victimized by acts of white supremacy. On the other hand, students of color (and black students in particular) experiencing some of the same emotions display resentment toward white students, all white people, and us (especially if we are not black) for opening up the wounds of racism. But risk-taking in education practice focused on a critique of domination lies at the heart of transgressive pedagogies of race and gender grounded in feminist critique of racism and (hetero)sexism, defying the premise that the classroom ought to be a "safe" space for learning. (Lemons 1996a, 160)

In The Whiteness of Blackness, we read and write about five to seven novels, depending upon whether I offer it as a first-year writing class or as an upper-division literature course. The first of the selected novels, read in chronological order, is Harriet Wilson's *Our Nig* (1859, rpt. 1983), a "fictional autobiography." According to Henry Louis Gates, it is the transformation "of the black-as-object into the black-as-subject" Wilson represents in the novel that is the archetypal domain of the black woman writer. However, in addressing the theme of miscegenation in *Our Nig*, as well as the other novels we read, it is the very idea of the "black" object/subject that I ask students to question—particularly with regard to the biracial (subject/object) character. By whose definition of blackness should we consider the biracial individual "black"? If a (trans)racial character in a novel of passing can indeed cross the color line without detection, who has the right to refuse her or him? What does the "one-drop rule" have to do with any of this? (Historically, in white supremacist thinking on the subject of miscegenation, one drop of black blood in an individual would disqualify her or him from claiming white racial identity.) These, and many more, complex questions come up during the semester as we push against the boundaries of skin color, which are interrelated with gender, class, sexuality, the institution of slavery, and laws of racial segregation.

In each novel, students deconstruct the politics of the color line represented in the social construction of (bi)raciality, as the (in)visible signifier of racial transgression. Always attempting to get at the ideological apparatus that (con)figures the mixed-race body, we look everywhere for insightful clues. William Wells Brown's *Clotel or the President's Daughter* (1863), the next work we consider, is composed of two narratives. One is the story of the "quadroon" Clotel; the other, as the novel's preface, is Brown's own memoir of his life as a fugitive, racially mixed slave. We examine in it the political relationship between its author and the protagonist he creates. The remaining novels all feature an interracial main character confronting the harsh realities of the color line. They include *Autobiography of an Ex-Colored Man* (1912) by James Weldon Johnson; two Nella Larsen novels, *Quicksand* (1928) and *Passing* (1929); *Plum Bun* (1929) by Jessie Fauset; and *Black No More* (1931) by George Schuyler, published at the close of the Harlem Renaissance.

Black Leaves, Twigs, and Branches on White Family Trees

Through studying bi-raciality I have come to realize . . . the irony of the possibility that all "whites" may in fact be passing for "white" (according to racial laws still on the books in certain states that adhere to the "one drop of blood" theory). Thus, there may be few "Caucasians in the great republic who can trace their ancestry back ten generations and confidently assert that there are no Black leaves, twigs or branches on their family trees"—George Schuyler (author of *Black No More*).

—Anonymous student response

Contesting accepted ideas of white supremacy and patriarchy inherently poses an ideological threat to what many students hold as sacred. Pedagogy in critical opposition to racism and male supremacy necessarily (en)genders pain, especially when students have to confront the race and/or gender privilege they possess.

—Gary L. Lemons

When I first began teaching the novel of passing, I did not employ the term "transracial" to discuss the politics of color-line crossing in it. It would come some years later with the enrollment of transgender students in the course. In the essay, from which I excerpted this section, students and I employ "biraciality" to reference the subject of miscegenation in the texts.

Remembering the first writing assignment I gave at the beginning of that semester in which students were to explain why they enrolled in the course, one wrote, "I distinctly remember the response that I carefully composed: 'I was tired of talking about race issues in clichéd-revolutionary terms with Blackfolk or in politically correct safe-zones with whites.' I'm not tired anymore; I'm fatigued and weary. I can't get over, under, around or by the feeling that I'm saying the same thing over and over and no one's listening. . . . [S]omeone needs to tell the truth: we ain't moved and things ain't changing and we sure ain't saying nothing new." This student, expressing her desire for a truly liberatory discussion of racial problems without falling into traps of dogma and clichés, voiced a common sentiment among students first entering the course. Each time I have taught it, confronting student cynicism about the chances of race relations improving in the United States has made me more urgently aware that a radical pedagogy of race is not only desirable in the classroom but also necessary. To combat the increasingly pessimistic feeling many students voice that no one is listening, that things have not changed, that no one is saying anything new about a solution to the problem, I have pushed myself to take more risks pedagogically, to be more politically vocal in the classroom about the necessity for student commitment to struggle against racism.

As a subversive narrative contesting racial purity (i.e., white supremacy), the novel of passing representing (trans)racial characters moving across racial categories not only works to destabilize racial distinctions but also calls into question the entire concept of race itself as a natural phenomenon. When boundaries of race break down at the level of skin color—complicated by gender, class, and sexuality—the fallacy of white power is exposed. I insist that for student critiques of racism to be most effective they must illustrate the effect of white supremacy on the biracial figure in terms of the interrelation of oppression. Methodologically, students learn to decipher the profoundly pervasive and systematic ways racism operates in racially mixed space.

Framing class discussions and writing assignments that help students to actively erase the line between fact and fiction, between the world of the text and the "real" world they inhabit, empowers them to talk and write more openly about the influence of racism on them—across race, gender, class, sexual, and ethnic borders. One female student writing candidly about the particularities of her mixed-race background had this to say: "When you asked the first day of class who considered themselves 'white,' I hesitated raising my hand for the fact that I am not just white yet I look it . . . I must cling to my color—because of my pale skin and my facial features . . . I look in the mirror sometimes and . . . I see my Irish grandmother's pale skin and my Korean heritage in the slant of my eyes, my African blood in the weight and texture of my unconditioned hair, yet I am "White.'" Another white female talked about the nonracialized view of whiteness she had before our class and the impact critical consciousness about race and racial inequality had on interaction with other people outside the classroom:

> It is true that I never considered myself a [part of a] race. I really only took the identities I was oppressed by, such as gender and class. I never considered "white" a race. I always have said I wasn't a racist; therefore, I thought I didn't need to examine

"whiteness." . . . Discussions about this extended beyond the walls of the classroom. My roommates and I have gotten in bitter arguments about race, which was amazing to me because these arguments were not about being racist but how to deal with racial inequality. I often left class confused about where I should fit into this discussion: whether I had a right to an opinion or not; whether I was a stupid little white girl who thought she could save the world or a concerned *woman* who knew the actions of her race affect her, too. I grappled with this during the semester.

Creating an arena for students to imaginatively participate in the lives of biracial characters is another means of achieving a form of sympathetic identification. When this happens, students experience a sense of freedom to let down their guard, to let go fear, anger, resentment. At this moment a process of healing can begin. To make this happen, I will ask students to write a paper (in any form or style they choose) in which they assume the persona of a mixed-race character from one of the novels we read. This exercise draws them into the narrative, getting them to feel, see, taste, hear, and touch the effects of racism on the biracial body. Facilitating an understanding of the fallibility of race, the hegemony of whiteness, and the ways racist thinking dehumanizes all people, I ask students to imagine traversing the border of the racial identity they inhabit, to experience the ambiguity of *being* between two (or more) races.

In negotiating the unstable, shifting boundaries of (trans)racial space, students in The Whiteness of Blackness bear witness to the dehumanizing effects of racism on the body, mind, and spirit of the mixed-race person we read about. Affirming my belief that African American narratives of racial passing provide a radical space in which to argue against white supremacy (at the intersection of sexism and homophobia), a white female student wrote: "Biraciality as the course's theme helped me come to the conclusion [that] [t]he application of gender . . . sexuality . . . and class [in the texts studied] seemed to create a space for a white person to actively critique white supremacist ideology. If this biracial person can exist, serving as a go-between in the discussion of equality, then certainly a white person could also add to the discussion." When white students come to understand that racism is the most salient feature of American life today, they comprehend the pervasive ways it operates in every aspect of all our lives across divisions of race, gender, class, sexuality, and almost every other line of separation we configure. But while exploring racial tensions in the narrative space enlivened our discussions, those same tensions charged the classroom space creating an air of distrust, contempt, disillusionment, and despair. Intervening against the emotional roller coaster students frequently felt I had strapped them into, I encouraged them to meet the emotional demands the course, texts, and their peers required of them.

However, one black woman student in class who had during the term persistently doubted the relationship of the biracial text to the reality of her daily life and the liberation struggle of black people wrote passionately about her feelings of frustration regarding race and class injustice, as they affect the lives of poor black women and men. She opened with a question about life in the real world:

> Were those Blackgirls in that free clinic I passed or was everyone wearing a mask? Did I just hear that white boy say he only pays $1500 a month for rent or did someone slip me an acid tab and I didn't know it? . . . What, exactly, have we accomplished? There are unemployed or illegally employed Blackmen on my corner from sunup to sundown. . . . And when I pass making my rounds— "Whatup Dex? Hey Keith. How you feelin' Blackman?"—and they ask me what I learned in school today, what do I tell them? That we-talked-about-how-fucked-up-shit-is-and-how-it-got-that-way-and-isn't-it-terrible-simply-horrible-and-we-can't-let-stuff-like-that-go-on-any-longer-cuz-it-ain't-right-it-just-ain't-right-goddamit. No, I smile and say, "Racism and shit like that." They smile back knowing that—I'm not fooling them or myself—somebody's paying for me to sit up in a class and talk about what they already know and live.

Articulately remarking on the economic and gender politics in the language of the neighbor"hood" where she lives, this student spoke pointedly about her way of justifying her own privileged position as a black woman enrolled in a course on race at a private university to a group of black men living out the frustration of racially inequality that she feels. Reading her reaction made me wonder as she had—"What exactly had we accomplished?" In what way(s) could antiracist feminism intervene in the situation she described above? Placing her commentary back into the context of the classroom, it strikes me that students talking about and listening to their own experiences with racism offers a moment of critical intervention where the activist teacher can initiate dialogue about education practice committed to teaching social responsibility. Had we been able to talk again, I would liked to have told this student that her frustration (and guilt perhaps for attending an expensive private school) could become the catalyst for thinking about ways to politicize her feelings in terms of social activism. Not having had this conversation with her left me feeling exasperated, realizing the limits of time and space in relation to the classroom.

Yet the class had produced moments of personal liberation for some students. An outspoken white female wrote about her personal struggle to contest the borders of race, as she claimed a racially "bicultural" identity—"either one . . . I am cursing those who say I do not belong in the places I go because I'm white. I grew up in the arms of black society—let go from a white womb—raised in a sea of blackness. I was raised as a 'sistah' even though you will never see me as one, outside my old neighborhood. Color does not always tell the truth. . . . [T]his class has forced me to deal with a lot of deep-rooted issues that have been inside me for a while." However, the most culturally liberatory moments in the classroom cannot guarantee that students will apply what they have learned there outside its walls. The same black female student who had written the sobering passage about "life on the street" also wrote about what she perceived had been a breakdown between "theory and practice" in our class. She noted her experience with a white woman student from the course in another class:

> One day in another class that I share with one of the girls in our class, we were having a discussion about the politically correct terminology for Latinos. I commented that there is a reasoning behind the demand to be called Latino. This girl said, "Well, I don't care what the reasoning is. I'm just going to call them Latinos. Who has time to learn the history behind all of those words?" She shrugged cutely and went on discussing eyebrow pencils. I had to grab a wall for support: Wasn't this the same girl who was talking about how wrong things are for the marginalized classes in America? So much for budding intellectuals. . . . There are so many Black story lines and I'm afraid that for many of my white classmates our study of the novel of passing was just that, another Black story.

The same black woman questioned the success of the course objective, measuring it by a sense of failed expectation that for her meant that The Whiteness of Blackness (one class on racism predominated by "liberal white kids from who-knows-where trying to understand" the immense problem of race in America against an enormous history of racism in America) simply could not have borne the sole responsibility for coming up with the solution for ending racism. I will always remember the outspoken way she took me on and her classmates, insisting that our racial optimism was frozen in theory and void of practice. I will remember her certainly not because this view affirmed my "liberatory" vision of race, but because the reality of the pessimism she bore made me realize the limitations of my work in the classroom.

The words she wrote followed me from the classroom. They speak poignantly to all progressive educators who may or may not employ feminist thinking to critique racism, but believe the classroom can serve as a transformational site:

> Many a time, while reading the text or looking around the room at my white classmates, I would be floored by how out of hand and absolutely absurd racialization in this society has become. (People get paid a whole lot to talk and talk and talk about race!) Here I am sitting in a class with a whole bunch of liberal white kids from who-knows-where "trying to understand" a phenomenon that didn't come to us by way of a classroom and won't be leaving that way either. What's wrong with this picture? Is it just me; am I imagining white kids living life "as usual" once they walk out of the classroom?

I have asked myself the same questions as a black professor (teaching mostly white students over the course of seventeen years), wondering whether white students in my "race classes" leave them to live life "as usual." "What is wrong with this picture?" she asks. Perhaps a partial answer may be found in the exam response of a white woman student who was not so sure how much transgressive ground we had covered in class by the end:

> The stories of the struggles of biracial individuals or black men and women who could pass serve to bring to light the dichotomy of white and black, but they do not carry us any closer to a resolution. I walk away from this class wondering if there is a resolution. What positive outcome can result from a recognition of racial difference? . . . Even in a [post]modern context, when "diversity" is all the rage and difference appears to be valued, such value does not feel truly honest. . . . [A]n end [to racism] seems desparately far beyond the scope of my own imaginings.

Resisting my own intense feelings of pessimism when reflecting upon the present state of race relations in the United States, I imagine Frederick Douglass and W. E. B. Du Bois waging war against both racism and sexism. Remembering their struggle as antiracist feminists reaffirms my vision of the classroom as a site for social transformation. And for one student leaving The Whiteness of Blackness, it had made a difference in her struggle to make a connection between racial and sexual oppression: "That I am a woman who has been grappling with growing up in a sexist world . . . I can almost see racism. Almost. And so I have viewed with feminist eyes the arbitrary privileging of 'white' and light-skin in the novel of passing and have come out of this course . . . with the hope that my voice, that so often gets caught trying to climb over my teeth, will serve me better than it has in the past." Her words affirmed my conviction that the practice of education ought to compel students toward critical consciousness as the first step in a commitment to progressive antiracist politics founded on a believe in the liberation of all people. In a course where so many complex issues, problems, and questions around how to strategize an end to racial oppression remained unattended, in the end a vision of antiracist feminism survived.

"Skinwalking"—Living in the Skin of an Other

[W]e all 'skinwalk'—change shapes, identities, from time to time, during the course of a day, during the course of our lives. . . . [L]ine-drawers have the authority to describe the world for everyone in it. They are exercising enormous power, power they have grabbed or earned or received or simply found. But they have it, this power to locate the line, to decide who stands where in relationship to the line, and to divide community resources based on that decision.

—Judy Scales-Trent

Reading Judy Scales-Trent's memoir, *Notes of a White Black Woman*, was the first time I had come across the term "skinwalk." Scales-Trent notes in her use of it that the term is a translation of a Navajo belief that "there exist certain powerful creatures who, although they appear to be mere human, can change shape whenever they wish by taking on animal form. . . . They are called 'skinwalkers'" (1995, 127). Thinking about her employment of the term, coupled with my thoughts about teaching antiracism through an exploration of (trans)racial subjectivity, I have appropriated it as a provocative idea to engage the notion of students emotionally committing to understanding the life experience(s) of individuals living on the color line—as if the experience(s) were their own. To move students toward an empathetic imagining of the (trans)racial life of an other, I crafted a course on contemporary narratives of interraciality. In the class, students read and write about contemporary autobiographies of individuals who possess a lived knowledge of mixed racial identity. I encourage them continually to evoke personal memories of having been marginalized, discriminated against, ostracized, hated for being different—"an Other." It is through empathetic imagination that students come to know intimately the (trans)racialized lives of the writers we read.

I selected five autobiographies and an anthology of (bi)racial biographies called *Black, White, Other* (Lise Funderburg) as course readings. Of the five memoirs we read (*The Black Notebooks*, by Toi Derricotte; *Beyond the Whiteness of Whiteness*, by Jane Lazarre; *The Color of Water*, by James McBride; *Life on the Color Line*, by Gregory Howard Williams; and *Notes of a White Black Woman*, by Judy Scales-Trent), I chose *Beyond the Whiteness of Whiteness* as a rhetorical model for teaching the "memoir of race." The manner in which Lazarre weaves together personal narrative and social critique is intellectually rigorous but designed for a broad audience. Moreover, it is the very self-conscious/self-critical way she multiply positions herself as a "white mother of black sons" at the intersection of gender, (Jewish) culture, and education practice that makes her life story so instructive in teaching racial healing. Lazarre accomplishes exactly what I want my students to do in the autobiographical race narratives they produce—to be always critically aware of the integral relation between the social context of race and the personal experience of it. In the prologue of her memoir, Lazarre brings much clarity to her attempt to link autobiographical narratives of race to an incisive social critique of white supremacy:

> In all my work . . . especially in this book, I have tried, in a way to use memoir to transcend itself; not only to recall and describe experience but to understand its significance beyond the self. Indeed, the unnatural split between individual and historical consciousness, where the one seems to emerge and prevail wholly independent of the other, is part of a distorted vision resulting from privilege, part of an ideology of individualism fraught with false stories which are dangerous to personal as well as to political life. The link between an individual life story and the collective story which gives context to that life is a defining formal and thematic aspect of African American autobiography. (1996, xviii)

As a white woman writer/educator acknowledging the power of African American autobiography that is so much about the fundamental importance of the personal to the political, Lazarre's memoir shows the germinal influence of the tradition upon its form and content. White students and students of color writing against racism need to know the lived experience and practice of antiracist white people, firstly because still too few white people identify as *anti*racist or practice antiracism, and secondly because most whites still believe antiracist education is the sole proprietorship of people of color.

I have argued that there exists an integral relationship between the tradition of African American autobiography and the contemporary memoir of mixed-race subjectivity that continually subverts the power of *whiteness* as a sign of racial invisibility (no race) and *blackness* as the preeminent marker of racial hypervisibility. I maintain that it is blackness that gives whiteness color; without color whiteness would continue to exist as invisible, an empty sign (of race)—even as white people continue to benefit from its institutionalized power. Thus, a pivotal task in teaching the memoir of race is to make whiteness visible so that white students come to acknowledge and go on to become self-accountable for the privileges that come with being white. In her essay, "White Privilege: Unpacking the Invisible Knapsack," Peggy McIntosh speaks about the necessity of whites becoming critically race conscious: "I think whites are carefully taught not to recognize white privilege . . . I have come to see white privilege as an invisible package of unearned assets, which I can count on cashing in each day, but about which I was meant to remain oblivious. White privilege is like an invisible weightless knapsack of special provisions, maps, passports, codebooks, visas, clothes, tools and blank checks" (1988). For students of color, acknowledging and becoming accountable for internalized racism rooted in white supremacist colonization also means coming to know the liberatory power of critical race consciousness. Though the critique of racism is situated in a pedagogical context authorized by people of color, (trans)racial, and progressive white voices, students of color, in particular, feel empowered to speak and write freely about the effects of white supremacy in their daily lives.

In part 2, I write about the interconnections between being a childhood survivor of domestic violence, a black male outside the script of black heteronormative masculinity, and a black student educated in majority-white classrooms from high school through graduate school. In chapters 3, 4, and 5, I represent the ideological tensions that inform my gender and racial identity, which is related to my conservative religious upbringing and the germinal influence of black feminist thinking in my classroom practice.

⇻ PART 2 ⇺

From the Margin to the Center of Black Feminist Male Self-Recovery

≫ 3 ≪

Learning to Love the
Little Black Boy in Me
Breaking Family Silences, Ending Shame

Over the past decade, the question of domestic violence against women—including black women—has emerged as a major concern in the fight against women's oppression. This is a controversial subject because, unlike other aspects of the subjugation of black women that target racism and economic exploitation, the burgeoning problem of battered women at first appears as an individual problem: a man beating a woman. Too many blacks still think this is a divisive issue that should not be aired in public. However, the problem of battered women is a social phenomenon, not an individual one, and combating this expression of social malaise must be approached with as much vigor as those rooted in the vagaries of a racial and class society.

—Beth Richie

The results of woman-hating in the Black community are tragedies which diminish all black people. These acts must be seen in the context of a systematic devaluation of Black women within this society. It is within this context that we become approved and acceptable targets for Black male rage. . . . This abuse is no longer acceptable to Black women in the name of solidarity, nor of Black liberation. Any dialogue between Black women and Black men must begin there, no matter where it ends.

—Audre Lorde

In this chapter, I confront my own internalized wounds of male supremacist thinking rooted in the personal experience of patriarchal violence. I am a childhood survivor of domestic violence. Owning these words publicly is about openly acknowledging my fear of breaking silence about how deeply wounding the experience of patriarchal violence can be, not only for women (particularly in a domestic context) who are most often its direct targets but also for children witnessing it. Telling my story of survival marks the end of years of silence and secret shame. Openly writing about my childhood experience of family abuse in this chapter represents a personal journey of inner healing initiated by my exposure to black feminist thought. First and foremost, black feminist critique of the wounding effects of patriarchal abuse in black communities opened my eyes to the fact that my experience of it was not unique. Second, black feminist critical focus on domestic violence and its impact upon the lives of black women and children provided me language to construct my own path toward a vision of feminist male self-recovery.

This chapter demonstrates the transforming power and healing agency of black feminists in the self-recovery process I began over fifteen years ago of writing a dissertation on feminism's impact on black men. I had no idea, at the time, that that writing process would lead to this one revealing my struggle to overcome the damaging effects of internalized self-loathing as a black male. Neither did I fully comprehend while writing the doctoral thesis that it was, even then, a crucial element in my becoming a self-proclaimed, feminist black man. The emancipatory writings of black feminists I read while in graduate school at New York University enabled me to break free from the bondage of silence, of shame, and self-hatred that had severely undermined my sense of self-worth and the lack of self-esteem rooted in my childhood.

Who Will Cry for the Little *Black* Boy (in Me)?

During my routine Sunday afternoon newspaper reading time, I was struck by one particular front-page headline of the *Newark Star-Ledger* (August 17, 2003). It read in bold letters: "Anguish over Two Stolen Lives." To my surprise and ensuing sadness, the article and accompanying photographs covered the funeral service for two young black women. One was the daughter of celebrated poet Amiri Baraka. Her sister's estranged husband had shot both women to death. The photographs dramatically captured the outward display of black male pain. In the larger of the two color photos, Baraka's son Ras, the deputy mayor of Newark, was shown stooped over with one hand covering his face (as if the grief was too much to bear). The smaller picture below depicted the other victim's young son. Embraced by a woman identified in the caption as his grandmother, with eyes averted from the camera, he, too, outwardly shed tears for the lost of his mother. Together the pictures illustrated the force of excruciating sadness that domestic violence works upon its surviving victims—for the living remembering the dead.

Questioning the senseless murder of his sister and her friend, according to the newspaper article Ras Baraka exclaimed during the eulogy: "Can anybody explain why this happened? Has anyone seen my baby sister? He killed my baby sister. My God, he killed my baby sister." A family friend, Sonia Sanchez, read a poem at the funeral denouncing black male violence against women: "[B]rothers, stop killing the sisters. Don't you know the difference between human and animal behavior?" When "dawg" (the slang expression for "dog") is a popular term of endearment among young black men, is there any wonder why inhumanity toward females in our communities continues to be such a marketable commodity in gangsta/misogynistic rap (and why so many young black males die early deaths)?

On a Saturday evening in 2003, when I saw the movie *Antwone Fisher*, it evoked in me strong memories of childhood abandonment I was not prepared to handle in the theater, on what had been an otherwise lighthearted evening with my wife and friends. Deep and hidden away, childhood feelings gripped me with such a searing inner pain that only the expression of tears could contain it. In the darkened theater, no one saw my tears.

In one particularly moving scene in the movie between Fisher (the perennially angry young black-male title character) and the military psychologist (played by Denzel Washington) assigned him (due to Fisher's repeated outbursts of violent aggression toward his shipmates), they meet each other's eyes in a moment of kindred (father/son?) recognition. In the psychologist's office, Antwone Fisher recites a poem about his childhood memories of being orphaned at birth. It set off a flood of tears bursting forth from a wounded place deep within me. I was that little boy in the poem.

Beth Richie addresses black resistance to dealing with domestic abuse publicly. For many blacks, doing so represents a communal breach—an airing of our dirty laundry. There is, however, a high price we pay for making family abuse a secret. Our silence is a most dangerous form of complicity, and serves to protect the abuser. Is racial loyalty worth the price of a black woman's struggle (often fatal) against her partner (most often a husband or a boyfriend)? What happens in the mind of a child witnessing a mother's abuse at the hands of a violently angry father? What is the emotional, psychological, and sometimes physical price a child pays in a home where domestic violence is a constant feature of family life? Why can't he or she tell? Why is it a secret? Will he or she pay if the secret gets out? What if he kills her? What will become of me? These questions hover over my narrative like vultures zeroing in on the carcass of a recently dead animal. I will tell . . .

In *Rock My Soul: Black People and Self-Esteem*, bell hooks writes of the critical role of liberatory education in the development of healthy self-esteem in black people:

> Education as the practice of freedom has never been available to any significant body of black folks. Learning how to be a conscious critical thinker places any individual in an *outsider position in a culture of domination that rewards conformity*. In the contemporary world black identities are diverse and complex; consequently we need a variety of educational settings to make education for critical consciousness the norm. More antiracist progressive teachers, of any race, are needed if schools and colleges are to participate in the holistic self-recovery of black folks and affirm the reality that it is possible to achieve healthy self-esteem within the existing culture of domination. (hooks 2003, 92; emphasis added)

In all the varied ways, in the course of my life growing up as a "black boy outsider," I always come back to that feeling of abandonment. When I have felt most connected to and disconnected from black men, there exists the fear that they will abandon me like my father. While my father never left our family physically, I felt abandoned by him emotionally during the years of his abusive behavior at home. Feelings of childhood abandonment connected to my father lie at the heart of much of my emotional insecurity and self-esteem as an adult male. Feelings of inner helplessness, stored-up shame, and guilt turned into anger, turned into rage, turned into depression, turned into the urge to continually self-destruct. In posttraumatic domestic violence recovery, I recognized that I brought all my feelings of abandonment into my marriage over twenty years ago, and it is clear to me that there could be no meaningful recovery without my partner's persistent call for rigorous honesty in our relationship, especially concerning my self-identity issues. Fear of becoming the abusive man my father was for so many years kept me locked for years within the cycle of silent inner abuse. I feared it one day would outwardly manifest itself—causing the end of my marriage.

Without a soul-searching form of self-inventory that critically examines the relationship between patriarchy, (hetero)sexism, and misogyny (male *dis*eases that fuel the root causes of domestic violence), male survivors of childhood family violence cannot hope to break the cycle of abuse. Denying one's feelings of self-woundedness experienced as a child will only continue to subvert the possibility that we can have healthy physical, emotional, and spiritual relationships with women, children, and other men in our lives. Through some heavy-duty soul-searching work in private and group therapy, I am only now able to articulate what happened to me growing up in a home of domestic violence. Male feminist self-recovery in resistance to violence against women requires that I maintain an active engagement in antisexist men's groups—as a leader and participant. It means that the feminist-antiracist agenda I set forth inside and outside the classroom must critically oppose (hetero)sexism as well as homophobia. Moreover, my spiritual practice as a gender-progressive minister must also reflect my stand against domestic violence and misogyny. Working with men of color in a substance-abuse recovery ministry, I am (more often than not) confronted by walls of silence and denial concerning issues of female abuse, particularly in the context of domestic relations.

"There is NO Excuse for Domestic Violence"

Above my desk, penned to the wall, in my small basement office space at home, there is a black-and-blue bumper sticker that reads in white letters: "There is NO excuse for Domestic Violence." Every time I sit down at my desk, I stare at these words. There is NO excuse, but it happens anyway—to many women everywhere, every minute, every hour of the day. One of my best women friends, Linda Rohrer Paige, a professor at Georgia Southern University (in Statesboro, Georgia) gave me the sticker. On her office door, she has posted the same one. For many years at Georgia Southern, she has led a vigorous campaign against domestic violence. Next to the sticker on her door is a newspaper picture of a battered white woman.

Several years ago, Linda invited me to campus to give a paper. The week I arrived in Statesboro, a former student of Linda's (a young white mother of two young sons), was being tried for the murder of her husband. While in town, I attended two days of the woman's trial. I met her sons during a recess. The smaller of the two asked me if I played basketball (probably because of my height of six feet four). Linda introduced me to her parents, an older white couple. The father introduced himself to me as "Evangelist ——." I introduced myself to him as a minister and a teacher. He and I pleasantly exchanged cards. "What am I doing here?" I asked myself when I got back inside. Here I am the only black person, surrounded by a crowd of white people, at a murder trial of a white woman. I told myself that this was all a dream, that I was not in a courtroom (one of two black people; the other was the bailiff, a black man), not among a crowd of blood-thirsty, angry-looking white men and women, not witnessing the trial of a battered white woman accused of murdering her husband (revered as a "good ol' boy") in a small Southern town.

On the last day of the trial, during the closing arguments, a dramatic turn of events occurred. The prosecutor called to the stand a young black man, in his late teens, who had just been brought into the court-room. Upon asking the witness if he was acquainted with the defendant, the prosecutor accused the young black man of having been sexually in-volved with her, citing this as the primary reason she killed her husband. He admitted his guilt, and for a young black male to be in a sexual rela-tionship with a (married) white woman apparently was enough (in and of itself) for the all-white jury to find her guilty of murder—whether or not she had been a victim of domestic violence. I kept thinking about the white woman's sons. What did they think of their mother, their father, the young black man who had entered their lives? What would become of them? Would they become batterers of women?

Never having personally witnessed a trial on domestic violence, the experience left me full of thoughts—not only about the dramatic play of its race and gender politics but also about memories I had long sup-pressed regarding family violence in my life. Remembering its occur-rences through the houses where we lived, I chart the geographical path of its existence over space and time from age six to sixteen, the year before I left home for college. Revisiting the trauma of that turbulent time in my family represents an important step toward accepting myself as a man raised in homes where violence ruled. Growing up, I never heard the phrase "domestic violence," even though it was taking place all around me. Nobody ever asked me what went on in our house (though certain relatives had to know), and I never told anyone. It was a secret. It was an awful, shameful, sad, painful secret. When it came to my father's repeated, physically brutal attacks against my mother (during the ten years of its occurrence), we lived in houses of secrets. We kept the truth hidden like a prized possession.

The first time it happened . . .

Geographies of Violence, Mapping Family Abuse Across Place and Time

Out of nowhere he comes home from work angry. He reaches the porch yelling and screaming at the woman inside—yelling that she is his wife, he can do with her what he wants. They do not understand what is happening. He is pushing, hitting, telling her to shut up. She is pleading—crying. He does not want to hear, to listen. They catch his angry words in their hands like lightning bugs—store them in a jar to sort them out later. . . . Yelling, screaming, hitting: they stare at the red blood that trickles through the crying mouth. They cannot believe this pleading, crying woman, this woman who does not fight, is the same person they know. She wants the woman to know that she is not alone. She wants to bear witness.

—bell hooks

Yelling, screaming, hitting; yelling, screaming, hitting. Pushing, hitting. Shut up, hitting, hitting—the red blood that trickles through the crying mouth (and nose). She is the pleading woman, the woman crying, the woman who does not fight (back). I do not understand what is happening, but I must bear witness. I must be present to witness the unspeakable. To name it, to call it out. I will no longer be silent. I will tell . . . Like hooks, I remember a mother crying, her screams, the blood, the accusations, things crashing, the sound of a fist meeting skin (even now my own thoughts of rage consume me). I will not stop the words from coming forth, the pictures long ago stored away in my mind, the horrifying images of a battered woman, a mother. I, too, bear personal witness.

There is no "first time," no initial moment, no place to point to that was the beginning of it all. In a boy's mind, it seemed to happen all the time. Never knowing when it would happen but being very sure that it would—from house to house and time and time again. Witnessing my father hitting my mother is about multiple memories of fear, about shards of broken scenes, about acts of a father's tormenting violence spread over days, months, years—over a decade; a montage of screams, tears, bloodied noses, and blackened eyes.

During those years when his abusive behavior followed us each time we moved from one house to another, from "downtown" to "uptown" and back again in the town where we lived, it was always accompanied by alcohol, his coming home late each evening, staying away from home on the weekends, arguments about his indiscretions with other women. And there was always his anger to deal with, the rage that preceded the hitting. What demon lurked inside of you? What made you do it? What force inside you made you hit her, always so brutally (more often than not in the presence of your children)? Did you ever wonder how we (your sons who came to fear your presence and the sound of your voice) felt as we witnessed you violating her voice, her body, her presence—every time you commanded her to hush, punched her, choked her, slapped her? Were you trying to teach us something about male power? But you were our father . . . You were also our enemy. Whatever demons were driving you, you unleashed them upon us—in your abuse of her.

They belittled her, publicly and privately humiliated her, marked her as the target of all that you could not accept in yourself. Did you love her during those years you hit her with so much consideration for the force of the blows against her face, eyes, head, and any unpredictable place where a blow might land? I could not help either of you—oppressor and oppressed caught up in a cycle of anger, screams, crying, and hitting, always hitting everywhere we moved; from house to house, one time or another, always violence.

During those years when violence in the houses where we lived resided like a favorite guest, I remember bits and pieces of life with and without my father. I remember evenings during the week when he would enter the front door, usually with the smell of liquor on his breath. I remember Saturday afternoons of solitary play as a six-year-old longing for his presence; years of Saturday nights fraught with paralyzing fear and anticipation, wondering whether this Saturday night she would come home with a bloody nose, a new dress ripped—the result of his jealous rage. For a decade, I watched, almost always through hysterical eyes, her nearly always failed attempts to defend herself against the force of his presence (and absence).

A shattered childhood laid bare—memories once (and still) so painful that to recall them (even now) brings forth a flood of tears. But men don't cry. I still can hear her screams, her crying. I still remember feeling the gut-wrenching fear of maternal loss. That my brother and I would be left motherless, abandoned to a father who would willfully end the life of the one who birthed us. What would happen to us? A child should never have to experience his mother being beaten—perhaps to death, to a thing to be thrown away, discarded. And men don't cry? It is difficult to comprehend the enormous weight of time in the mind of a child enduring the agonizing fear of living in houses where family violence exists as a constant feature of daily life, an ever-present threat. Would it happen this time or that time? Would the next second, minute, or hour begin with the end of her life? Tonight, tomorrow, next week, next month, or next year? Always thinking about her death—not by some dreaded disease or by a terrible car crash, but by his clinched fists or his strong hand positioned tightly around her neck, ever tightening until the last breath was squeezed out of her . . . I feared him from the age of six.

When I was six, I mostly remember him not being at home. Mom and I being at home on Saturdays together alone, without food. We lived on Mooney Street in a nondescript house at the top of the hill. I especially remember late one gray, cloudy Saturday afternoon playing in back of the house. Hungry, I went in to ask mother for something to eat. She offered me a bowl of oatmeal. It was all we had. Where was my father—

off somewhere again? Who knew where to find him? From age six to nine, he was a shadowy figure. Perhaps this is why today I am so sensitive about having enough food to eat—why I used to secretly gorge and hide food. In many of my childhood memories he is not there at all. We never did anything together as father and son. As a child, I did not think of him as my father but rather as the man in my life that caused me pain.

When I was nine, however, my father's presence seemed particularly ominous. This was a time when it seemed some of the worst violence occurred. Like the destructive force of a tornado or a hurricane, his presence when he was full of liquor would move through the house destroying everything in sight. At nine, I witnessed the destructive force of "Baby Fred" (as he identified himself to his friends). Roughly for the next five years, his presence wreaked utter havoc in the houses where we lived. I lived in constant fear about the next time he would choke, punch, or slap my mother, often with disdain or disgust for something she had (or had not) done.

When I was nine, we moved into a newly built house uptown near the end of a cul-de-sac on Muscadine, at the foot of one of the town's majestic pine-tree-covered mountains. I loved climbing that mountain, though I never quite reached the top of it. I remember during summer days, the intoxicating smell of pine sap would fill my nostrils, luring me up into woods. The woods became a sanctuary. Away from home, alone among the towering pines, I experienced safety and peace. I now realize it was my daily travel to the mountain that saved me from the heart-wrenching pain of a child witnessing domestic violence. The mountain became a place of escape. That mountain was the place where God lived, and God would save me from my father.

I remember vividly one Friday night when my mother appeared at the front door of the house—bloody. Clothes torn—with a cut in her forehead—how did that happen? The force of the blow must have been horrendous. What made him do it? I kept thinking. Was it something she had said? All I know is that the picture of her with the cut at the top of her nose was so frightening. And gunshots being fired in the pitch black outside our house that night. My mother's brothers came to the house with lethal intentions. They would save her. He would pay. Who would die that night? For a traumatized ten-year-old looking upon the body of a battered mother, the calculated revenge of angry uncles could be a terrifyingly welcomed response to a father gone mad. No one died that night, but the wound above my mother's eyes, in the center of her forehead, remained—and has remained even to this day. Now when looking at it (now only visible to those who know where to find it, namely me), I know a part of me died that fateful Friday night along with the belief that "Daddy" would protect me from evil in the world.

On another night (when my parents came to pick up my brother and me from my cousins' house downtown), suddenly, without warning, before we could get into the car, he started hitting her. As he was hitting her with unbelievable force, as if he were fighting another man equally as strong, I remember screaming out, demanding that he stop. How could he do this to our mother? It was an act of unbelievable cruelty. I came to relish his time away from home in those days—never home on the weekends, always out with his drinking buddies, always drinking, always drunk. Even during the weekdays he was always out with them, finally coming home late after having been somewhere drinking. That would happen especially on Friday nights, and there would be trouble when the weekend came. Many times it wasn't just the violent rage of the beatings of mother I witnessed, it was the way he treated me. Surely, you must have hated me? What did I represent for you? I remember him telling Mom and me (maybe he said it to Mom and I happened to overhear it) that we were not to eat any of the food he had bought that Friday night.

Sometimes I wonder how different my life might have been had I had the opportunity to be with other boys—to play basketball or other sports without the fear of leaving the house. Though I could not protect her, I could be there to witness. It seemed (except when at school or church), I was always at home, always there to witness. Leaving home meant leaving Mother to suffer alone.

At twelve, when we moved downtown on Crescent, I remember seeing my mother in the hours before dawn go to the back door of the house to wait for him with a butcher knife in her hand. It had snowed earlier that day. As he came in and he passed her in the dark, she drove the butcher knife into his upper shoulder. In the dark, all I could hear was verbal abuse mixed with groans of physical hurt—had she killed him? Maybe in his drunkenness, he really didn't even feel the pain. All I know is that no one was rushed to the hospital—no stitches would be applied to the long, deep gash in my father's shoulder. Years later a very visible keloid remained there to always remind us of that terrifying night.

When we moved from Crescent to Ivy, one block over, I was fifteen. One time there, I witnessed him choking mother in such a manner and with such force that I felt sure he would choke the life out of her. But she did not die then. And she did fight back. When I saw her stab my father in the darkness on Crescent Street, it reminded me of those awful years uptown when she had not fought back. This time she did fight back, and I was glad. When we moved from Ivy to Jackson across town I was sixteen entering my junior year in high school. My father's drinking (weekdays and through Friday and Saturday) and the physical abuse continued.

Whether domestic violence continued in the house on Jackson after I left for my first year of college at seventeen, I don't know. If it did, no one at home ever spoke about it—not even my brother. It was at the beginning of my college years that my father started going to church with my mother. My father's conversion to Pentecostalism would mark the beginning of the end of family abuse in our house, as I had known it the years before. My father had been "saved"—converted from being an unadmitted alcoholic wife beater with a cigarette habit to being a churchgoing, self-avowed, serious Christian practitioner. He would eventually become an ordained minister and soon thereafter a pastor of a small church around the corner from our house on Jackson.

When my father died of lung cancer in 1997, he died a changed man. Whatever demons from his past possessed him—at thirteen he had left home and had lived on the streets—he had conquered. When he died, hundreds of people came from all over to pay their last respects, for he was known as a good man, a friend, a hard worker, a pastor, a man of God. The ministers who eulogized him spoke about his love, compassion, and care for those he knew. Everyone loved him—blacks and whites. There were few places in our town where his name was not known. And so, at the end of his life, he had become all that God wanted him to be; I loved him and my mother, his faithful and dutiful wife for over forty years, loved him.

I remember the places and times that mark a different kind of man— one who was loving, particularly toward his friends and extended family, one who worked hard as a ditchdigger for the town's water company for many years, and one who was known for his good looks (very dark skin and muscular body) and the stylish clothes he wore. Mapping the places of domestic violence in my life over the span of a ten-year period, I realize that each of us in my family, having survived that horrible period of our lives, had found ways to deal with it. But the "church" (both as a physical and a spiritual place) functioned as a source of healing—for my parents, my brother, and for me. It "saved" my father and us from the inner demons that had tormented him and us for years.

As long as I can remember, my mother has been a believer in the Pentecostal faith. It was through my mother's persistent influence that my father, who had embraced Catholicism as a young child, would later in life convert to Pentecostalism. Her faith, she still reminds me, brought her through a troubled marriage to my father and for many years allowed her to be the sole moral guide for my younger brother and myself. While never having overtly admitted it, a very real reason she endured my father's abuse during those troubled years is that my mother had no independent means of support; she had had no formal education beyond the eleventh grade and had never lived on her own. Thus, typical of battered women, she believed remaining in an abusive relationship with a man was her only option.

My mother never left my father at any time during the ten-year period. She never reported any of the incidences of abuse to the police. Over the years, however, the trauma of domestic violence left my brother and me emotionally and verbally paralyzed, unable to share with each other its devastating impact upon our lives as children or as adult survivors. We had no language to express our fear, our pain, our shame, our anger. Why had our mother *chosen* to stay with my father? Not until reaching adulthood did I ask my mother this question. Mother told me she stayed with him because of my brother and me, but that hardly mediated the agonizing pain of her ten years of silence. Apart from all the other complex emotions my brother and I kept bottled up inside of us, even as adults, her answer left me with deep, unresolved feelings about the sacrifices she had made for us. My feelings were fraught with emotional contradictions of guilt and anger. On the one hand, what a selfless, all-giving mother she had been to risk her life for the welfare of her children. On the other, how could she jeopardize her own life or her children's at the hands of my father whose violent rage could have resulted in her death or ours, had we ever attempted to stop him?

Even years after the abuse ended, my brother and I still suffered emotionally from internalized feelings of shame associated with domestic violence survival. Neither my mother's faith nor my father's spiritual conversion could wash away the memory of the small scar my mother bears on her forehead today, a permanent sign of the skin-splitting blow to the face she sustained long ago in an encounter with one of my father's powerful fists. Before feminism, it was the church (as my brother reminded me recently) that kept us both from becoming the violent man our father was before his spiritual conversion. Even so, my brother and I agree that we still bear psychic and emotional scars from our childhood.

When my brother and I revisit the years of family abuse we endured, neither of us remembers anyone from my father's family intervening on our behalf. There were times when we both felt like outsiders in it. My mother often told us for years she felt like an outsider in his family. I wonder to what degree it had to do with her having light skin and marrying into a family of dark-skinned siblings. My father, as earlier stated, was a dark-skinned black man. While he never admitted it, I think he was attracted to my mother because of her skin color. "Colorism" (the preference for light skin, a feature of internalized white supremacy in people of color) is common in black communities. I believe family members on my father's side held having light skin against her. In fact, sometimes I have wondered whether they allowed my father's abuse of her to go on—precisely because they resented her skin color. While neither my brother nor I ever told anyone about the abuse in our home, we knew for a fact our father's sisters and brothers knew about his violent behavior. On occasions over the years, they witnessed it against our mother. They did nothing to stop it. Did any of them ever wonder what the violence was doing to my brother and me emotionally? Instead they talked about us—said we were sissies, punks, because we were quiet and mild-mannered. I will never forget that when nine or ten years old, one of my father's sisters chided me for being "timid." She said it to make fun of me in front of her daughters. Did my aunt or her other sisters and brothers not know the psychological toll their brother's violence was having on us? Why I seemed so withdrawn from grade school through high school? Why I had no desire to do "boy" things? Why, growing up, I stayed at home so much? To this day, deep within, I harbor resentment for the ways they made my brother and me feel like family outsiders—and failed to see the signs of our abuse.

As adult men, in the last five years my brother and I have begun sharing our pain with each other, looking back at our family circumstance. We talk with amazement about the odds against our having survived the abuse. We also talk about the pervasiveness of domestic violence within a larger familial context. We also know that some of our father's sisters were victims of spousal abuse. Many of the cousins we grew up with—female and male—did not survive as we have. Many of them are drug- and alcohol-addicted, and suffer from their own emotionally tortured childhoods.

Ending the silence about my abusive past first came as a graduate student at NYU when I entered the feminist classroom of Professor Rena Grant (a radical young white woman born in Scotland and trained at Yale). Her class on contemporary feminism introduced me to the work of bell hooks. It was my first course in feminism. I was one of only two males in the class; the other was a white male much younger than myself, in a room of over fifty white women. I read hooks's *Feminist Theory: From Margin to Center* with particular interest. Here was a self-proclaimed black woman feminist writing about feminism as a liberatory location for men to understand sexism. Not only that, but in chapter 5, "Men: Comrades in Struggle," she challenged men to enter the struggle against female oppression—maintaining that we were also victims of "patriarchy," a term that in growing up I had connected only to male figures in the Bible. More importantly, hooks's analysis of patriarchy and sexism helped me to comprehend the ideology of women's subjugation in a culture of male supremacy.

For the first time in my life, feelings of helplessness that had surrounded my inability to make sense of my mother's plight had given way to a powerful feeling of knowing. In my mind, what had seemingly been my mother's *choice* to stay with an abusive husband was in actuality a complex situation tied up in issues much larger than one woman's individual experience. What hooks helped me understand, in ways I could not have before, is that violence against women is about an institutionalized and systemic devaluation of all women and womanhood. Moreover, her belief that "[a]s long as men are brainwashed to equate violent abuse of women with privilege, they will have no understanding of the damage done to themselves, or the damage they do to others, and no motivation to change" (hooks 1984, 76). This incisive analysis of gender oppression made me realize that my father's actions against my mother—while unacceptable on any ground—were comprehensible in feminist terms.

bell hooks formulates a critique of sexism that exposes it as a dehumanizing perversion of black manhood and masculinity. It helped me understand that domestic violence is an insidious form of male supremacist behavior that reflects a system of patriarchy that promotes male battering of women. The work of hooks and that of other black feminists (among them Audre Lorde) significantly influenced my understanding of sexism and misogyny in black communities in two strategic ways: (1) it made me analyze critically my own experience as a black *male* domestic violence survivor, and (2) it made me challenge black men in my life to break the bonds of sexist and misogynist thinking and behavior. Living a life committed to pro-feminist spiritual, social, and political transformation in black life means actively challenging black men and myself to resist the traps of male supremacist behavior and misogyny.

"One Oppression Does Not Justify Another"

As black women and men, we cannot hope to begin dialogue by denying the oppressive nature of male privilege. And if Black males choose to assume that privilege for whatever reason—raping, brutalizing, and killing Black women—then ignoring these acts of Black male oppression within our communities can only serve our destroyers. *One oppression does not justify another*. (Emphasis added).

—Audre Lorde

I, like most Black men I know, have spent much of my life living in fear: fear of white racism, fear of the circumstances that gave birth to me, fear of walking out my door wondering what humiliation will be mine today. Fear of Black women—of their mouths, of their bodies, of their attitudes, of their hurts, of their fear of us Black men.

—Kevin Powell

In *Sister Outsider*, Audre Lorde argues that "[i]t is for Black men to speak up and tell us why and how their manhood is so threatened that Black women should be the prime targets of their justifiable rage" (1984, 60). Like Alice Walker, Lorde does not view the feminist project of black women in gender-divided terms: "We recognize the fallacy of separatist solutions" (61). Principally as a response to black sociologist Robert Staple's inflammatory article in the March/April 1979 issue of the *Black Scholar*, Lorde calls black men to account for their misguided and wrongheaded attacks against black women. Rather than brutalize black women as our enemies, we need to redirect our "justifiable rage" toward the institution of "white supremacist capitalist patriarchy" (in the words of bell hooks).

Lorde calls for black men to take responsibility for ways we *feel* wounded by racial, gender, and economic injustice. Moreover, she emphatically contends that our emotional welfare is not the responsibility of black women in our lives. We must begin to dialogue with each other about what ails us. Relying on black women to carry our emotional burdens is not a compliment to their "enduring strength" but a totalizing, sexist signifier of the myth of the "strong black woman." Insistently, Lorde maintains that a cross-gender, dialogic process must be engaged in between black men opening up to each other about the psychic and emotional wounds we bear: "Black men's feelings of cancellation, their grievances, and their fear of vulnerability must be talked about, but not by Black women when it is [at our] expense . . ." (61). Until we black men allow ourselves to be vulnerable with each other and share progressive, antisexist survival strategies, we cannot hope to convince the women in our lives that we are serious about a vision of black liberation struggle. We have to be actively engaged in the process of liberating ourselves from white supremacist, heteromasculinist, homophobic notions of our manhood.

As stated in the introduction, for two years I helped run a church-sponsored addiction-recovery program for men and women. The program serves not only persons in recovery from drug and alcohol abuse but also individuals dealing with domestic violence (either as victims or perpetrators), incest, depression, and overeating, among other things. The "Program" (as we call it) works on the belief that recovery from any form of addiction requires spiritual self-transformation. Through weekly group meetings, employing the twelve-step principles of Alcoholics Anonymous and Narcotics Anonymous, we share our recovery process. One of the core tenants of the process is the factual evidence that "one addiction feeds another." Based on accounts of recovering addicts, dependency on drugs, for example, is often linked to other forms of dependency. Leading men's groups, I found that while males in them were successfully recovering from one form of substance addiction or another, many of them held on to their "addiction" to abusing women in their lives. In other words, men could celebrate "clean time" (that is, no longer being actively addicted to drugs and alcohol), while remaining bound to sexist and misogynist behavior. For many of them, this was not a problem. Such attitudes are precisely what Audre Lorde has in mind when she argues, "One oppression does not justify another."

In my men's recovery group, listening to the gut-wrenching stories of men with substance-abuse problems was always painful. My heart ached for them and their struggle to stay clean. Sometimes I wept silently as I listened, unable to fight back the tears. Sometimes they wept for me. Our collective weeping was good. The outward tears symbolized an inner washing. Perhaps we were also weeping for the long silences between us and for the wounds we had inflicted upon each other—for fathers and sons who had lost each other. Like Antwone Fisher, I ask too: "Who will weep for the little boy" (in each of us)? I must weep for the little black boy in me who still yearns for a father's love and protection. On fateful Wednesday nights, in our recovery meeting, women and men gathered to learn about the nature of our addictions. To confront and overcome our addictive behaviors and to share our struggles "to stay clean" were the reasons we came together—to be as honest as possible with each other (and ourselves) as we recovered. Personally, recovering from years of depression rooted in childhood abuse has meant getting in touch with that past in ways such that its power over me is neutralized. This is a life's work.

To end the silence. To disrupt the cycle of seemingly endless bouts of depression. The never telling, for fear of public exposure. Working the "Fourth Step" helped me to know that the personal sacrifice of sharing my past of family abuse publicly is far more valuable in my recovery process trying to keep it a secret. The more rigorously I search within and the more openly and honestly I share, the more I allow myself to embrace the process of self-healing. Outward weeping during "sharing" (individual disclosure time) in the meeting—by either the member of the group telling the story or by a member listening to it—is a sign of solidarity, an empathetic gesture of personal connection, as in "(Girl/man), I can relate to your pain." In moments when we lay the wounds of our life bare for everyone to see (and hear), collective tears become a critical agent in the struggle for recovery—making the process of us putting the bits and pieces of our lives together again a collective effort. We are connected to each other's struggle through the belief that inner healing is about understanding the place of divine intervention in our lives. In group meetings, we say the recovery process "sometimes happens quickly; other times, slowly."

As black men in a white supremacist capitalist culture, our sense of "brotherhood" is stuck in the racist image of us as an ever-present menace to (white) society. Rather than taking the responsibility for creating a truly liberated, nonsexist vision of black male self-determination, many of us have instead internalized racist, misogynist representations of us. More than ever, our common ties as black males are knotted around a totally capitalist, hypersexualized commodification of our masculinity—represented as spectacle in the entertainment industries of sports and hip-hop. In popular culture today, the essentialization of black manhood and masculinity in the form of gangsta imagery is a moneymaker for any black male willing to work on the plantation of white supremacist, capitalist, homophobic patriarchy, as bell hooks has asserted. I maintain that the truth of our being *black* and *male*—in a nation that continues to deny our humanity—is about our coping by repressing a lot of pain, anger, and inner woundedness. It is not our inner hurt that we show. Rather, the badge of our manhood is a show of self-denial—denial that we hurt at all. Some of us are full of unacknowledged (self-)anger and rage—of pain locked away behind years of silence about internalized hurts. "It is," as Audre Lorde said, "[time] for Black men to speak up and tell us why and how their manhood is so threatened that Black women should be the prime targets of their justifiable rage. . . . Black men themselves must examine and articulate their own desires and positions and stand by the conclusions thereof (1984, 60, 62).

Pro-feminist black men have taken the lead in black male conversations about domestic violence in our communities and its impact upon lives. Kevin Powell is among the leaders of the dialogue with his book *Who's Gonna Take the Weight: Manhood, Race, and Power in America* (2003). In this slender volume, Powell shares his thoughts about the huge personal weight he feels as a young black man in the United States struggling for meaning in his life beyond the death-grip of black machismo. Writing in the hip-hop style that has become the signature of the speech, clothing, and attitudes of Generation X, he places his life history on the line in this book. Composed of three pithy essays, it captures the mind-set of a young black man caught up in the spectacle of hip-hop culture. As a memoir of gender, race, and power driven by white supremacist capitalist greed in the music industry, it is the story of the rise, fall, and redemption of a talented black male "hip-hopper in exile" (Powell 2003, 64). Of the essays, the one that unabashedly demonstrates the transforming power of black feminism in a man's life is "Confessions of a Recovering Misogynist." It underscores the need for men working to become gender-progressive in their thinking and actions and to admit their failure when they fall short.

Powell introduces us to the life of a black male sexist in the making, a man whose memory of childhood is indelibly marked by the absence of his father. He recalls its imprint as a formidably signifying force in the misogynist development of his ideas about black women. His experiences as a misogynist college student exemplify all the negative ways females are made to serve (hetero)masculinist fantasies of manhood power. He is now a popular antisexist lecturer on college campuses, and he says, "[C]ollege is simply a place where we men, irrespective of race or class, can—and do—act out the sexist attitudes entrenched since boyhood. Rape, infidelity, girlfriend beat-downs, and emotional abuse are common, and pimpdom reigns supreme" (2003, 58). Powell changed his womanizing ways in a moment of critical self-reflection: "[M]y ex-girlfriend stepped up her game and spoke back to me. . . . My world said women were inferior, that they must at all costs be put in their place, and my instant reaction was to do that. When it was over, I found myself dripping with sweat, staring at her back as she ran barefoot out of the apartment" (61). Powell admits: it took "raising my hand to my girl friend, and . . . two other ugly and hateful moments in college, one where I hit a female student in the head with a stapler during the course of an argument, and the other where I got into a punch-throwing exchange with a female student I had sexed then discarded like an old pair of shoes" (67), to understand the dehumanizing impact of misogyny on the women in his life *and* himself.

Deeply guilt-ridden and remorseful about the incident—and after entering therapy, reading black feminist critiques of male violence, having ongoing dialogues with feminist women, and doing much soul-searching reflection on his relationship with his mother, other women (in and absent from his life), and men (especially his father)—Powell determined he had to change: "I struggled to understand terms like *patriarchy, misogyny, gender oppression*" (62). A year later, he would write about the incident with his ex-girlfriend for *Essence* magazine. Admitting that he remains in a struggle to overcome the sexist in him, Powell continues to write and speak about his commitment to ending sexist and misogynist violence against women. I appreciate his work as a recovering sexist.

"Saving" Ourselves: The Feminist Work Black Men Must Do

Black males who refuse categorization are rare, for the price of visibility in the contemporary world of white supremacy is that black male identity be defined in relation to the stereotype whether by embodying it or seeking to be other than it. At the center of the way black male selfhood is constructed in white-supremacist capitalist patriarchy is the image of the brute—untamed, uncivilized, unthinking, and unfeeling. . . . *Anyone who claims to be concerned with the fate of black males in the United States who does not speak about the need for them to radicalize their consciousness to challenge patriarchy if they are to survive and flourish colludes with the existing system in keeping black men in their place, psychologically locked down, locked out.* (Emphasis added)

—bell hooks

While writing the earlier section about my memory of childhood domestic violence, I felt a visceral kinship with bell hooks and her narrative of family abuse in the memoir *Bone Black.* Her willingness to share openly the traumatizing impact of her father's abusive behavior toward her mother is precisely why I chose to open my narrative with lines from it. I was amazed by the power of hooks's telling, and it invoked in me agonizing memories of my past. Like hooks and her siblings, I stored images of the violent father deep in the recesses of my mind. The images of my father as a violent man followed me into adulthood. Through the heart-wrenching lines of her story, I reentered the trauma of my own. Remembering times my father struck my mother was like having to remember the first time I almost drowned, struggling helplessly without the benefit of knowing how to swim—feelings of dying helplessly with no one to save me. I realized that breaking silence about domestic violence in my family was the first step toward ending the shame associated with it. This was the work *I* had to do to begin my recovery.

While publicly breaking family silence about family abuse issues has been personally liberating, allowing me to arrest the emotionally self-deprecating demons of my past, being openly vulnerable continues to be difficult. I have come to know in recovery that male (self-)transformation —toward breaking the cycle of internalized sexism and misogyny—is not the work of women. As much as my wife loves me, she cannot save me from myself. No matter how many public lectures I give, articles I write, or books I compose on being a pro-feminist black man, I will not change until I deal with deeply rooted issues of black male self-esteem that keep me bound in heteronormative, sexist, homophobic masculinity. Without remaining actively involved in recovery, feelings of worthlessness, self-hatred, and low self-esteem (intertwined with years of rage and anger toward my father's abusive behavior, and feelings of utter helplessness in the face of it) would continue to sabotage my desire to break free of the self-destructive hold of black machismo. As an adult male, feelings of manhood failure torturously haunted me until I began to understand from a feminist standpoint masculinity, manhood, and the abuse of male power. Elsewhere I have written about the necessity of a critique of racism and black male liberation that does not collude in the perpetuation of black female oppression:

> All Black men need to understand that antiracist strategies which uphold sexist, patriarchal dictates of Black empowerment doom themselves to fail, for they ignore the historical centrality of Black women in the movement for racial justice. Louis Farrakhan's call for Black men to "atone" for not having owned up to a patriarchal version of manhood (to be "respected as men") falsely leads many of us to believe our manhood resides in the power to dominate women. Womanist Black men reject masculinist thinking rooted in the idea of male superiority. Without acknowledging the ways Black men can oppress women and be racially oppressed simultaneously, Farrakhan refuses an analysis of white supremacy that would expose the relationship of power between racial and sexual domination. (Lemons 2001b, 82–83)

Even as I began confronting feelings of low self-esteem from the past, feeling as if salt was being poured into an open wound, I knew no woman in my life should have to shoulder my pain. I recognized that black male self-recovery in a culture of white supremacy is hopeless without its link to spiritual inner transformation.

Uncovering the excruciating pain of the recovery work I had to do as a child survivor of domestic violence left me feeling that the entire world was able to see my wounds (translate "weaknesses"). But this was and continues to be the work that *I* must do. To transform I must be vulnerable, not only breaking family silences about black male misogynist abuse, but also black manhood silence about ways heteromasculinist and homophobic notions of our identity as men hurt, wound, and undermine our relationships with one another and with women and children in our lives. On an intellectual level, having studied the feminist critique of patriarchy and sexism for almost twenty years, I understand domestic violence. On an emotional level, however, for years shame, guilt, and embarrassment kept me from confronting ways I had internalized them and their effects upon my marriage, relationships with other women, and men in general. I have never physically abused my partner of nearly twenty-five years. For a man who has identified as a pro-feminist man for twenty years of marriage, it completely shocked me when Fan recently revealed that my silence (refusal to dialogue with her) when we disagree is a form of (psychological) violence against her. At first, my response was denial. How could she say this when my life with her has been about resisting (rather successfully in my mind, I thought) abusive male behavior? What Fan made me understand is that refusing to engage her in mutual dialogue when we disagree is as painful for her as if I had struck her.

For years, silence was the only way I knew how to deal with marital conflict. I would never hit my partner, and I abhorred men who abused women. It did not take long for me to understand Fan's interpretation of my behavior as a passive form of aggression, for it was the exact same strategy I employed growing up to show my father how much his abusive actions really hurt me and our family. Coming from a family where physical violence was nearly always the means by which conflict was dealt with between my parents, I learned that the best way to control my temper was simple: be silent. This is how I responded to conflict in my marriage. Justifying my behavior, I reasoned that silence was not the same as physical aggression. After times when my father would have physically attacked my mother, weeks and months would pass before I would even utter one word to him. The absence of words spoke very loudly and clearly what my thoughts were about him. While resistance to his behavior never manifested itself in physical retaliation from my brother or myself, I experienced power in refusing to talk. He did not (and could not) ever force me to speak to him. I used silenced against him to hurt him, to make him feel disregarded, unloved, worthless, erased from my consciousness. Fan told me these were the exact feelings she felt when I used silence against her.

My shutting down hurt Fan, and I knew it. Being a pro-feminist man is about more than a *self*-proclamation, much more than an acceptance of women's equality. What I now know from Fan's critique of my behavior toward her is that silence can be, and is, a weapon of abuse. Even as a self-proclaimed feminist man, I can use it against my partner to devalue her opinions and feelings, to simply tune her out. Having learned that domestic violence can manifest itself in varying ways—and that I have been a perpetrator of domestic violence in my own marriage—shattered the self-righteous image of myself I held as an exceptional male model of antisexism. Being committed to feminist struggle against sexism and misogyny as a black man means being critically conscious of the traps of male supremacy—on a daily basis. Like Kevin Powell, I am in active antisexist recovery through personal and group therapy to understand the root causes of my sexist ways.

My partner has never left me. We have never been separated except for those times when she goes away for extended periods to act or to work professionally as a teacher of acting. Most likely, if asked, Fan would say that I am a good husband, father, lover, and spiritual partner. She would also say that being married to a "feminist black man" is about having to continually remind him of the integral relationship between theory and practice; she would say that his practice does not always line up with the feminist principles he espouses—even when he is relentlessly defending them.

For we black men who are childhood survivors of domestic violence, silence about the psychic and emotional wounds many of us have buried deep within is killing us *and* the women and children in our lives. Are the sacrifices we invest in the reification of black machismo worth our humanity? The patriarchal vision of manhood many of us have endorsed, as espoused by Louis Farrakhan in the form of new black manhood nationalism, is not the answer for our liberation as men. We have become lovers of things more than of ourselves. How can we freely and fully love the women in our lives, when we cannot express our love for one another and our own selves? We survived the holocaust of slavery in mind and body, but for many of us, our spirits suffered near fatal attack—though the black church would have us believe otherwise. What price our humanity—or the humanity of the women and girls in our lives—that we would choose a form of life-threatening manhood power over the lives of our "sisters"?

In black churches, the words to the traditional gospel song "We Will Understand It Better By and By" speak to the unfolding truth about the human struggle transformed by the power of divine intervention. The song's theme of hope is articulated in the words: "We will tell the story of how we've overcome . . ." In recovery meetings, individual "sharing" produces a critical space for vulnerability where telling *the story* represents a collective triumph over adversity. Everybody in my family was "saved" from the destructive power of domestic violence—including my father. Yet it was understanding feminism as a critical tool against domestic violence that enabled me to lay bare my mother's story as a battered woman, that became a necessary, albeit deeply painful, step toward my own self-healing.

In telling my story as a survivor of domestic violence, I have ended years of secrecy, years of shame, years of silence. I have begun to love myself in different, radically black, *pro*-feminist spiritual terms. I have transformed my past as a "black boy outsider" into a strategic location of empowerment as an adult male having become a "professor" of feminism inside and outside the classroom.

White Like Whom? Racially Integrated Schooling, Curse or Blessing?

The only question which concerns us here is whether these "educated" persons are actually equipped to face the ordeal before them or unconsciously contribute to their own undoing by perpetuating the regime of the oppressor.... These "educated" people ... decry any such thing as race consciousness; and in some respects they are right. They do not like to hear such expressions as "Negro literature," "Negro poetry," "African art," or "thinking black"; and roughly speaking, we must concede that such things do not exist. *These things did not figure in the courses which they pursued in school, and why should they? "Aren't we all Americans?"* (Emphasis added)

—Carter G. Woodson

The oppressed, having internalized the image of the oppressor and adopted his guidelines, are fearful of freedom. Freedom would require them to eject his image and replace it with autonomy and responsibility. Freedom is acquired by conquest, not by gift. It must be pursued constantly and responsibly. Freedom is not an ideal located outside of man; nor is it an idea which becomes myth. It is rather the indispensable condition for the quest for human completion.

—Paulo Freire

Writing about my journey of black male feminist self-recovery means also revealing how ideas of white supremacy shaped my ideas of intelligence, culture, and success. It means revisiting the history of my education in majority-white schools for more than thirty years. My decision to become a pro-feminist black man is integrally connected to the evolution of my racial identity.

While teaching at the college, I developed a course called "Pedagogy of Race." Beverly Daniel Tatum's book "*Why Are All the Black Kids Sitting Together in the Cafeteria?" and Other Conversations about Race* was a required reading. It introduced me to the work of the black psychologist William Cross. In *Shades of Black: Diversity in African-American Identity*, Cross names five stages of racial identity development in blacks: "*Pre-encounter* (stage 1) depicts the identity to be changed; *Encounter* (stage 2) isolates the point at which the person feels compelled to change; *Immersion-Emersion* (stage 3) describes the vortex of identity change; *Internalization* and *Internalization-Commitment* (stages 4 and 5) describe the habituation and internalization of the new identity" (1991, 190). Through racial-identity development theory, I examine the influence of whiteness as a precipitous ideological force in my internalization of white supremacy. In this chapter, I focus on my "preencounter" with whiteness via schooling. It maps my racial development as a product of years of integrated education in majority-white institutions—from high school to graduate schools in the South and Northeast.

On the Margins of Blackness, Whiteness, and Masculinity

In *Why Are All the Black Kids Sitting Together in the Cafeteria?* Daniel Tatum utilizes Cross's theory to illustrate patterns of black students in integrated schooling. Beginning with the "preencounter" stage, Daniel Tatum observes: "In the first stage, the Black child absorbs many of the beliefs and values of the dominant White culture, including the idea that it is better to be White. The stereotypes, omissions, and distortions that reinforce notions of White superiority are breathed in by Black children as well as White. Simply as a function of being socialized in a Eurocentric culture, some Black children may begin to value the role models, lifestyles, and images of beauty represented by the dominant group more highly than those of their own cultural group" (Daniel Tatum 1997, 192). I learned the myth of white supremacy as a little boy growing up in the South watching much more television than should have been allowed. Television taught me that being white was indeed better (than being black). Reared in a culture of white supremacy, I internalized the racist belief that white people were superior to blacks—as role models, in lifestyle, and in images of beauty. As Cross clarifies, internalized racism in black children is about socialization; rarely is it a conscious act: "In being for-mally educated to embrace a Western cultural-historical perspective, Pre-encounter Blacks cannot help but experience varying degrees of miseducation about the significance of the Black experience. . . . One reason the need for nigrescence is such an ubiquitous theme in the dis-course on Black identity is that it is very difficult for *any* Black American to progress through the public schools without being miseducated about the role of Africa in Western civilization and world culture in general, and the role of Blacks in the evolution of American culture and history in particular" (1991, 192). While I had begun to internalize the myth of white supremacy before beginning school as a young child, I had not really formed any set opinions about whites or blacks by the time I began attending the segregated Catholic school in my hometown. I had no con-tact with whites other than the nuns who taught me in school. By age nine, however, after having been taken out of Catholic school at the re-quest of its white "sister" in charge because I was an incorrigibly slow learner, I had begun to understand the power of white women. Even though my parents placed me in the segregated elementary school known as Goldstein, where all my teachers were black women, I learned from television that white women wielded infinitely more power than black females. In fact, this was one of the first lessons I learned about race, gender, and class. My earliest memory of the idea of white superi-ority first materialized in the form of an elite white woman on television. That woman was Jacqueline Bouvier Kennedy.

Beginning with the preencounter stage of my racial-identity devel-opment in this chapter, I will discuss how images of elite whites on tele-vision—particularly those of white females—facilitated my internalizing white supremacist thinking as a young black boy in ways that would "color" how I perceived black females and males well into adulthood. But it would be the experience of education in integrated, majority-white institutions—from high school through graduate schools in the South and Northeast—that *mis*haped my vision of *blackness*. In this chap-ter (and the one that follows), I demonstrate the experiential inner workings of race- and gender-outsider positionality. It would create the deep psychological sore spots and scarring wounds that resulted from black heteronormative, homophobic notions of masculinity I experi-enced in my childhood and teenage years. As central to its theme, this chapter examines the role of white supremacy, black machismo, and re-ligious fundamentalism as principal factors that contributed to my becoming a "black boy outsider"—growing up on the margins of black-ness, whiteness, and masculinity.

My Earliest Memory of Race, Gender, and "The White House"

> Every boy who comes here [the White House] should see things that develop his sense of history. For the girls, the house should look beautiful and lived-in. They should see what a fire in the fireplace and pretty flowers can do for a house; the White House rooms should give them a sense of all that.
>
> —Jacqueline Bouvier Kennedy, 1962

Growing up in Arkansas during the 1960s in a black working-class family where domestic violence was a common feature of life, I used our black-and-white television as a form of anesthesia to escape its emotional torment. I willfully entered TV land, a place where *whiteness* ruled. Little did I know then how much it would (mis)form my ideas of *blackness*. I learned from hours tuned in to television sitcoms, commercials, and dramas that whiteness was synonymous with *high* culture, success, wealth, intellect, and the supremacy of white skin. I lived less than fifty miles from Little Rock, Arkansas, where in 1957 federal troops had to be sent from Washington to accompany nine black students into all-white Central High School. In my mind (and that of many other blacks in the small resort town where I lived), the end of "black" schools signified racial progress. I equated being schooled with white students and being taught by white teachers with a form of "higher" education. While neither I nor any other black person in my community ever voiced it aloud, many of us believed that "if it was white, it was right." *Whiteness* at home on television, *whiteness* in pictures of a white Jesus at church, *whiteness* in the images on product labels in supermarkets and department stores, *whiteness* at the movies, *whiteness* on billboards—WHITENESS everywhere.

As a child, long before I knew what "internalized racism" meant, before I began my first day in a classroom, I knew it was the way of the WHITE world. I would judge the value of everything and everyone by it—myself, other people of color, *and* even lower-class whites (who lived outside the norms of white middle class respectability). I learned about whiteness from white people; I learned it well, well enough to *pass* . . . across the color line.

In 1962, like the imprint left from a rubber stamp, whiteness was impressed upon my mind indelibly. I have never actually been to the White House, but more than thirty years ago, I entered it through the medium of television. Imagine on a sunny Sunday afternoon in February, a little black boy sits facing a black-and-white television watching a historic tour of the White House—conducted by the nation's "First Lady, Jacqueline Kennedy." (He is one of the "80 million Americans who would be tuned in," according to the press reports.) What he sees and hears during the tour that afternoon—in images of race, gender, femininity, power, of idealized white womanhood personified—would become imprinted in his *un*conscious mind, indelibly. In a hyperfeminine, high-culture, whispery voice, Jacqueline Kennedy guides the viewing eyes of the nation through the majestically appointed rooms of the presidential mansion. As she describes the luxury and the history that surrounds her, in the observant eyes of the impressionable little black boy it is her image alone that gives meaning to these things. Like Daisy, the young, rich, *white* heroine of *The Great Gatsby,* she speaks elegantly ("of the sounds of money"). Maybe it is in the calculatedly restrained way she moves, the educated gestures of her hands, or the perfectly well styled hair? All congeal into a portrait of perfection, of privileged womanhood, of refined culture, of inherited wealth—of *whiteness.*

She possesses all that his mother does not. At the age of nine, the little black boy in this story had no knowledge of "gender" or feminism. But, as he watched Ms. Kennedy conducting the tour, listening to the stories she told of how things came to be in the White House, he was very much aware of the absence of *blackness* in the historical anecdotes she recounted. Was everything and everybody connected to the White House *white?* All the great men and all the women? There were no images of blacks or people of color in any pictures in any rooms of the White House. Did black people have no rightful place in the White House? On that sunny day in February 1962, that little black boy learned more about the "whiteness of whiteness" than anything else the First Lady had to tell. It would take a lifetime for this little black boy to unlearn the history lesson on race and gender the "First Lady" taught that day.

Vividly remembering the televised tour of the White House (albeit not in the language of a nine-year-old), as the little black boy grown up to be a self-professed black *male* pro-feminist today, I think about it as *the* signifying moment in the development of my racial consciousness. Despite the fact that Jackie Kennedy Onassis's message to girls was steeped in the ideology of the nineteenth-century cult of true womanhood and that her lesson to boys reinforced the belief that historical knowledge is the province of a male (and that *his* story is what really counts), it was the message she communicated about the relationship between whiteness and femininity that was most telling. How this message came across to a Southern black boy is a different story of race, gender, and class.

Growing up black and Pentecostal in the South during the 1960s was like different sides of the same coin. The former had to do with coming into contact with white students for the first time in my life at the newly built, integrated high school. The latter had to do with my being a "church boy," a "Holy Roller," and all the other religious idiosyncrasies associated with the black "Holiness" church. Coupled with my status as a boy outside the boundaries of heteromasculinist identity, my gender, racial, and religious identities formed a triad of outsiderness. An often heard song in the church I grew up in was "How I Got Over." It is sung to a lively, up-tempo beat, and I have repeated its refrain more times than I can remember: "My soul looks back and wonders . . ." These words seem appropriate when reflecting on my education as a black male in integrated, majority-white schools from high school through graduate school. The allusion to Woodson's book *The Mis-Education of the Negro* (1933) and the epigraph from it that introduces this chapter also appeared especially fitting, considering its and the next chapter's focus on integrated schooling. I reflect upon my education in majority-white schools from a decidedly *black* standpoint. Precisely what this means has to do with the critical import of Woodson's phrase "thinking black" as an oppositional standpoint of reflection. As a critical viewpoint, "thinking feminist" (a phrase used by bell hooks) allows for an interrogation of the positional politics of *whiteness* related to the outsider gender identity.

Thinking black and thinking feminist (mapping ways being black and male positioned me on the margins of black, white, and masculine identity), I promote a critique of integrated schooling rooted in white supremacist thinking. Critical of the racist premise often associated with integrationist rhetoric, bell hooks maintains in *Black Looks* that "[r]acial integration in a social context where white supremacist systems are intact undermines marginal spaces of resistance by promoting the assumption that social equality can be attained without changes in the culture's attitudes about blackness and black people" (1992, 12). However, in a culture of white supremacist colonization, not only must whites' "attitudes about blackness and black people" fundamentally change, but also there must be a liberatory transformation in the racial consciousness of black people. As Woodson argued in 1933, a primary symptom of the "mis-educated Negro" is internalization of white supremacy. As a pro-feminist black male professor and based on my experiences of education in majority-white schools, I argue for a vision of radical education that opposes white supremacy—even as it rejects education invested in male supremacist and heterosexist thinking.

White Schooling and the End of Blackness?

In integrated schooling rooted in white supremacy, what happens to the mind, body, and spirit of a black child who learns to devalue blackness and all things associated with it? What happens to the body of a black child in majority-white classrooms who learns that the white body is valued above all others? Upon what spiritual plane does the soul of a black child soar in a Christian culture fixed on the superiority of whiteness—white souls, white angels, white Jesus, white Creator? Like "the little black boy" in William Blake's poem by the same title, I internalized the myth that my skin was black but my soul was white. As revealed in chapter 1, because I lived in constant terror that domestic violence would result in my mother's death, growing up I thought of home as a haven and a hell. From age six to seventeen, when I was not in church or school, free time consisted of television watching as a means of escaping from the psychic bruises of family abuse. There was no father figure to guide me into loving ideas of masculinity. As early as I can remember, through nightmarish experiences of a father's abuse and abandonment television functioned as a panacea against the pain.

My initiation into black boyhood school culture began what would be a long series of attacks from black males who pushed me to its very boundaries. I hated schooling with black boys in the all-black junior high school. They refused to give me the benefit of the doubt. Not behaving stereotypically male like the majority of them was enough for them to exile me to margin of masculinity. Couldn't they see the mangled wreck I was, a broken leftover of a severely dysfunctional home? I possessed no desire for the hurtful masculinity of the black boy culture of my school nor for the violence that my father perpetrated against me. I confess that I was ill fitted to the script of black boyhood masculinity in junior high school. No skill (or affinity) for sports, too awkward and uncoordinated. Voice always a register (or two) too high. Factor in shyness, timidity, and being overly self-conscious about having a tall, lanky body. Add the fact that I did not hang out with the boy gang at recess, after school, or on Saturday, that I liked school (and generally made good grades), and, to top it all off, that I wore glasses with ridiculously thick lenses to correct severe astigmatism. These deficiencies defined my outsider status, marking me as an easy target for ridicule, harassment, and erasure. I could accept erasure; being invisible meant not being subject to attack. I could have been the poster child for boy outsiderness. I became the butt of every joke at twelve years old—the one to bear their insecurity about emerging male (and female) sexuality. They called me a "booty-getter," a term for a homosexual boy. To this day, I have no knowledge of its origin. I knew that my attackers aimed to hurt me with it. They succeeded. It set me apart from the "real" boys.

For one thing, boys played sports: basketball, and football, for sure. But, more than this, stereotypical masculinity required real boys to act out in sexualized gestures. This called for "copping a feel" (cupping a girl's "butt," a sign of sexual daring that sickened me). It was my seeming noninterest in boy play around the sexualization (or objectification) of girls that made my outsider status overtly apparent. I never copped a feel, had never kissed a girl, and certainly had never had (or tried to have) sex with a girl. I was a virgin. It was as if all boys intuitively knew it. Not knowing, and having little information from me about what I did with girls, they had enough information (or lack thereof) to crucify me sexually.

Moreover, real boys swore. I did some, but apparently not enough to pass the test. Real boys hung out together during recess, after school, on Saturday afternoons; took woodshop (which I did); and practiced a cool style of walking, standing, talking, and the general display of as little feeling as possible. Richard Majors and Janet Mancini Billson describe this self-affirming posturing as the "cool pose." While suggesting that black males employ it as a mode of self-protection, they also point to its downside:

> Striving for masculinity presents dilemmas for the black male because it is so often grounded in masking strategies that rest on denial and suppression of deep feelings . . . being cool can become more important than life itself. Unfortunately, it can exact a price that seems destructively high. *We believe that cool pose helps to explain the fact that African-American males die earlier and faster than white males from suicide, homicide, accidents, and stress-related illnesses; that black males are more deeply involved in criminal and delinquent activities; that they drop out of school and are suspended more often than white children; and that they have more volatile relationships with women.* (Majors and Billson 1992, 2; emphasis added)

As a black boy outsider, the "cool pose" provided no form of self-protection. For all the reasons above, whiteness presented itself as the possibility to be myself without restraints of rigid, narrow notions of black masculinity.

I remember distinctly when I was fourteen, one of the ninth-grade teachers in my all-black junior high school told our social studies class that we would enter a different world at the new (white) high school. Preparing us for the realities to come, she told us we needed to improve our dress. She also suggested that we carry attaché cases instead of book bags and that we had to watch our speech and our behavior. We were going to enter the world of "white" people. She had socially and intellectually prepared us to engage whiteness. While feeling quite racially intimidated by her talk, I was secretly bursting with anticipation. Entering our town's new high school—where white students, teachers, and administrators would overwhelmingly outnumber us—would represent an escape from the excruciatingly painful and oppressive world of black boy masculinity I had suffered through in junior high school. I brimmed with excitement about the possibility of more humane treatment, based on my perception that white gender norms imposed less stringent rules of masculinity on white boys. Ironically, I would remain a virtual outsider to them during all three years of high school. I could *live* with that.

Crossing over to the white world of the new Hot Springs High School, the codes of masculinity were more liberal, more fluid, and less overtly homophobic. In the gender freedom of this new white context, what had been considered male outsiderness in the all-black junior high school came across as normal. In "HSHS," I was simply free *to be*. Looking and acting like an outsider appeared fashionable, trendy, a symbol of individuality. My personal differences of behavior and looks (except for my dark skin) blended into white individualistic ways of being. In fact, they worked for me. My standing among the black boys no longer mattered, as my status among the whites quickly rose. I was exceptionally black—sociable, funny, smart, nonthreatening. As far as I was concerned, in 1968, whiteness represented my ticket out of black male identity. Just as the "cool pose" operated as a coping strategy for black males I encountered in both black and white school settings, *passing for white* functioned as a strategy of advancement for me in the majority-white high school classroom.

The church played a big part in my life during these years. Like whiteness, it provided a place "to pass" in, a place to hide out from masculine expectations of adults (my parents, other relatives, and family friends). It also afforded a place to hide from black males who intimidated me. Yet hiding out in church had its downside. The church's views on education were contradictory. On the one hand, getting an education was applauded. On the other, older "saints" would caution young people about the limits of "worldly" education. "Don't let that education take you away from the church," they would say. Before integration, the church was the directional compass for my view of the world. Yet it encompassed a worldview in which nearly everything was sinful. Schooling with whites—even in the Bible Belt—loosened the grip of conservative religious dogma that for so many years I felt trapped by. It represented one long list of "don'ts." Being educated with whites signified personal freedom *to be*—free from the church's numerous religious/social restrictions in the name of "holiness."

Entering majority-white classrooms where few black males existed released me from their terrorizing attacks. Whiteness was not only a site of freedom; it was also a place of safety. It represented safety from all the black males who had tormented me. It also stood as an emotional sanctuary away from feelings of shame, guilt, and anger I experienced in a home plagued by abuse. In classrooms with white students, I fantasized about the happy, normal lives they led at home, fantasies based upon images from television sitcoms like *Leave It to Beaver, Ozzie and Harriet,* and *Father Knows Best.* It would be well beyond my high school and undergraduate school years before I realized that integrated education in majority-white schools was both a blessing and a curse.

The Oneness of Whiteness and the Class of '71

Race has an all-too-present master signifier—Whiteness—which offers the illegal enjoyment of absolute wholeness.

—Kalpana Seshadri-Crooks

Paging through my high school yearbook, the *Old Gold Book,* I stop after the first few pages. With photographs of blacks and whites together, intermingled narrative lines tell a story of racial unity. That racial integration in public schools in Hot Springs proved successful. The class of 1971 illustrated it. While photographs of integration visually suggest blacks and whites had worked through the problems of racial difference in three years, in truth (as I understand it now) racial integration at my school could only be photographed in such a racial culture of white rule. It defined racial unity without addressing politics of power and domination that determine who should (or should not) be helped in society. The text explicitly established a clear distinction between two types of students: militant (bad, troublemaking) students and nonmilitant (good, cooperative) students who eschew civil disobedience.

Through silence on *race* in my high school yearbook, white school hegemony masked itself—making invisible the mechanics of racial domination it willed. The absence of race in this text was not just about the will to hide white power; it also implicitly spelled out another message: "No *black* blacks allowed."

The introductory theme pages of my high school yearbook reveal a striking disjuncture between the visual performance of race (through photographs) and the textual misrepresentation of racial unity signified in its figurative use of the number "1." This analysis aims to show the fallacy of racial unity conceived in the politically correct minds of young, idealistic Southern white and black high school students experiencing racially integrated schooling for the first time in their lives. The same politically correct, de-racialized notions of racial unity held by Southern white and black students in the late 1960s in Hot Springs represent themselves in the postintegration, "color-blind" attitude many white students and students of color hold toward race, as I have confronted in my feminist-antiracist classes over forty years later. Critically scrutinizing passages from the yearbook text today, I am amazed how my ideas of race have dramatically changed.

The class of 1971 represented a number of racial "firsts." The high school class of 1971 in Hot Springs achieved something that no other graduating class had before it. Officially, this class was the first class that completed all three years of senior high at the new school. It stood for the efficacy of integrated public education in our town. To whites and blacks in the community, the new high school stood as a shining icon of racial progress—like the (now faded) embossed gold number "1" on the cover of the *Old Gold Book*. My black classmates and I made a number of racial firsts. In my senior year, I served as the first black editor of the school's newspaper. I was also the first black male to play the flute in the school band. One of my black male friends became the first to direct the "pep band." Two female friends of mine were the first blacks to dance on the school's coveted dance squad. Our football and basketball teams were stronger because of the first black males to play on them. In 1971, our racially integrated teams had achieved top spots in the state finals in both sports. In fact, that same year, our football team was rated number one in the state.

In our high school yearbook, terms like "first" and "one" stood as idealized, numerical signs of indisputable racial progress. For many of the black students being educated (for the first time in their lives) as "minority" students, integrated education in high school proved culturally, intellectually, and socially traumatizing. But no one spoke openly about it. Except for an assembly at the beginning of the 1968 school year, race was not openly engaged again. After that meeting, black and white students never came together to dialogue about issues of racial integration (as if none existed in our school). For the most part, white students kept to themselves and so did black students. There were those among us who dared to cross the color line. As this narrative painstakingly attempts to show, crossing over the racial barrier into whiteness became a personal goal for me.

Examining the text of the opening pages and images from my graduating class yearbook offers a revealing look into the systemic and institutionalized manner in which ideas of schooling in a postsegregationist

Southern high school remained tied to myths of white supremacy. To begin with, implicit in the school's goal of racial unity and harmony is the idea of racial homogeneity—that after three years of school together our race, class, and cultural differences as black and white students could be summed up in a single discursive and visual representation through the employment of a collective "we." It occurs to me now that I never read the opening pages of the text. I just internalized the model pictures of "diversity" (of which there was actually very few) through color-blind eyes all too willing to erase racial difference. Reading lines in the text makes me painfully aware just how uncritical and apolitical I was during those years. I believed in the promise of integrated education through a romanticized vision of racial oneness: "This was the year [1971] that . . . An entire community vibrated with involvement. Pride became a natural element in our lives as we suffered the bitter sweat of work and grew in the sweetness of success. We realized that winners were made, not merely through strength and ambition, but also through the fusing of minds and the binding of hearts. Fifteen hundred individual students linked hands, reached for the top, and made it. HSHS became ONE." (Hot Springs High School 1971, 3). "We" black and white students were "winners." All fifteen hundred of us "linked hands, reach[ing] for the top, and ma[king] it." Of course, that never really happened. Written in a discourse of racial sentimentality typical of such an occasion, the language is replete with terms that aspire toward racial equality—that aim to attain social justice. Did becoming "one" mean that black and white students had embraced a vision of racial equality? If such was the case, it remained veiled in the text. Racial equality is implied in the statement above, but race itself is never overtly stated.

On another page, with text in white set against a black background, the words read, "We marched in triumph—an undivided school, a union of friends . . ." (5). Imbibed with the fervor of eternal optimism, representing themselves as united warriors, the students fought together to defeat racism? It is never clearly stated what "we" were fighting. What a powerful statement against racism the passage would have made had this been the case. As illustrated, racial ambiguity in the students' minds could be read as a telling sign about the larger community's anxiety about the possibility of racial discord. Like the years of our town's silence in response to the issue of school desegregation, the yearbook speaks in muted tones—as if mentioning "race" itself would imply defeat.

There is a conscious, albeit generalized, recognition of a world with problems in the late 1960s, but again the yearbook of 1971 depicts (black and white) students (sans racialization) as a united front against social evils, even as it puts forth an overt rejection of militancy in the form of protests and marches (associated with violence). "We" could march together as an integrated school in "triumph" against social evils but never outside the bounds of reason (which obviously precluded any thought of violence as a strategy for battle). Unlike students who might resort to violence to attain social justice (which would be nonproductive), our approach (the one "we, the majority" favored) was "help[ful]," and therefore indisputably justified: "They [students advocating active demonstration for social change] tried to convince the world that their way was right through protests and marches, through violence for peace. But we, the majority, met the world face to face and decided to help it . . . to work undivided, to strive as one. Brimming with the optimism of yes, we reached out together. We found that our greatest accomplishments were achieved through unity. . . . And we discovered that our world's greatest purposes were fulfilled when we were—ONE." (7). The language of "we, the majority" in the passage above, promoting a pacifist vision of student social involvement, implicitly denounces a model of student activism supportive of civil disobedience as a viable strategy for social intervention. In this way, the text is politically ultraconservative in vision. But its conservatism is concealed through the illusion of innocent, youthful altruism.

Upon a close analysis of the text's explicit promotion of benign student *non*activism is the troubling advancement of a racially conservative ideology of school integration. It repeatedly erases students' racial difference, making any problems of racism invisible through language that belies its existence. (Racial) unity and solidarity is achieved once again through the evocation of "one"ness, which "we [the students] discovered." Now, what seems so tragic about this optimistic vision of racial integration through education is that its problematics could not be publicly voiced. The literal absence of race in the yearbook's introductory text symbolically states the defining problem of race talk in the majority-white classroom. In the de-racialized world of Hot Springs High, racial integration meant everything and nothing at the same time. "We" reached upward to attain and unite together to discover our common purpose through it. At the same time, however, "we" could not name it directly. For all our hard work, we had transcended *race*. Thus, it did not warrant even mentioning. It was as if the struggle to end racially segregated education had never existed in the United States.

Passing for White in a White Classroom

For many black families, full integration of the public school system came not only as a sign of racial progress, but also as a sign of a better, higher standard of education. Indeed, it may have been better, considering the fact that white schools in our town had been historically privileged to have *better* facilities and *better* materials. Before integrated public education in Hot Springs, being a black student meant getting the hand-me-downs of the white schools—books, football equipment, band instruments, and so on. My entrance into high school marked my entrance into the *white* world. We (black students) had crossed the railroad tracks that divided whites and blacks in my hometown.

As a black male student in majority-white schools, I learned three basic things about white power that would get me to the head of the class: (1) avoid race talk, (2) be racially color-blind, de-racialize, and (3) most importantly, *pass for white.* I grew up in the segregated South of the 1960s believing that integrated schooling with whites was the promise of a superior education. I believed the promise of integrated schooling in my hometown would bring about a better life for me personally. As an impressionable black child from a working-class family (neither of whose parents had graduated from high school), whiteness came to symbolize success. Images of blacks on television suggested that we were good for entertainment—singing and dancing mostly, joke telling, or serving whites. Except for images of black *male* basketball and football stars, representations of successful blacks on television and at the movies were few.

In the integrated classroom with majority-white students, I learned to like being around white people more than black—especially white females. All of the ugly myths of white beauty standards, notions of "high"-class femininity, purity, and intelligence maintained itself in the white female body. While there were white girls I had crushes on, I never dated a white female (nor a black female, for that matter) in high school. Given my antisocial religious background (no mixing with "sinners") and the outsider status among black males my age, my low self-esteem pretty well guaranteed that I was a community of one. As stated in the opening, all that I was learning about the myth of white superiority in the white classroom, television had already reinforced. In my colonized world of black self-hatred, images of whites in the classroom and on television complemented each other. I was not white; I never forgot that. But I desired the prestige of whiteness, though no white person in high school (as friendly as she or he was) ever invited me to her or his home. In classes with whites, I learned quickly how to imitate the stereotype of what being white represented—middle-class, carefree, intellectually grounded. Ultimately, acceptance into whiteness would mean replacing black role models with white ones—interactions with more white teachers, more white students, more white texts, and more tolerance for the unearned privilege(s) that came with being white.

As much as I learned in majority-white classrooms in high school how to pass for white, I also learned that whiteness (as well as embodying the badge of racial and feminine superiority) signified high-class status. This was apparent to me in class discussions of class. Middle- and upper-middle-class white students I associated with in high school had parents who were professionals—doctors, lawyers, bankers, "important" people. Secretly embarrassed about the menial jobs my parents held, I avoided class talk in school. While trying to ignore the politics of racism and classism at school, I was always aware of it at home in my parents' job discussions. Their experience as black manual laborers in a culture of white supremacy functioned as another source of learning that created a personal race and class mind-split. I really fed on the racial self-adulation that came with education in majority-white classrooms. The fact that I full well knew my parents' job struggles often made me feel divorced from them. I loved them but vehemently hated the race, class, and gender oppression they faced daily on the low-paying jobs they held.

As I have mentioned, for many years my father worked as a ditchdigger laying pipe or repairing it for the water company in town. Even when he would come home with the smell of liquor on his breath, his clothing and boots would be covered with mud. Particularly, during the hot summer months, I wondered how he endured the sun's blistering heat. Every now and then, he would complain about white men on his job—how they got promoted over him or paid more. I remember seeing him on occasion working in street trenches around town. He was always happy, laughing, and joking with the other men, most of whom were white. My father really enjoyed what he did for a living. I never got the feeling he was embarrassed by it. About two years before he retired, he received a promotion to the position of "assistant superintendent" at his job. I never knew exactly what that meant except that he got a little more pay. Years before that, however, he had gained the respect of almost every white man on his job. When he died, I met many of those men.

During the days before my dad's funeral, they came to my parents' home with food, offering to do whatever they could to help us prepare for the funeral. In a thick Southern drawl, on the day of the funeral they spoke publicly about how much they loved and respected him. I listened with surprise. My father, who had only completed the eighth grade and not educated in formal book knowledge, was a deep thinker. He was always reading. When he got "saved," he became a scholar of the Bible. Having become a man of great Christian conviction, my father never taught me to hate anyone on the basis of skin color. As someone who had endured years of racial discrimination on his job, he never held it against all whites. Unless I am mistaken, he is the only African American in Hot Springs to have a street named in his honor for his contributions toward racial unity in the community.

Like my father in his middle years, my mother became a devoutly religious woman. She completed the eleventh grade with work toward a GED (much later in life). For years she was a domestic worker in the homes of elite white people in our town and became a factory worker briefly afterward. Her views on race emerge from this history and from her experiences growing up in a rural community in Arkansas during the 1930s and 1940s where racist whites openly discriminated against and harassed blacks. Of my parents, my mother is the more vocal and defiant in her reaction to racism. While growing up, I was accustomed to hearing her talk forcefully about one of the most overt forms racial discrimination she experienced as a domestic worker: having to enter the homes where she worked through the back door. I remember what my mother had said to the white male president of the local bank for whom she worked when she decided to quit. She told him she was tired of coming to work through the back door and taking leftover food and clothing from his house. She said she had a son in college just like he did, and no, her own personal key to the back door was not going to make things better. And with that last remark, she left, never to return to his home or that of any other white person as a domestic worker.

Even to this day, I love hearing my mother tell this story. Each time she recounts it, she becomes even more animated in its telling. For a soft-spoken woman, even after thirty years she still possesses a sharp tongue and quick wit regarding her experience of racism. After leaving domestic work, she became a factory worker until some years later, when the company closed. While my mother worked in service positions for white people most of her life, she never failed to assert the right to be treated fairly as a black woman. While she never actively linked her stance to the plight of other black women in oppressive work situations (the terms "feminism" and "feminist" were absent from her vocabulary), I learned from her experiences that racism was real but so was sexism. Even in the face of domestic violence endured for years before my father's spiritual conversion, I learned from my mother's experiences that as a working-class black woman (combating abuse at work and in her own home) she had had to confront multiple oppressions. While my mother never taught me to hate white people, she did teach me to be vigilant about the subtle and pervasive ways racism functioned to deny the humanity of black people. For years, she did not know, however, what to tell my brother and me about the years our father physically abused her. Despite the process of internalized racism that was a by-product of integrated education in majority-white schools and television shows that glorified middle-class white identity, I held on to my parents' basic belief in racial equality. The indelible memory of the triple oppression my mother endured as a working-class black woman became the experiential grist for my profession of feminism.

Each morning, instead of walking four blocks to the former, black school (which was actually relatively new compared to the old white high school), black students crowded onto city buses to make the trek out to the suburb. In contrast to the city buses we rode to school, cars driven by white students filled a huge parking lot. And while we "mixed" in our classes during the day, at 3:15 p.m., we went back to our separate worlds. There was never a "racial incident," a race riot, or a race-motivated protest . . . whites and blacks crossed the color line to make integration work in mostly superficial ways. Some things were noticeable, others not. Why did we have to have a white principal and not a black one? Why did so many black students drop out after the first year at HSHS? Why were so many black students tracked into lower-level classes? According to Beverly Daniel Tatum, "In racially mixed schools, Black children are much more likely to be in the lower track than in the honors track. Such apparent sorting along racial line sends a message about what it means to be Black" (1997, 56). We had been thrust among throngs of white students and white teachers who had little to no social interaction with black culture beyond the school building.

Before integration, we were all black together. Schooling with whites would mean our blackness would always be filtered through the cult of whiteness. We discovered to our surprise that none of the white students at HSHS wore suits or carried attaché cases. Even so, many of us were still determined to dress better than they did, because many of our parents believed we had to in order to compete with our white counterparts. To the surprise of them and the white teachers who taught us, we were smarter than many of them—though many of us never fully realized it. "Why," Daniel Tatum asks in her book, "are all the black kids sitting together in the cafeteria?" For black students in my high school, "sitting together in the cafeteria" could be interpreted as a racially separatist act. However, the "black table" was a sanctuary away from the forced imposition of whiteness everywhere around us. The "black table" in the cafeteria symbolized the one place in school where blackness obtained, and where it ruled. No matter how racially integrated school life at HSHS seemed, lunchtime represented the time for racial separation. Beyond this overt form of black solidarity, no show or exhibition of nationalist or radical form of blackness existed.

Against the history of white racist resistance to desegregation in Arkansas, at Hot Springs High no federal troops had to descend upon our town to enforce desegregation, though full integration in our public schools did not actually occur until nearly fifteen years after the infamous struggle to desegregate Little Rock Central High School. Perhaps the racist taint associated with the state's name contributed to why integrated public school education in our town happened without incident—albeit over a decade after federal troops had convened in the state capitol's city. While this midsize Southern resort town (known for its hot water springs and horse racing) of about forty thousand people appeared to effortlessly transition into the acceptance of desegregated schooling, the nation itself was in a state of racial turmoil. In 1968, Martin Luther King Jr. was assassinated. Cities across the country burned for days. Only months later, we witnessed the assassination of Robert Kennedy. While the 1960s was a decade wrought in turbulent civil upheaval before and after their deaths—from the public slayings of John F. Kennedy and Malcolm X to militant resistance to the Vietnam War by college students across the United States and the rise of the black power movement—I lived in an idyllic town that had insulated itself from the world beyond the mountain range that surrounded it.

Reflecting on the history of my high school education with white students over thirty years ago, I understand now that passing as white as a "black boy outsider" was a survival strategy. On the one hand, it compensated for my outsider standing in black boy culture—though it never secured me a place in the culture of white boys in school. On the other, passing as a *white* black male at the time symbolically represented a ticket to academic success. Psychologically, assimilating into whiteness allowed me to deaden feelings of deep racial self-hatred bound up in issues of black masculinity. In my life, it represented all that hurt me; it kept me feeling like a "boy" failure because I liked being smart, sensitive, artistic, and religiously grounded. I had contempt for black males who employed machismo tactics to assert themselves, usually at the expense of black females. I may not have passed the cultural test of masculinity proffered by the black boys in junior high, but I would become a vigilant student of whiteness (to fit into the social and intellectual norm integrated schooling offered me).

My preference for "white ways of being" developed largely unmediated, uncontested, and unresisted by anyone. As one close black woman friend with whom I graduated from high school termed my race and gender dis*position*, I was the "invisible man." Like Ralph Ellison's title character, I cloaked myself in invisibility. I concealed myself within the myth that being educated with whites was about becoming more cultured, more civilized—less *black*, less scrutinized in masculinist ways. Black racial invisibility allowed me to "lighten up," to be free to learn white middle-class codes of accepted behavior in school. It required speaking in a manner that was culturally nonthreatening to white people (read: standard English). It called for a style of dress that suggested middle-class standing (my Sunday-best slacks, shirts, and shoes). Moreover, it mandated a politically correct attitude about race (to be color-blind, avoiding its discussion altogether). I conformed to the stereotypical codes of whiteness, adopting them to appear "whitclike." Having gleaned the race, gender, and class criteria by which I could excel in an integrated educational setting, I self-consciously represented myself as the exceptional black male. In my interactions with white students and teachers, I aimed to appear nonthreatening (as in "not racially aggressive"); witty (as in "able to take or defuse a racist 'joke' by whites without responding with racial accusation"); intelligent (as in "believing that studying and making good grades was a good thing"); and racially neutral (as in "not a black troublemaker," as in "capable of *passing for white in the white classroom*").

A *Pre*-Integration *Post*script: "Given the Choice, They Would Not Have Gone"

On Sept. 3 [1968], a group of school kids got off the public buses, made their way along Emory Street and entered Hot Springs High School for the first time. The school was new, but the tradition was all Trojan black and gold. *Their new schoolmates were white. Their teachers were white. The administration was white. They were black* [emphasis added]. They were to be the Langston classes of 1969 to '72. Instead, they became the first classes to integrate Hot Springs High School. These students have been silent about those years.

—Victor Whitman

While writing this chapter, Sue, a female cousin I grew up with, gave me a copy of an amazing article by Victor Whitman that appeared in our hometown newspaper on Thursday, September 3, 1998. The article was two full pages long and was entitled "Langston's Lost Years—Given the Choice, They Would Not Have Gone." It is a story commemorating thirty years of integrated schooling in Hot Springs, Arkansas. It focuses almost entirely on black perception of the historic integration of Hot Springs High School. Based on a forum held at the Emma Elease Webb Community Center, a landmark of black life in Hot Springs for many years, former black students of HSHS and Langston met to share thoughts about the impact of integration on them.

Reading the story with amazement, as if I had acquired it through an act of divine intervention, I savored every word and visually feasted upon the accompanying photographs that traced the all-black school's history back to its beginning in 1881. Like a missing link from my past, this newspaper article provided me a larger context for understanding the racial forces at work that led to the end of segregated schooling in my hometown. According to the news story, Langston began as Rugg Academy for black students in 1888. It was renamed "Langston School" in 1904 for John Mercer Langston, a black Virginian congressman known for his contribution to education. The school graduated its first high school class in 1910. After fires destroyed it at two locations, a new Langston was built at 316 Silver Street in the 1920s (Whitman 1998). When I first attended it in 1965 as a seventh grader, the historic (Gothic-designed) main building had already been torn down and replaced by a new, architecturally uninspired structure. The new building stood behind where the old one had stood—out of visual range on Silver. No longer was there a visible landmark of black education in our town. In fact, as the article reports, "[v]ery little remains of Langston High School from the glory days of the blue and gold and the Langston Bulldogs [the school mascot]. The trophies are gone. Even the old clock in the gym—which remained for years after Langston closed—was replaced recently." Even as a child fascinated by building design, I remember seeing the "new" black school for the first time. Facing a narrow nondescript side street (Chestnut), it had no recognizable facade—no signifying entrance except for the large industrial-looking fence that enclosed its long, low, two-story central building. Adding to its factory-like look, beyond the big metal-sheathed gym/auditorium/cafeteria that was now the visual center of the campus, there was not a single tree or any sign of grass in the entire gated entrance—just concrete pavement.

Like so much of what segregated education in Hot Springs had been prior to 1968, the "new" Langston, while new in construction, looked like a hand-me-down. In all truth, I am surprised that black parents, educators, and citizens of the community did not rise up against its pitiable, less than inspired design. Ironically, while Langston was rebuilt on a low-lying plot of land (much lower than the elevation of the multistory building it once was on Silver Street), the multistory high school white students attended (officially known as "Hot Springs High") stood on a high elevation, in a central part of town (visible from a number of vantage points in the area). Like the Langston building, the white high school was Gothic in style, only much, much bigger and more visually impressive. While the aesthetics of the physical structure of Langston paled in comparison to the white high school building, according to Wilberdine Howard (a close family friend and 1968 graduate of the all-black high school) learning in a black environment was inspiring: "They expected you to be twice as good. You heard it in my house from kindergarten on up. From my first days, I can remember my mom always saying you are expected, even if you want to be a dishwasher, to be twice as good as the worst [or best] white guy or you won't get a job." She emphasizes how in the time before integrated schooling there was a community politics of black education: "Everybody kind of knew each other. What you did at school got home before you did. It was kind of checks and balances—'I know your father or I know your mom or I am in church with your mom.' It kept you in line" (qtd. in Whitman 1998).

Life changed dramatically for every student who entered HSHS in September 1968. For many of the black students, it was racially traumatizing. The news story reports those black former graduates of the integrated high school, "The message [from them was]: They didn't want to go. They wouldn't have gone, if given the choice. And they are still angry about those lost years." While leaving Langston represented a form of gender freedom for me personally, as I have recounted, it is clear that for black female and male students not having suffered overt harassment from their peers at the segregated school, the memory of forced entry into a white-dominated school system—under the guise of integration—rightly represents a legitimate source of anger. In comments throughout the news story, mostly from black female graduates but with one black male speaking out, the sentiments are the same. Integrated schooling with white students at HSHS had more damaging than positive effects on black students in general. Minnie Nolen Lenox (class of 1969) emphatically notes, "They were just going to infuse us into the system like a blood transfusion. . . . We went from not having a choice at a school we dearly loved to not having a choice at a school we didn't care anything about. That was what was tragic about it" (qtd. in Whitman 1998). Lenox's statement speaks to the "tragic" implications of life for many of the black students entering the white world of education for the first time. Lenox further laments: "There were chapters in my life that were made at Langston. They knew nothing about those chapters at Hot Springs High School. They wanted us to conform to everything they had. They wanted us to lay down everything we had, everything we had done and move over to their side. But we had to do it on their terms."

Perhaps, had my experience of black boy culture at Langston not been so mired in the hurt of having been made a symbol of gender outsiderness, I might have felt the same way. But for a black boy (already psychologically assimilated into whiteness via television) whose academic proclivities leaned more toward art and music, integrated schooling symbolized a way out of the oppressive script of heteronormative black masculinity. Another of the black females who shared her feelings at the forum (and whom I remember fondly from high school), Gladys Jones (class of 1971), spoke about the educational disparities between the black and white schools: "Where we felt loved at Langston, we felt hated at Hot Springs High. We knew the teachers at Langston loved us and were strong at disciplining us. At Hot Springs High, they really didn't care" (qtd. in Whitman 1998). In spite of the ways white supremacy remained a normalized feature of my experience as a classmate and friend of Gladys, I bonded with two white female teachers in particular—one in art, the other in journalism. In reality, my relationship with them probably had as much to do with the idealization of white femininity on television I had internalized as the fact that they took a serious interest in my artistic and writing abilities. Their mannerisms reminded me of Jackie Kennedy in the White House—they were soft-spoken, cultured, and intellectual. They embodied the myth of whiteness (in female form). In Ms. Jenkins's journalism class in eleventh grade I first thought about becoming a teacher.

While retaining the school colors and mascot of the formerly all-white teams, the school's sports programs transformed with the inclusion of black male athletes. Undoubtedly, on the football field and basketball courts, black and white schools united. Even there, however, racism was a hurdle to overcome. Frank Cooper (class of 1969), the only black male mentioned in the article, played on the school's football team. He states, "[T]he black football players almost quit the team, believing they were treated more like blocking and tackling dummies" (qtd. in Whitman 1998). The year he played, the football team's record was 8-1-1. With each year after integration, the teams improved dramatically. So much can be said about the racial politics of sports and the exploitation of black male athletes in a culture of white supremacist patriarchy that reifies certain myths of black physicality. In truth, Hot Springs High rose to unprecedented athletic heights when the black and white schools merged. But in so many ways, Langston lost in the educational arena. What about the display of black talent in the academic and artistic arenas of the integrated school's programs—such as the honor society, music, drama, art, and journalism, for example? Black talent only existed on the ball court and field?

It cannot go without mentioning that while the period from 1968 to 1971 saw no major race-related violence at the school, six years after integration, an article about racial problems appeared in the Hot Springs High School yearbook under the title 'Salt and Pepper.' There were fights and incidents where the police were called to patrol the halls that year" (qtd. in Whitman 1998). While debates about integrated schooling will continue as long as public schools wrestle with testing, curriculum, and teacher education, the end of white supremacy and equal opportunity in the classroom for students of color will remain a volatile issue. When I try to assess the psychological toll education in majority-white classrooms had on me beginning in high school, I remain conflicted. On the one hand, like the other first black survivors of integrated schooling mentioned in the article, I too feel angry that being successful in classrooms with white students called for me to de-racialize—to lose my blackness or any trace of ethnic identification. On the other, I adapted to the racist script of white supremacy as a means of survival outside a culture of masculinity in which I did not fit. Considering my marginalized gender status (and, by default, racial standing) in black masculinist culture, what would have happened to me had not Langston closed?

While I have never had reason to question the merits of its curriculum, particularly because it mirrored the academic standards of learning promoted by a white-dominated educational system, I wonder whether the oppressive weight of black boy culture would have eventually crushed me—mentally and emotionally. In my mind, even today, I think of the idea of racially integrated schooling as a curse and a blessing. Over the course of the thirty years and more since the integration of Hot Springs High School, the vantage point of former black students who experienced it firsthand has not changed—"[T]hey are still angry. Few attend reunions of Hot Springs High School. They are Langstonians. They also feel the black community lost something with the school's closing—an agent for cohesiveness and identity in a once thriving black community on the east side of town" (Whitman 1998).

I have never attended a reunion of the class of '71 and most likely never will. But I have never attended a reunion of "Langstonians" either, as many former black students back home have, whether they graduated from Langston or not. I do not hold the memories of schooling there that those in the news article possess. Technically, my three years of high school were spent in the "new" Hot Springs High School where—for better or for worse—I learned the ways of white folk in the South that prepared me in 1971 to enter Southern State College, a majority-white public institution two hours away from my hometown.

✤ 5 ✤

"There's a Nigger in the Closet!"
Narrative Encounters with White Supremacy

> Since a person's ongoing identity will defend itself against identity change, the person usually has to experience some sort of *encounter* that has the effect of catching him or her "off guard." The encounter must work around, slip through, or even shatter the relevance of the person's current identity and world view, and at the same time provide some hint of the direction in which to point the person to be resocialized or transformed.
>
> —William Cross

"[B]eing the 'right kind of Negro'" as a teenager in the late 1960s had enabled me ideologically to pass for white in high school, as a "high" black male achiever. However, a series of racial "encounters" in higher education would "shatter" my preencounter with whiteness. They began in 1972 in undergraduate school at (what was then) a small, majority-white college (now Southern Arkansas University) two hours from Hot Springs. Transforming my ideas of race *and* gender as a black male, they continued into graduate school when I entered the University of Arkansas in 1978 and later as a doctoral student at New York University in the mid-1980s. In *Shades of Black*, William Cross—delineating the transition from first-stage de-racialized consciousness to the second stage of nigrescence precipitated by one's experience of "racist encounters"—maintains:

> . . . Blacks who have somehow managed to avoid or escape racial incidents at earlier points in their lives often begin nigrescence after a startling racial episode in college or at their place of employment. Having worked so hard at being the "right kind of Negro," racist encounters can shatter a Pre-encounter person's conception of himself or herself and his or her understanding of

103

Black America. . . . Giving credence (i.e., personalizing) to this information may challenge someone radically to rethink his [or her] conception of Black history and Black culture. Even in such instances, however, a negative side to the Encounter is often introduced, *for it is almost inevitable that the person will become enraged at the thought of having been previously mis-educated by white racist institutions.* (1991, 199–200; emphasis added)

As Cross defines the second stage of racial-identity development in blacks, he notes that the encounter stage begins with a "startling racial episode in college or in their place of employment." Having passed the test of whiteness in high school, I firmly believed that being invisibly black made me a good student. With a music scholarship, a grant, and student work-study, I enrolled in the small, majority-white college because I was financially unable to attend my first choice, the University of Arkansas at Fayetteville. With the success of high school behind me, I was sure a bright future for college achievement lay before me. I was determined to avoid "political" involvement in anything remotely connected to the student unrest that characterized college experience on many campuses across the nation in the 1970s. As a model student, I would not protest, march, or draw attention to myself for any purpose that created racial division. However, my second year in college proved to be as traumatizing as the three years I had endured in junior high school.

Editing Out Blackness:
A Picture Is Worth a Thousand Words

The first eye-opening encounter occurred in my job as coeditor of my college yearbook. It is ironic that the racial politics of this "book" in high school and college would have so great an influence in the development of my racial consciousness. The glorification of student (racial) unity in my high school yearbook, critiqued in the previous chapter, is similar to the sentiment on race illustrated in my college yearbook when I became its coeditor along with a white female student from the North. However, the vision of *inter*racial harmony we conceptualized as the yearbook's theme would come under blatant attack by our white male faculty adviser.

I remember that on a Friday afternoon near the end of the spring semester, when all the student yearbook staff workers had taken off for the weekend, the faculty adviser summoned Linda and me to his office. In an angry, clipped tone, he demanded we remove from the book what he considered was an excessive number of blacks in pictures with whites. Unless we agreed with his demand, we could consider ourselves fired (from the paid positions we held as editors). He gave us until five o'clock that afternoon to return to his office with our decision. We never went back. In our minds, we faced a no-win situation. At this point in the semester, with a month remaining in the semester, three-fourths of the yearbook's content had already been proofed and returned to the printer. That evening turned into days and weeks of an ongoing battle to protect our vision of racial unity . . .

Maybe my coeditor and I had forgotten our vision of multiracial harmony had been conceived in 1973 at a small, majority-white, Southern liberal arts college in Arkansas. When we assumed editorship of the *Mulerider*, our shared "politically correct" notions of racial diversity led us to believe that the yearbook's theme should be "United we stand; divided we fall." It would be reflected in as many photographs of white and black students together as possible (at least one per page)—eating together, partying together, studying together, in class together, and just hanging out together. Symbolized in bold white letters embossed on a black cover, the word "Vision" (reprinted front and center, several times in three different font sizes) stood for our desire to showcase racial unity. Before the yearbook adviser overrode it, we reveled in our unabashedly idealistic celebration of interracial harmony. Inspired by the 1960s pop artist Peter Max, the cover also featured a black-and-white, stylized graphic design of a field of human figures standing hand in hand before a setting sun.

Linda (my white liberal, hippyish partner in crime) and I were a model of interraciality, living out our personal ideals of diversity through the yearbook. We were the cocreators of a new, more powerful, more realizable dream of racial unity at the small Southern college we attended. It appeared that students on campus would not be opposed to the "cool" portrait of racial diversity we aimed to depict, even though blacks represented a small student "minority." In our visionary zeal (and youthful naïveté, looking back with thirty-year hindsight), not once did we ever pause to think that our righteous effort to model campus diversity through images of interraciality would lead to its very undoing . . . Our crime: there were *too* many pictures of blacks in the yearbook. I remember Linda crying angrily during that visit to the adviser's office as she unrelentingly questioned his ultimatum. Who was this white man who wielded so much power to crush our dream? He had threatened to fire us, to take our jobs. Linda and I needed the money . . . That day an intense hatred rose up in me for this white man that made me want to kill him, for killing our dream. Where would we go? Who would we tell? Would anyone help us?

That evening after leaving his office, not clear where we were going, we walked aimlessly down a road at the edge of the campus. I remember the day being abysmally cloudy, as if personifying the bleakness of our plight. The campus seemed deserted. As we walked along that road, I recall that everything around us looked flat, gray, and lifeless. That Friday would be the beginning of one of the worst few days of my life, I remember thinking. This was the thanks we received for our "noble" work. Monday morning came, however. Linda and I had decided to request a meeting with the school's vice president for student affairs, a slender, middle-aged white man. He agreed to meet with us. After we explained the dilemma facing us, he concluded (based on the percent of minority students) that we had, indeed, overrepresented the number of black students at the school. His mathematical formulation of how many pictures should show black students per page seemed ludicrous at the time, appearing to have been concocted on the spot. He suggested that our intentions were good, but nevertheless sided with our adviser in the end.

No one or any mathematical formula could convince us we were wrong. While garnering little support from the administration, faculty, or from students (black or white), we refused to alter the yearbook's photographic content. We were fired. The adviser replaced us with another student on our staff, a nonconfrontational white female. As soon as the yearbook came out that May, Linda and I combed its pages to discover what had been changed. Nothing—not one photograph! Only pages in the index including new pictures of "student life" had been added. The new editor's name appeared above ours on the opening page of the book, ours appeared below hers in alphabetical order. Ours was a Pyrrhic victory. On the one hand, we had lost our jobs as paid editors. On the other, the vision of racial diversity we had fought for had remained untouched. Linda did not return to school the next fall, transferring to another school. The yearbook adviser also did not return. I returned with a completely different academic agenda that further solidified my ideas of race and the attainment of whiteness. I changed my major from journalism to art and English, deciding to leave the problems of race behind for the colorless world of aesthetics and the literary universe of great (white) writers.

Transcending Racial Politics

Art and literature transcended racial politics, so I thought. In my junior year of college, British and American literature became a passion, though I never liked reading books as much as I loved drawing. Already filled with elitist notions of literary study from high school, English became a second major, giving my artistic studies some serious credibility (stereotypical notions had it that art was not academically rigorous enough). Literary studies was about the sublime world of texts. Few black males majored in English at my school; only one other did so during the time I was there.

I remember my freshman English class. For someone who grew up loving to draw more than anything and reading few books (outside of required reading in school), the idea of studying the "great books" of literature appealed greatly. I learned to love the idea of being a devoted reader of them as a part of my vision of whiteness materialized in the form of the young, tall, always very stylishly dressed white female professor who taught me freshman composition. She embodied the "high" class and cultured whiteness of the white women I saw on television. Needless to say, she evoked the indelible image of Jackie Kennedy. My teacher was also an artist; she loved to draw. I loved her sophisticated way of being white. In fact, this white woman professor was the reason I majored in English—not books. As an English major, I took four of this professor's classes—to be around her, to study her. Was I in love with her? No, I was in love with what she represented in my mind. I read the great books, but I could continue to draw also. Because she validated my love of drawing, I became passionately interested in art.

I became an art/English major, a member of two cultures. Being an art major in a department of all-white faculty and only three students of color (all black: two males and one female) was about as far away from racial politics as one could get. I recall once, at the height of a black student protest on campus, my pro-black-power cousin Patricia (who had prompted me to attend this school) called me to join in. I refused, not wanting to be associated with anything to do with *black* radicalism. Being one of a few black English majors meant joining a literary, cultural, white elite in an all-white faculty department in which white females who were bookish and snobbish predominated. As one of only two black males, however, I felt special, unique, and intellectually superior. I was the only black male admitted to Sigma Tau Delta (the national honorary English society) and the only black male to graduate in the department during my time there. Except for the one black female student in the art department, all the others were white.

Surrounded by white people at school, I had become accustomed to being the *exceptional* black student—the one who could pass for white. When I returned home during holidays and summer vacations, I wore my "outsider" status like a badge of honor (by choice). Being in college elevated my standing above that of many of the black males who had taunted me in junior high school, who had either not graduated from high school or had decided not to go on to college after graduating from high school. Older black folk in my community (inside and outside the church) admired me. In actuality, having left home for college, I left behind vestiges of heteromasculinist black identity that "othered" me and the church dogma that sexually bound me. Though I did not attend church while away from home during the four years of college, at school I maintained a reputation as a tried-and-true fundamentalist Pentecostal. My father—who by then had joined the church and become a devoted Bible student—enjoyed the "intellectual banter" of the religious debates we shared at the dinner table during those times when I came home from school. My parents praised the good grades I made. They relished my academic achievements—while never questioning my white racial politics. If anything, like many working-class black parents, they viewed being college-educated (especially in white schools) as a ticket to achieving economic success.

"Nigger Lover" Is Not a Term of Endearment

If the first encounter with race in my second year of college taught me that the racist politics of the *color line* were alive and well in Magnolia, Arkansas, the second encounter with racism the year after I graduated schooled me in the ways of Southern white racists. Having graduated with a bachelor's degree in English and art education, I returned to Hot Springs with hopes of teaching at my alma mater. No such luck. I interviewed, but nothing came of it. Without an alternative plan, I hastily decided to reenroll at the college from which I had just graduated. Another semester there, I figured, would save me the embarrassment of having to explain to relatives and family friends why "all that education" had not landed me a job. Because I reapplied to school so late in the summer, a dorm room could not be reserved until the term began after Labor Day. I arranged to stay the holiday weekend with Ellen (one of my best white female friends, who also had just graduated with a degree in English). Not from the South, she had remained in Magnolia over the summer.

I remember that on a scorching Saturday afternoon, I followed her directions to a large two-story house outside of town on a deserted country road. I recall how scenic the drive was, field after field of open farmland. Arriving at the house after driving around to the rear of it, I immediately noticed how remote it seemed, as if in the middle of nowhere. Ellen, having spotted my car, rushed out to greet me. Excited, we embraced without reserve. I never imagined we would be seeing each other so soon after graduation. Grabbing a few things from the trunk of my car, we entered the back of the house through a small, neatly kept kitchen. Most of the clothes I had brought along were piled high in the car's backseat. As Ellen and I walked up the back staircase off the kitchen to her second-floor apartment, she told me she rented the apartment from an elderly, single (white) woman. The two of them were the only two residents of the house. For that reason, it was always quiet around the place. The apartment was simply furnished and quite spacious, ample room for at least two or three people. As I settled in in the living room (where I would sleep on the couch), Ellen made tea. While I do not remember the specifics of our conversation, as we sat together seeping the herbal brew we must have talked about our friends, my recent misfortune on the job market, and her future plans.

Before we turned in for the evening, Ellen told me that she had to leave town the next morning to visit a close friend, but that she would return late that Sunday. She showed me where bath and kitchen necessities were, and said I was welcome to anything of hers in the refrigerator but to clean up after myself if deciding to cook. She shared the kitchen with her landlady, who Ellen thought would not mind my using it as long as there was no mess. Ellen told me she never locked the door to her apartment, since the owner was elderly and never came up the stairs leading to it. Again we shared how good it was to see each other, even though the circumstances could have been better for me before turning in for the night. As I lay on the couch that night, it occurred to me that Ellen had been my one true friend since my relationship with Linda. Was I attracted to her? Undoubtedly, particularly because she fit the part of the perfect English major—well-read, quick-witted, and just all-around scholarly. Probably most males would not consider her physically attractive. She was short, small-breasted, and rather boyish-looking, with dark brown hair. But I enjoyed her company. Did she find me appealing sexually? If so, she never expressed it. I fell asleep to the sound of crickets communicating with each other outside the open living-room window just above my head.

In the morning when I awoke, the house was still as quiet as the day before. It was early, about 8 a.m. Ellen had already gone before I had awakened. Just as the day before, the sun shone brightly. One thing Ellen had said the night before caused only a slight personal concern: the first floor would probably be full of (white) people. The landlady's family had planned a surprise birthday celebration for her on Sunday. Ellen had cautioned me to be as quiet as possible so as not to disturb anyone downstairs. I found this instruction somewhat strange, but decided to follow it. Until voices of male and females signaled the arrival of people downstairs, I spent the time reading and making sure that I walked softly in my socks through the apartment—not even having ventured down to the kitchen to take a peep in the fridge. By midafternoon, the first floor was filled with the voices of men, women, and children—all speaking joyously with the melody of Arkansas twang. How long would the party last? Here I was on the second floor of a house full of raucous white folk in the middle of nowhere.

Feeling ill at ease as the excitement of the people below heightened, I began to feel trapped, a prisoner, and began conjuring up images of the Ku Klux Klan in a world inhabited, except for me, only by white people. I quietly walked to the entry door to the apartment, locking it just in case someone accidentally wandered up the stairs. Who knew I was here (except for Ellen)? Who would find me? I could hear everything from the first floor—a baby crying, children and adults laughing, the surprise of the elderly landlady when her daughters brought out the birthday cake; the noise grew louder and louder, until someone inquired about the beige car with men's clothing in the backseat out back. Whose car was it? Where was its owner? Was he upstairs? "Let's go up there." "Get the key." Who was this man who had entered their mother's house unknown? Did she (Ellen) willfully let him in? "We will find him." I could hear the movement of feet below rushing through the house, searching for a key. They would find me. What would they do to me? I should confront them, meet them face-to-face at the door. I should challenge the right they felt to enter a tenant's locked apartment. I was the hidden menace—waiting to slaughter an innocent family, an elderly white woman. Maybe I had already raped and murdered Ellen, the young white woman who had lived upstairs. They had to find me. An angry mob, they charged up the stairs—irate white men, hysterical white women, frightened white children. I could not face them. The fearfully paralyzing monologue I carried on in my head matched the willfully terrorizing dialogue they generated.

I was the culprit, the rapist, the murderer—the savage violator of all white womanhood. What should I do? Where could I go? Where was Ellen? She would tell them, but why would they believe her? How could she bring a "nigger" into their mother's house? She would get hers, once they finished with me. I tried to think whether there was any way to let Ellen know that she could never live here again, that she should not even return, that this never happened, that she never lived here, that she never knew me. They enter the apartment. I rush to the closet in the living room. They search the bedroom—under the bed, in the closet. Next they charge into the bathroom. But they know I am still in the apartment. Can they can smell me? Instinctually, they smell their way to the living room. A slender, brown-haired, medium-height white boy (about fourteen or fifteen) opens the closet door. All six feet three inches of me is crouched in fetal position in the dark closet, holding my breath, anticipating the door's opening as the beginning of my end. The light of the setting sun filters quietly into the closet as the door is flung open by the boy's white pale hand—"There's a nigger in the closet!" he frighteningly yells. In a split second, without thinking, I bolt through the crowd of contorted young and old white faces. Only one goal in mind—get to the front door of the apartment.

Amid screams and shrieks of white women and children's horror, white men yell in rage, "Get a gun before he runs." With no time to spare, all I could see was an image of myself hanging bloody, brutally beaten with a noose around my neck somewhere in the woods behind this house on a deserted road outside of town. Darkness had come. To this day, I am not even sure I left with my shoes on. The one thing I knew rested deep in my front pocket was the key to my car. Did they come after me down the stairs? Was there a gun? A gunshot? Reaching the car in the darkness, I fumbled to get my hands on the key. I jumped into the driver's seat, shifted the transmission into "reverse," and sped backward, barely breaking to shift into forward. From the drive to the roadway was only a short distance, but in the pitch-dark night distance seemed relative. Where was I? Transported back in time. Like a slave tasting freedom for the first time, I fled the plantation and the old master's lash. I was free, free. No hanging that dark night for me.

Driving back toward town on the dark road, I did not want to imagine what Ellen would encounter when she returned home. In a daze, not knowing where to go, in town I stopped at a public phone to call a white couple Ellen and I had gone to school with. Shocked to hear what happened to me early that evening, they told me to come straight to their house to spend the night. We called Ellen's apartment. Answering the phone in a frightened voice, Ellen told us she arrived home to find all of her belongings out on the front yard. The landlady's family let her know in rather strong terms they had chased the "nigger" away. The racist insults they hurled toward Ellen like daggers could be summed up in two words: "nigger lover." They demanded she collect her belongings and leave that night. She refused. On the grounds that she had done nothing illegal and could not be forced out, in protest Ellen stayed the night. What a nightmare that must have been for her. While lying in bed in the couple's guest room, I stayed awake the entire night wondering if those angry white men would physically harm Ellen. A myriad of emotions flooded my head. I trembled with anger at the thought of having hidden in a closet fearing what those white people would have done to me, and agonized about causing Ellen to be unjustly evicted. Got what she deserved, like Linda, because she transgressed the boundaries of whiteness? Where would Ellen stay tomorrow? Dare I go back to her apartment to help with the move? Would she fight them legally? So many questions . . . I could never tell my parents, who while never teaching my brother or me to dislike white people had warned us about getting too close to them. Moreover, my brother and I had heard my parents tell story after story about racist white people's treatment of them.

School began that Monday. I got a room in one of the dorms. Ellen moved in with our friends until she found another place. There was no legal action against the landlady, who reluctantly returned Ellen's deposit. Ellen never looked for another apartment. Instead, after a brief stay with our friends, she moved out of state shortly thereafter. My parents thought I had begun work on a master's degree in education. Had they seriously investigated what I told them, they would have discovered that the school offered no master's degree in education. I was a student again back in Magnolia, taking more English courses but without any plans of pursuing any kind of degree. In fact, I began school again to hide out—no place else to go, nothing else to do. If I could not teach, no other job would satisfy me. That one semester at school was the loneliest I have ever spent. Nevertheless, I preferred loneliness to the feeling of worthlessness that living in Hot Springs would mean. In spite of my feelings, I moved back home at the end of the semester.

Toward the Myth of a *Whiter* Whiteness

After working for six months in Hot Springs as a social worker for single mothers on AFDC (Aid to Families with Dependent Children), in 1976 the school district hired me to teach junior high school English and reading. I taught at Central Junior High School for two years (formerly the all-white Hot Springs High School from which Bill Clinton graduated). Years later, as faculty adviser for the school's literary anthology, I stood on this same sidewalk for a photograph in front of the school with my eighth-grade advanced English class that created the anthology (they were all white except for one black female). I remember as a boy many times walking by (without racial attack) the imposing Gothic building on the hill during Sunday afternoons with a group of my cousins, imagining what school was like inside its old redbrick walls. Who would have guessed that years after desegregation, I would teach there? My meager salary of $7,000 in the late 1970s forbade having an apartment of my own. I lived with my parents for two years while teaching at CJHS.

My life changed drastically in 1978—I resigned from teaching at CJHS. I left Hot Springs bound for the University of Arkansas at Fayetteville, home of the Razorbacks. I had been accepted into a master's program in English at the school of my dreams. Fayetteville, probably one of the whitest towns in the state, was also its intellectual capital. The summer before school began, during my first visit to the picturesque college town nestled high up in the Ozark Mountains, I saw no people of color anywhere. Later, after settling into the community, I discovered that blacks in this lily-white town lived in the "hollow"—a low-land, small, rundown section of town. During the two years I lived in Fayetteville, none of the whites I associated with ever mentioned it. Fayetteville was *whiter* than white racially. No people of color on the English department faculty. I was one of two black graduate students in the entire program; the other was a black male creative-writing student. Not once during the two years did we ever exchange more than a casual hello.

At first, the whiteness of the university and the town filled me with a heightened sense of racial self-consciousness. White students and professors everywhere. As in high school and undergraduate school, I had learned one valuable lesson about being successfully black in majority-white educational settings—blend in, de-racialize. But it never worked completely, because when not in school I was at home or in church—in a black world where few white people entered except through television. Most white people I had encountered in majority-white schools showed no interest in race talk. I learned not to engage in it. Adopting a race*less* identity in Fayetteville posed little personal difficulty. Since junior high school, learning the rules of whiteness in majority-white schools came easily. In this small, majority-white, mountainous northwest Arkansas town, dominated by its majority-white university, I *re*immersed myself in whiteness—white English professors (the majority of them male), white friends, white students in the freshman writing classes I taught, and centuries of white-authored texts.

In a world so far away from home (in actuality only four hours by car), the two years I spent in Fayetteville represented the most experimental period of my life. Whereas religion had controlled and constricted my sexual desires as an asexual "nerd" in high school and undergraduate school, graduate school with liberal white intellectuals in Fayetteville exposed me to the freedom to dress, speak, act, and *to be* in a completely uninhibited way. No church, no Bible reading—no religious ties. I was free *to be*. Boundaries only existed to be broken—racially and sexually. What I wore on any given day was dictated by how I felt, and seldom did anything match—that was the idea, indeed. The Afro I grew framed my face like a giant black mushroom cloud—I was visually a cross between Jimi Hendrix and Frederick Douglass. During the week, I acted the part of the complete intellectual—a studious literary critic in the making. As a TA (teaching assistant), I ran my classes as seriously as any of the department's most respected senior faculty. When 3 p.m. came on Fridays, along with several other of my white cohorts, caution was thrown to the wind and we took College Ave. by storm. College Ave. offered itself as the hub of the nightlife scene in town—bars, bars, and more bars. We took advantage of them. I learned to drink liquor with a passion, beer excluded. In retrospect, deciding to go to graduate school in Fayetteville represented another opportunity to escape masculinist, religiously conservative notions of blackness that so severely policed my gender identity back in junior high school. Living in racially white Fayetteville and attending the prestigious, flagship university of Arkansas was like socially reliving my life in high school—only at this school in the late 1970s, I knew no other blacks on campus.

Of the white students whom I met in the English department of the University of Arkansas at Fayetteville, one became a lifelong friend—Linda. In my first year at the university Linda and I took a liking to each other immediately as "freshman composition" TA office mates. We quickly became inseparable as soul mates. We did everything together, except sleep together. Rarely did anyone see one without the other during the two years and a summer we were together. We both had taught previously in public schools before enrolling at the university. Telling me about the close relationships she had developed with black students in her classes, particularly with one black female student, led me to believe that Linda really cared about them. In my mind, her past "racial encounter" with black students lent her a level of racial credibility that laid an easy foundation for our relationship. That was over twenty-seven years ago. While we went our separate ways after finishing our master's degree program, we have maintained a close relationship. Linda remained in the South, married a good white man, had two children (of whom I am the godfather), finished her PhD in English at the University of Tennessee, and currently teaches at Georgia Southern University.

The histories of our marriages, our children, our academic careers, and our feminist activism in antiracism and domestic violence have kept us connected. Regardless of the depth of our passionate commitment to the feminist critique of domestic violence, it must be said that in the history of racism in the South a black man is always viewed as a sexual threat to a white woman, even if the two of them are professorial colleagues or long-standing feminist friends of the deepest kind. Impressed upon my mind as a child growing up in the South, scenes of racist violence related to the myth of black male defilement of white womanhood have remained in my consciousness as an adult. Since publicly identifying myself as a feminist in the late 1980s, I have struggled with the whiteness of feminism as a black student and pro-feminist professor.

Black Literature, a Consuming Passion: Stage Three, Immersion-Emersion

By the time I entered New York University in the mid-1980s intending to pursue a PhD in English, the idea of being an English major as a signifier of intellectual and racial superiority (as in ideologically *passing for white*) had become a way of life. Having had no previous courses in black literature at the undergraduate or master's level, I was steeped in the European literary tradition. In fact, neither undergraduate nor graduate schools I had previously attended offered black literature courses. This was also the case in the graduate English department at NYU when I began. Neither was there any full-time or part-time black faculty in the department while I was there from 1984 to 1990. Moreover, it was white male dominated. William Cross states that the third stage of racial identity development, known as "immersion-emersion," "represents the vortex of psychological nigrescence." He continues, "During this period of transition, the person begins to demolish the old perspective and simultaneously tries to construct what will become his or her new frame of reference. . . . *Black literature is consumed passionately*" (Cross 1991, 201–3; emphasis added).

I would come to know the power of literature written by African Americans through my association with three highly esteemed African American writers—bell hooks, John A. Williams, and Calvin Hernton. I met the black novelist John A. Williams in 1987, three years after first meeting bell hooks. Williams was a visiting professor during the spring term. I did not actually meet Calvin Hernton until years after I had finished doctoral work in the English department but I came to know Hernton's writing as a "self-proclaimed" feminist literary critic. Not only did writings by these three individuals have a profound impact on my views of American literary study, but as intellectual mentors they helped to shape my professional identity as an African Americanist. Indeed, having since experienced the joy of fostering mentoring relationships with students of color and white students, I know the influence a faculty member of color, can have in the life of a student of color, especially at a majority-white institution.

John A. Williams opened my mind to the joy of reading the black literary text. He came to the English department for one semester as a visiting professor in the creative program. Apparently, having gotten my name through the department chair, he contacted me about covering several sessions for him in an undergraduate African American literature class he was teaching. I agreed, while (as stated) possessing no formal knowledge of black literature. Both excited and afraid, I met with the students during the week he had to be away. The class was small and majority-black. While I have no recollection of the texts Professor Williams assigned for me to teach, I recall the students' enthusiastic response to the reading assignments during class discussion. I made no mention of my ignorance of the selected writers they read or the field of black literature in general.

Upon Professor Williams's return, he thanked me for taking over for him, told me that the students liked me, and presented me with a check for $350. I was completely caught off guard; he had not given any indication that my services would be compensated. What would I spend the money for, what did I need? Like the suddenness of a revelation, it occurred to me that I had no books by black authors, except for hooks's *Feminist Theory*. I decided to begin my own library of black books with Professor Williams's check. I began with his novel *The Man Who Cried I Am*, Richard Wright's *Native Son*, Paula Giddings's *When and Where I Enter*, Angela Davis's *Race, Women and Class*, Ann Petry's *The Street*, Ralph Ellison's *Invisible Man*, Zora Neale Hurston's *Their Eyes Were Watching God*, Langston Hughes's *Selected Poems*, Alice Walker's *The Color Purple*, Ntozake Shange's *For Colored Girls*, and Calvin C. Hernton's *The Sexual Mountain and Black Women Writers*, among others.

I keep in the top drawer of my writing desk at home a letter Professor Williams wrote to me in April 1991. It came toward the end of the first semester of my first full-time college teaching job in New York City. I had seen him briefly one evening at a production of a show on Broadway called *Black Eagles*, and he writes, "Dear Gary. . . . It was good to see you and bask once again in your enthusiasm for [black] literature." We had corresponded a couple of times previously about a paper I had written on blacks in Shakespeare and a piece on William Blake's antislavery poem, "The Little Black Boy." For an author of his stature, I was amazed that he maintained a writing connection to me. I marveled at his enthusiasm, interest, and considerable knowledge in the subjects I was writing about in graduate school. Never telling him how the check he had given me was spent, I simply noted in the inside cover of each: "Purchased with funds from John A. Williams." Little did he know in 1987, $350 went a long way toward not only in establishing a library of noteworthy black writers, but also in marking my place in the tradition of African American literature as a student and professor of it. As brief as my association with John A. Williams was, during the one semester he taught at NYU, it was enough time to ignite in me a passionate love of black literature I possess to this day.

One of the books I purchased with Professor Williams's check was Hernton's *The Sexual Mountain and Black Women Writers*. At the time, having read little pro-feminist criticism by black men beyond that of Arnold Rampersad, Henry Louis Gates, and Houston Baker (among a few other lesser-known names), this slender volume further opened my eyes to the possibilities of black male feminism. Its title essay had appeared as a separate essay in 1984. The essay provided me an initial historical reference counterpoint to masculinist versions of the black literary tradition. I also credit the essay for helping me create the list of black female-authored books I initially purchased. Moreover, Hernton's ardent, pro-feminist defense of black women writers in the essay so inspired me that I changed my dissertation topic from art and politics in William Blake's poetry to an exploration of the impact of feminism on black female and male writers. In the process, having began a historical search for other black male proponents of feminism, I discovered the pro-feminist writings of Frederick Douglass and W. E. B. Du Bois, among others. Reflecting on the racial implications of the literary education I received in majority-white English departments (from undergraduate school through graduate school), it was clear to me that the white (male) writer and critic had functioned to reify whiteness in my literary imagination. However, because of the literary mentorship of bell hooks, John A. Williams, and Hernton, before I left NYU I had begun to *re*imagine my racial and gender identity through the experience of black literature.

Like the student racial and gender ratios of the English departments in undergraduate and graduate schools I attended in the past, NYU's department was dominated by white females. Except for me at the doctoral level (for almost all of the five years I was in the department), there was no full-time black student (female or male). For the most part, I had little to no association with white male students in English at NYU. In most of the classes I had with them they were myopic, literary stuffed-shirts, and boring, quite frankly—the epitome of a sedate, sterile whiteness. Thus, the students with whom I formed collegial relationships were white and female. Feminist talk came easily among the majority-white female graduate students I knew. Some of us had taken the course on contemporary feminism together in 1985, the year Professor Rena Grant (the young, white radical feminist from Yale) joined the faculty. Nevertheless, the liberal vision of feminism among these white women was far from radical or liberatory. They may have thought otherwise, considering their acceptance of me in the graduate "feminist" group in the department called the "Women's Alliance." Outside of its periodic meetings, there was no political platform supporting its foundation. Perhaps the most radical thing we accomplished was to change its name to the "Feminist Alliance." In the mind of a black male reveling in the acceptance of feminist white women, being a part of this action was proof that I had a right to call myself a feminist.

While the politics of gender was never an issue between us, neither was race, until the one time I raised it. Before then, I do not think white women in the group spent a lot of time thinking about my racial identity. I was black, but more importantly to them, I was feminist. During my first year in the department, I along with several other new female and male grad students served as office assistants in the department. Our duties varied. On occasion, we served as in-house caterers and cleaning help for department faculty functions. I didn't complain. The work was easy—until the head GA (graduate assistant), a small white Jewish woman student who had been in the department a number of years, informed us that we all had to serve the faculty at one of its upcoming get-togethers. No one could have ever told me that being a doctoral student at a prestigious school like NYU would mean literally having to serve at faculty parties as part of my assistantship. None of us wanted to do it, and felt insulted at such a request. Yet no one was willing to complain until I spoke up to say how personally degrading the task seemed. It didn't seem proper on the basis of gender *and* race. I asked for a meeting with the acting department chair. He consented. At the meeting, he sympathized with my position (as a black male) and stated that it would, indeed, be inappropriate for me to serve. He made it clear, however, that the other female and male students would have to serve. They didn't resist, not even the one feminist among them. They served; I didn't.

In a graduate English department where there were so few students of color—black or otherwise—being black, male, and feminist was like being the "brother from another planet."

In truth, the way I felt then, as one of few students of color in an overwhelmingly white department, is much like the way I feel now teaching in a majority-white female college classroom. My feminist sincerity and sympathy, and the "male position" I occupy in this space, are always *colored* by race. In black feminist thought, I can never separate my gender from my race. Any consideration of the problematics of "male feminism" without analysis of the implications of race is blind. This is precisely the point I maintain in my profession as a pro-feminist educator—particularly in all-white or majority-white college classrooms. It underscores the fundamental problem I have with whiteness not only as the reigning signifier of racial privilege, but also of white supremacy.

Confronting whiteness in a black male pro-feminist classroom necessarily means demonstrating analogously that the normativization of male

privilege (in a culture of male supremacy) is tantamount to the natural-
ization of white skin privilege (in white supremacist ideology). As all men
who uncritically accept the sexist oppression of women stand to benefit in
a culture of male supremacist values, so all white people blind to the
"whiteness of whiteness" continue to reap the benefits of *not* seeing themselves as racialized beings who are undeserving of race privilege simply because they are *white* people. If the life-changing academic associations I
began with bell hooks, John A. Williams, and Calvin Hernton as a student
at NYU influenced my decision to become an African Americanist and
characterized the immersion-emersion stage of my racial- (and gender-)
identity development, then the reclamation of my identity as a "black boy
outsider," related to the evolution of antiracist feminist pedagogy I teach,
represents the final stages of Cross's theory of nigrescence. Cross notes
that in the fourth and fifth stages (often combined), blacks "devote an
extended period, if not a lifetime, to finding ways to translate their personal sense of Blackness into a plan of action or a general sense of commitment" (1991, 220). My work in the classroom as gender-progressive,
antiracist professor has become a lifelong pursuit.

Teaching as a *Commitment* to Self-Engagement

Reclaiming my "outsider" past in black feminist terms became a strategic
means to *re*identity with blackness in a progressive framework. While this
process has been personally transformative and rewarding, my struggle
teaching majority-white students demonstrates the viability of black feminist thought in their lives. It is more than a "course" of study, and I desire
to represent its liberatory power in education conceptualized for self-
recovery. bell hooks clearly points to the need for teachers to self-actualize
in what she refers to as "engaged pedagogy"—a "progressive, holistic education [that] is more demanding than conventional critical or feminist
pedagogy." For teachers, it means that we open up to being vulnerable in
the classroom (hooks 1994, 11, 13). Teaching black memoir writing that
assists students struggling to express guilt, sadness, anger, bitterness, or
other feelings associated with the wounding effects of domination gives
way to an experience of self-healing for those who are willing to self-
engage. I have realized over the years that my pedagogical aims must promote education as the practice of personal, social, and spiritual liberation
for all students who enroll my classes. Among white students and students
of color, they have a reputation of being controversial. Yet the classes I
teach at the college are always full on the first day of the semester, even
though none of them are required courses.

I have made it a practice to let students know up front, on the first day of classes, that my courses focus on black studies in a feminist context, and that they are driven by an antiracist premise. Despite my fear that white female (and male) students (as well as students of color) will blacklist the "race classes" I teach, because they confront whiteness, my courses have remained popular with students. Their popularity exists for varying reasons. In the feminist antiracist courses I teach, white students often exoticize people of color as the bearers of race, as "native informants." As a black male professor of feminism confronting whiteness, I embody difference, which on the surface makes my classes chic, trendy, and even titillating. They are the spice that livens up "the dull dish of whiteness," as hooks would say. In the rumor mill, students sensationalize them, expecting they will be "edgy," "intense," "dangerous," "frightening," "confrontational." White students and students of color who take my classes quickly learn that I employ confessional writing as a strategic starting point for critically confronting white supremacy as a complex self-reflective process—not as a minstrel show for white entertainment.

Yet having experienced the ways education in majority-white schools has continually marginalized black identity associated with radical expressions of blackness, I found that, black feminist critique of racism helped me understand that white supremacy is not the only threat to black self-recovery. Having embraced black feminist thought as a man in my early thirties meant that I had to understand that sexism was as dangerous to the survival of black people as institutionalized racism. Moreover, becoming an ally in black feminist struggle against sexism not only calls for me to condemn the oppression of females of color but of *all* females. It continually lets me know that I must denounce the homophobic assault against *all* lesbian women and gay men, of any colors—particularly those among them without race and class privilege. hooks emphatically states in *Killing Rage, Ending Racism*: "There will be no feminist revolution without an end to racism and white supremacy. When all women and men engaged in feminist struggle understand the interlocking nature of systems of domination, of white supremacist capitalist [homophobic] patriarchy, feminist movement will regain its revolutionary progressive momentum" (1995, 107). More than any of hooks's memoir-based works, *Teaching to Transgress* (a book I have taught continuously in a course on her ideas of engaged pedagogy) grounded my *re*education as a gender-progressive educator— toward *thinking black and thinking feminist*, simultaneously. After teaching black feminist literature a decade and more in all-white and majority-white college classrooms, I have become certain of the pedagogical necessity of black feminism in them.

❧ PART 3 ❧

From Theory to Practice:
Classroom Case Studies

❧ 6 ❧

Complicating White Identity
in the Classroom

Enter Color, Gender, Sexuality,
and Class Difference(s)

The successful resolution of one's racial identity conflicts makes it possible to shift attention to other identity concerns . . . the Internalization stage marks the point of dissonance resolution. . . . *The person feels . . . more at ease with self. . . . One of the most important consequences of this inner peace is that a person's conception of Blackness tends to become more open, expansive, and sophisticated* [emphasis added]. As defensiveness fades, simplistic thinking and simple solutions becomes transparently inadequate, and the full complexity and inherent texture of the Black condition becomes the point of departure for serious analysis.

—William Cross

Teaching outside heteronormative ideas of masculinity as a gender-progressive "brother" is about ending my fear of emasculation in black communities. As a pedagogical overview, chapter 6 represents the beginning of a series of classroom case studies that defy black machismo. Having developed memoir-writing pedagogy that confronts patriarchy, white supremacy, and gender-conservative ideas of blackness, in the case studies that follow, I chart its evolution over a decade and more.

The Grammar of (Self-)Liberation:
From Object to Subject

In the late 1970s, when I first started teaching, I taught seventh- and eighth-grade English and reading for two years in my hometown. I remember

distinctly drilling my students on the fundamentals of subject/object relationship in sentence structure: grammatically, the "object" of a sentence is
acted upon; the "subject" is the performer or that around which the sentence revolves.

Narrating the history of my education from a segregated black elementary school and junior high school through majority-white institutions
of higher learning to teaching in all-white college classrooms is about re-
structuring the syntax of my life—from object to subject. In theory, parts 1
and 2 illustrated my transition from black boy outsider to pro-feminist professor teaching for social justice. Having had an immersion experience
reading black feminist writers while a graduate student, I learned to be far
less concerned about passing the litmus test of straight black manhood
than about comprehending a much more complex, progressive form of
blackness black feminism offered. The goal, in William Cross's words, is to
partake in a "more open, expansive" form of blackness predicated upon an
inclusive vision of black humanity—where no member of black communities is devalued because of gender, class, and/or sexual difference.

William Cross describes the stage of racial-identity development in
which an individual has found inner peace with a black self-concept as internalization. As the classroom case studies attest, the pedagogy I practice involved an immersion-emersion process grounded in the feminist
theory of black women and men. If coming to know the work of bell
hooks, among other black feminists, and gender-progressive men like
John A. Williams and Calvin Hernton in graduate school at NYU signified my movement through Cross's immersion-emersion stage (transforming my vision of blackness and black masculinity), then teaching as
a committed advocate of black feminism would characterize the fourth
and fifth stages of nigrescence—internalization-commitment. Cross
notes that these stages are interrelated and may be summarized in the
fifth stage, in which a person may "devote an extended period, if not a
lifetime, to finding ways to translate [her or his] personal sense of Blackness into a plan of action or a general sense of commitment" (1991, 220).
Committed to gender-progressive black male pro-feminism as a foundation for male self-recovery in our communities, in my essay "To Be Black,
Male, and Feminist" I responded to what is a psychosexual fear in many
black men of emasculation (rooted in white supremacy):

> [I]t is the fear of feminization in the minds of many black men
> that has led us to over-determine our sexuality, believing that
> our identity as men resides only in the power of our penises.
> Against the inhumanity of our past, we must create a place/

space to make ourselves over again in our own image. This place/space must not reconstruct the very mythology that sexually demonized our bodies as the scourge of white womanhood; rather, it must free us *to be black* in the most radically revolutionary manner, *to be male* in the most nonoppressive, antisexist way, *to be feminist* in the most supportive, nonpatriarchal way to bring about an end to the domination, subordination, and mistreatment of women because they are women. (Lemons 1998b, 46).

Sexual Difference, What *Race* Has to Do with It: "GLBTQ" is Not Simply a "Queer" Label

Moving from an exclusive focus on Black women to a broader one that encompasses how the politics of gender and sexuality frame the experiences of women and men alike creates new questions for investigation and, perhaps, a new antiracist politics that might follow.

—Patricia Hill Collins

The only helpful way to teach about difference is to teach about sameness at the same time. Only if our students are able to see others as they see themselves, able to care about the issues of others as they care about their own issues, will they then be able to answer in a generous way "Why does it matter? Why should I care?" Only if we teach sameness at the same time will they see themselves implicated in the answer. They must learn that they can stand—indeed, are standing—on both shores of the river at the same time.

—Judy Scales-Trent

During thirteen years of teaching at the college, in my pro-feminist classes on race there were white students (female, male, and transgender) who spoke out against racial injustice; they were openly willing to challenge white supremacy in solidarity with outspoken students of color. These courageous white students, together with the students of color, exhibited an understanding of the *inter*connection between white supremacist thinking, sexism, homophobia, and class oppression. Many of them did not identify as heterosexual, and they articulated a form of resistance that opposed the additive model of social justice. Rather, they boldly declared the necessity for a politics of liberation that recognizes the critical importance of sexual difference in the struggle for personal and political freedom for all people. As a black male reared in a black Pentecostal church who has contested many years of sexist, heterosexist, and homophobic indoctrination, I learned from the students mentioned in this chapter (among them some of the best students I taught at the college) that unless one's voice is heard speaking out against oppression (in whatever form), it remains complicit with forces of power that seek to silence it. Especially because of the courageous antiracist voices of students of color and white students I taught who did not identify as heterosexual, I have become a stronger, more committed advocate of antioppression politics founded upon an alliance with gay, lesbian, bisexual, transgender individuals, and people who question heteronormative ideas of sexuality.

This chapter analyzes selected excerpts from students' autobiographical narratives collected over the years in courses I taught where memoir writing was the central feature. It reveals how students of color and white students write through feelings of "outsiderness"—of being positioned on the margins of white supremacist, normative constructions of race, gender, and sexuality. Outsider identity is a common theme in the narrative excerpts I have chosen. But how does sexual identity impact not only students' race, gender, and class, but also their ability and body image? This is the primary question this chapter seeks to engage. In my experiences teaching feminist antiracism to classes composed of gay, lesbian, bisexual, and transgender students, and other students questioning heterosexual identity, I found that the GLBTQ white students were generally more outspoken on race than many of their straight white counterparts. Of the small number of students of color at the college who took my classes—among them gay, lesbian, and bisexual individuals—those who questioned heterosexuality were highly politicized about the politics of white supremacy in nonheterosexual communities (inside and outside the academy). Additionally, these students of color and white students—more often than not—not only embraced black feminist thought on race, white supremacy, and white privilege, but also challenged straight students (white and of color) to interrogate heterosexual identity politics. The race, gender, and sexual justice politics of the black feminist, antiracist pedagogy I practiced in the classroom aimed to be inclusive. Even as it sought to decenter heterosexism and heterosexual privilege, within a critique of sexism, it remained critically focused on the deconstruction of white supremacy.

My defense of black feminism in the classroom, as I have described, relies on memoir writing about race to oppose white supremacy and its interrelation to other forms of domination. In my approach to teaching antiracism through black feminist thought, particularly courageous students of color and white students who are not heterosexual have found my classes to be affirming spaces to speak and write against white supremacist thinking, heteronormative ideas of gender, and heterosexist notions of sexuality. During the years I taught at the college, what made teaching memoir writing for social justice personally rewarding for me was that most of these students responded in amazing ways. In the memoir-writing process, many crafted memoirs of race that capture with incisive poignancy the struggle to examine oneself across the boundaries of race, gender, class, and sexuality—complexly and in complicated terms.

The GLBTQ students most often possessed a nuanced, critical understanding of the interconnected nature of domination. In a white-dominated institution, there were a small number of students of color in my classes who did not identify as heterosexual, and most perceived white supremacy and white privilege to be major barriers to open dialogue about sexuality in the classroom. As part 1 discussed, one of the major obstacles I continually encountered with white students was their silence on race. When white students had to discuss race, whiteness, white skin privilege, or white supremacy (related or unrelated to sexuality), many of them responded with silence. White students' silence signified a range of complex emotions associated with fear of being perceived as racist by students of color, me, or other white liberals. White students and students of color who did not identify as heterosexual found the progressive sexual politics of black feminism liberating. Its multi-identity theory offered both groups a critical location to interrogate the politics of gender, class, and the heterosexist constructions of liberation struggles in communities of color.

I hold on to the belief that whiteness, white supremacy, and white skin privilege remain major obstacles to feminist solidarity across lines of race, gender, class, and sexuality—especially for students of color who are not heterosexual attending these majority-white institutions. "White silence" (on racism, *white skin* privileges, and white class status, for example) in the classroom represented a pervasive, ongoing issue in nearly every course I taught at the college. The next section, which examines students writing to confront the ideology of white supremacy, makes a power statement about the benefits of antiracist education. I begin with the work of a student who identifies herself as "a queer white woman from a working-class background."

Speaking Truth to (White) Power:
White Students Talking Back to White Silence

When white students begin to speak about themselves in terms of their relationship to white skin privilege, whiteness, and its relation to white supremacy, they will begin a process of self-recognition that is about self-transformation. White silence in the classroom not only threatened to disrupt class discussion, its seemingly arrogant posture attempted to silence the voice(s) of students of color—as well as my own. For white students to break white silence on race opens space for a critical dialogue aimed to "decenter" whiteness as *the* signifier of white supremacy. In my experience, far too many white students claimed silence as a way to deal with race. Of the white males who took my classes over the years (and the numbers were consistently small, indeed), few possessed the courage to openly disclose their feelings about being white and male.

In all-white and majority-white classrooms, *whiteness* loomed large, functioning as an ever-present subject of controversy. Whether interrogated in its association with the ideology of white supremacy, analyzed in the "novel of passing," or linked to white skin privilege, confronted in the media, or written about in students' memoir writing, *whiteness,* as students of color argued consistently, was always trying to center itself in classrooms at the college that were already overwhelmingly white. As the class studies also reveal, my focus on white supremacy in this context was always a source of tension not only for students of color but for white students as well. For many white students, over the years, the subject of race itself was controversial—particularly when it required them to discuss it *personally.* There were white students who courageously addressed *white silence* in the classroom. In fact, during the last year I taught at the college, one white female student voluntarily took on the subject as her final paper in my course Hollywood and the Education of America (spring 2004). It took the form of a "question-and-answer" dialogue in which I posed five questions for her to answer on the subject of white student silence about race in her class. Having taken several other antiracist classes I had taught, the student had experienced the racial silence of white students in these classes.

Here are some excerpts from our dialogue:

Q: In a course on race where "whiteness" is being interrogated, what issues surface most often for white students that keep them from speaking openly about their relation to this subject?

A: "The first rule of white club is that you never talk about white club" (anonymous). [A primary issue in keeping white students from talking about whiteness is a feeling of] general disconnection from the history of whiteness. . . . [M]any white students want to see whiteness in other people, and not themselves. Some students don't want to believe [that it exists]. To them people of color [represent] race. The question [you asked the class], "How have you experienced your own racialization?" seems to baffle many white students because we are taught to think of race as something that only affects the lives of people of color in their communities. . . . What many [white] students do not want to hear is, "You are white; you are getting power through that, and you are accountable to do something about it." Even if students are willing to hear this, they are sometimes frozen when it comes to figuring out what "doing something" might mean.

Q: How do issues of ethnicity, gender, class, *sexuality*, and religion (among other identity formations) factor into "white silence" in the race classroom?

A: I think an identification with an ethnicity, sexuality, or lifestyle that is marginalized within whiteness can lead to fruitful and complex conversations about it, about points of solidarity with people of color, and political motivation. In my years at the college, the white people I have seen most often speaking up about racism, about their own identity and its construction, are those people who have an "un-ideal" white identity. As a queer white woman from a working-class background, I have felt that I am not suited to the priorities of the school in some ways; however, I receive skin color privilege and many others that make my position here easy to get through. . . . I think it takes understanding one's own marginalization (not victimization) to begin to see other people's immediate life options in a new way, or to begin to see oneself as "othered." We, as white students, need to recognize how different it is for us to be silent [on race] than for students of color—especially at a predominately white school where people of color are watched, made a spectacle of, and speculated about. Students of color bear a lot of weight in a majority-white college classroom. White students, by talking about racism and speaking from our own experience, can begin to take on some of that weight. Many of us [white females in particular] are initially taught the lie that feminism is about white, middle-class, feminine women [searching for fulfillment] beyond their household duties in a heterosexual framework, and that Black American, Asian, Latina, and American Indian women had no part in formulating feminist discourse.

The student's responses yielded a number of critical insights regarding the interconnections between white students' silence on race and its relation to gender and sexuality. To begin with, her observation that there is a binary construction in the white liberal media between "good white people" and "bad white people" demonizes working-class and poor white people, absolving the middle class and elite whites of the onus of racism. Racism is considered by them a class matter, about so-called white trash and the Ku Klux Klan. Few white students I have taught over the years have been as candid as this student. She asserts that the willingness to speak openly about race marks her "move past initial [racial] paralysis to a [place of] fractured vulnerability." Based upon my experience confronting white silence in the classroom, I understand her point about white students' resistance to identification as "white" has as much to with media misrepresentation of white racism as it does with a lack of knowledge regarding the history of white supremacy in U.S. history.

When I asked the question, "How have you experienced your own racialization?" in all-white or majority-white classes, most white students invariably freeze. For many, the question represents the first time they have had to contemplate their identity as white people. White students, as this student points out, are taught that race "only affects the lives of people of color." This is a form of white supremacist thinking I confront continuously. Even when white students read and study texts by whites and people of color on whiteness, there is no guarantee that knowledge of its ideological formation will empower them to feel secure enough to engage openly in racial dialogue—particularly when linked to the issue of sexuality and black identity. The critical awareness this white female student displays regarding the necessity for white students to question the gender, class, and sexual politics of white identity is something I have endeavored to teach for years. Many white students in classes I teach have discovered in memoir writing about race that they are marginalized within whiteness. I argue that even the "whitest" of white students cannot bear the mantle of perfection white supremacist ideology demands. This same student notes, "[T]he white people I hear most often speaking up about racism, about their own identity [as white people] and its construction, are the people who have an 'un-ideal' white identity." She complicates her identity as a "queer" white female "from a working-class background."

It is precisely the idea of finding the "other" in oneself as a white student that initiates the process *of coming to voice* about ways he or she is set up to fail the whiteness test. Even membership in the "white club" and obedience to its code of whiteness will not save the white student from wrestling with demons within—struggling at the margin of idealized white superiority. In this way, white students free themselves from its *de*-humanizing weight. Cornel West, contextualizing his observation within the racial politics of the music industry and the arena of sports, makes a cogent point about the humanizing power of blackness in the lives of young white people: "The Afro-Americanization of white youth—given the disproportionate black role in popular music and athletics—has put white [youths] in closer contact with their own bodies and facilitated more human interaction with black people" (1994, 121). As the student above adds, white students speaking out in the classroom about (internalized) racism also take some of the load off students of color—who (more often than not) bear the mantle of "native informant" (authorities on race/ethnicity via racial otherness) in a majority-white class. Finally, as an outspoken, young white feminist, she exposes what I have perceived in many classes of young, majority-white feminist students: the fact that many white feminist students are being erroneously taught the myth that feminism emerged out of a white, middle-class, "feminine," heterosexual history—independent of any role by women of color in its evolution. I appreciate this student's willingness to take on the subject of white silence in the classroom. I recall her presence in more than one of my classes as that of a critical ally toward challenging white students to open up about race, so that students of color or I did not always have to bear that burden alone.

Another white female, Jewish student (who also does not identify as heterosexual), emphatically writes that being white *and* Jewish—aligning oneself with antiracist people of color, antiheterosexist actions, non-Christian, or pro-immigrant movements—is tantamount to being a traitor to whiteness ("'blackened' or 'niggerized' in whiteness"). While resisting the notion that one form of oppression is equal to another, she maintains that the stories of white students contesting whiteness must be told and that

> white people do suffer for their transgressions at the hand of white supremacy. We must remember though, that striving for empathy through comparing experiences does not necessitate equalizing them in any way. Certainly, white people suffer from white supremacy in some fundamentally different ways than people of color. Being vigilant not to buy into reductionist ways of addressing this, I can say that we are all being forced toward an ideal model of whiteness we cannot achieve without harming ourselves. . . . Speaking to the complex lived realities of [individuals involved in anti-domination struggle].

In an advanced memoir of race writing class I taught in fall 2001, the student above (initially having taken my first-year memoir-writing course on bell hooks two years earlier) writes about her memory of not being "the right kind of white" female in high school:

> Because I am white, it wasn't apparent to me [in high school] that I was being read in relation to a kind of whiteness that I didn't properly embody—the right kind of white. I am only now able to name the ways that whiteness alienated me. My body was wrong, my culture was wrong, my mannerisms were wrong, my gender was wrong. . . . Nothing added up right to me or anyone else. In my mind, comments people made verbally or implicitly circled around me, maddeningly: "If you're Jewish you have to work your ass off to prove you're still white, and if you're a white girl you shouldn't be talking so loud and moving your hand so much anyway. . . . Your face might be white but you've got a ghetto ass. . . . If you're a fat girl who's white, you should be quiet and shy and embarrassed all the time, but if you're eating disordered it's because you're a perfectionist, and are you a dyke or not? . . . Don't you know lesbian is the only important part of lesbian identity? What are you? I was a contradiction. I was Jewish, queer, white, fat, loud, female, and visible. Most importantly, I had a sense of empathy with systematically disempowered people and I felt an immediate connectedness to resistance struggle, having grown up with knowledge of oppression and resistance in my personal history . . .

Even within a progressive school in terms of sexual difference and educational philosophy as she describes it, this student—secure within a middle-class environment—was made to feel like an outsider in multiple, stereotypical ways that were at once anti-Semitic, sexist, and white supremacist. To fit the white female ideal of femininity required her to deny her not-so-white body type ("ghetto ass"), rid herself of any cultural signifiers (connected to being Jewish), and conform to "feminine" gender norms of the model white girl (thin, soft-spoken, and invisible). Moreover, in a white-lesbian-identified context, she was made to feel that that single identity superseded all others.

As the student writes above, being politically conscious and empathetic toward the struggles of "other" people placed her on the margins of whiteness in the school community she inhabits. Her point about white people transgressing the boundaries of whiteness is well illustrated. In a white educational environment where sexual transgression was acceptable for young white females, being Jewish, overweight, loud, and possessed of a "knowledge of oppression and resistance" compounded her feelings of white outsiderness.

"Stranger in Another Village": A Black Gay Male Student's Critique of Life in Greenwich Village

When students of color have enrolled in my classes over the years, they invariably shoulder the burden of race talk. Because my courses on race are taught from a black feminist standpoint, they have drawn female students of color in particular. However, as I have already written, the absence of males of color in my classes was striking. In the thirteen years of teaching at the college, I can count on one hand the number of males of color who have studied with me. It is not so much that male students of color were not interested in feminism or feminism taught from an antiracist standpoint (of those who took my classes, they chose them because of that focus). Rather, the critically small number of male students of color coupled with the small number of female students of color graphically demonstrated the underrepresentation of nonwhite students at the college.

I can remember every male student of color who registered for my classes. While intrigued by their reasons for taking my classes, I wondered even more why they had decided to enroll in a majority-white-female college (even as I pondered on more than one occasion my decision to teach at such an institution). While none of them described themselves as pro-feminist, one student (an openly gay black male student) had taken the course I teach called "Womanist Thought." He was the only black student in the class (otherwise composed of white females, two white males, and a "queer Filipina-American," as she identified herself) who had taken more than one of my classes. I remember his work on sexuality in another course with me on memoir writing and race in the fall of 2001. He was the only black male student in that class as well. The memoir he wrote for that course is one I will always remember.

He had moved to New York City to study in Greenwich Village while experiencing its fabled gay community, and in his memoir he draws upon James Baldwin's well-known essay "Stranger in the Village" to critique racist white attitudes he found prevalent in the sexual politics of "the Village" he had idealized before moving there. He begins,

> I moved to Greenwich Village three years ago for the same reasons that most migrate to this area—I believe it to be, if not the center of the universe, at least the cultural capital of the United States. I came to New York City because I thought that I could lose myself in the crowds of gay men that flooded the streets in newscasts of the Pride Parade and find myself a niche among them. I, like most gay teenagers, thought that New York City (particularly, Greenwich Village) was a neo-Garden of Eden. . . .

It never occurred to me that in my exaggerated fantasy all of the characters were white.

Pondering the racist skin-color politics of the gay community of Greenwich Village, this student, like Baldwin (who discovered he was the first black person that whites in the small village of Switzerland he visited had seen), realized that his skin color was *the* signifier of difference in an otherwise all-white community. As he and Baldwin experienced, their "blackness" was a sight framed in racial otherness. Of his entrance into the all-white Swiss village, Baldwin writes, "From all available evidence no black man had ever set foot in this Swiss village before I came. I was told before arriving that I would probably be a 'sight.' . . . It did not occur to me—possibly because I am an American—that there could be people anywhere who had never seen a Negro" (1955, 159).

While the student's experience of racism shattered his vision of a racially inclusive gay community, he continued to believe that New York City would offer a more accepting environment, in spite of his alienating experience of whiteness: "I was the only colored phenomenon occurring in my world and everyone/thing else was white. But even after realizing this, I continued to go on unconsciously thinking that this discovery did not matter because I was in New York City. The place that defied all of the prejudice and self-loathing that being gay, and often times being Black, had caused me to experience at home. Trying to lead an ordinary life was even reduced to Black and white." Baldwin notes that even though he had returned to spend more time in the village a year later in the winter, it was as if it were his first time: "Everyone in the village knows my name, though they scarcely ever use it, know that I come from America—though, this, apparently, they will never really believe: black men come from Africa. . . . But I remain as much a stranger today as I was the first day I arrived, and the children shout *Neger! Neger!* as I walk along the streets" (1995, 161).

Like Baldwin and this student, I too know the pain of being "othered"—inside and outside of black communities. I felt this black male student's feeling of outsiderness and longing for acceptance. I know the painful feeling of being the only black male in majority-white spaces, and felt it particularly when I lived in an all-white community while a graduate student at the University of Arkansas in Fayetteville. I never felt completely comfortable there; I was always conscious of my blackness like a spot on a blanket of snow. Longing to be accepted by white students and professors as an English major in undergraduate and graduate school, I became obsessed with the notion of "passing" as white—until I realized that a knowledge of centuries of white-authored books would never change the color of my skin. The student writes about his sense of race, gender, and sexual isolation in visceral, imagistic terms:

> There are very few men at my small, liberal arts school in the West Village; there are even fewer gay men, and less than that of Black men. As much as I thought that New York City would solve the problem of everything being so Black and white, it did not. I was a double-sided subway token—Black on one side, gay on the other, and a big hole in the middle. Compounding the absence of racially liberated white gay men in the "Village" and the underrepresentation of black males in the college is the student's experience of colorism perpetuated by white *and* black gay males. The reality of the racial politics of Greenwich Village's gay community is that it mirrors the internalized racist attitudes of the larger, hetero white and black communities.

Preference for "light" skin remains a problem for black and white gay men. Cornel West has said, "[The antiracist] demythologizing of black sexuality is crucial for black America because much of black self-hatred and self-contempt has to do with the refusal of many black Americans to love their own black bodies—especially their black noses, hips, lips, and hair [and dark skin color]" (1994, 122). As a dark-skinned black gay man, the student refers to a form of internalized black (and white) racism as the "Dark Complaint." "[This] is the sentence of gay color in the Village— exoticization or invisibility." Having experienced what William Cross would describe as the "encounter" stage of racial identity development, the student reflects on the similarity between his racial experience with whiteness (and blackness) and that of Baldwin: "After almost four years of living in the Village, I can agree with Baldwin that '. . . I remain as much a stranger today as I was the first day I arrived.'" Cornel West has said, "Yet the paradox of the sexual politics of race in America is that, behind closed doors, the dirty, disgusting, and funky sex associated with black people is often perceived to be more intriguing and interesting, while in public spaces talk about black sexuality is virtually taboo. *Everyone knows it is virtually impossible to talk candidly about race without talking about sex*" (1994, 120; emphasis added).

Crossing Lines of Race, Sexuality, and Gender: *Trans*identity Politics in the Classroom

Students studying *trans*racialism through multiple lenses must think about the personal in complicated terms. The exploration of inner sources of racial anxiety analytically linked to an interrogation of gender, class, and sexual oppression is the primary work of the *trans*racial memoir. Over the years, the novel of passing course has attracted a number of students from mixed race backgrounds. Without positioning these students (mostly female) at the center of the study of transracial identity in the novels as "biracial informants," as with other students, I challenge them to think through the thematic implications of the texts related to the realities of their own cross-racial experiences.

One of the most complex representations of race, gender and sexuality came out of the same advanced memoir-writing class that was attended by the student above, and it was written by a transracial, lesbian-identified female. In her "auto(race)critography" she narrates the complicated identity politics that come with being "biracial," lesbian, and muticultural:

> It is difficult to bring a clear mind to my battles. I am fighting hard against oppression in the U.S. as a lesbian in a heteronormative society. I am also working to find a space of acceptance within black spaces of heterosexuals. The most difficult challenge is accepting myself as a biracial woman who considers herself black in a [non-U.S. cultural] context that discourages my sexual identity. How do I begin to feel at home in my blackness when my American culture denies my sexuality . . . to attach myself to Black people who see not only my whiteness as *other*, but my Americaness, and my sexuality? Perhaps, the luxury of heterosexuality would cloud my ability to recognize the tension between these groups. These groups are all of me. I am Black American—my complexion says I am biracial in a Black family photograph. I am lesbian in my heterosexist non-white neighborhood. I [embody the culture of my non-U.S.-born father]. I am on a search for a name for the complexities that represent me. As it has been known historically and told to me by my classmates, if you aren't white, you are *other*, and if you are *other* in any area of white imperial terrain . . . you are Black. I am Black.

In the excerpt from the student's memoir above, she captures with amazing clarity the position of multiple jeopardy that informs her identities—as a racial, gender, and sexual outsider. She is at once inside and outside the hetero(sexist), racist, and cultural borders of both black and white communities inside and outside the United States. The transracial, multipositionality of this student leads her "on a search for a name for the complexities that represent me."

In *Notes of a White Black Woman: Race, Color, and Community,* Judy Scales-Trent imaginatively "names" the complexities of transracial identity in this way, borrowing from indigenous mythology:

> In Navajo cosmology there exist certain powerful creatures who, although they appear to be mere humans, can change shape whenever they wish by taking on animal form. These are supernatural beings. . . . They are called "skinwalkers." And I think about them, and this name, when I think about how we all "skinwalk"—change shapes, identities, from time to time, during the course of a day, during the course of our lives. I think about how we create these identities, how they are created for us, how they change, and how we reconcile these changes as we go along. (1995, 127)

While there may be no single term that can capture the complicated identity formations the transracial student above inhabits, that she has begun a journey of self-naming represents an act full of liberatory possibility. Scales-Trent has come upon a term that works to "reconcile" the seemingly irreconcilable, multiple differences many of us embody. As "skinwalkers"—shape changers and identity shifters—we can possess the power within to the defy racist, hetero(sexist) ideas of fixed identity. I think of the student above, whom I have come to know very well, as a "skinwalker." Her decision to "identify" as "Black" is not about a reduction of the complicated "trans"positionality she occupies. Rather than being tragically *black* and female (in all the ways blackness is inherently always already hypersexualized in white supremacist heterosexist culture), I read the student's decision to identify herself as black as a radical stance of defiance against internalized (and externalized) racism and heterosexism in black and white communities. "Skinwalking" is a visionary term for that which defies what is "natural" in the eyes of men (*and* women). In this way, we can begin to see each other in *super*natural ways, ways that enable us to envision liberatory communities beyond the limits of categorization. When I have taught novels of racial passing within a larger conceptual framework, I have employed "skinwalking" as a theoretical platform for students to imagine life in the skin of "an*other*" person's identity. This concept is pedagogically provocative for me precisely because it embodies the critical underpinning of my approach to teaching transraciality through memoir writing—from slave narratives on miscegenation, "black" autobiographical fiction of passing (from the nineteenth century through the Harlem Renaissance), to the contemporary period representing what I call the "memoir of the multiracial subject."

In fall 2003, I offered The Novel of Passing course (discussed more fully in the next chapter). Of the students in the course (all white with the exception of one black female student), a white, Jewish, transgender male student wrote an amazing memoir on the fictions of whiteness *and* gender: "I came to this class looking for comrades, people to nurture my struggle, the allies of *trans*racial characters in novels about *trans*raciality, queer desire, female oppression, and class struggle to help me destabilize the boundaries that keep us all fixed, to connect their *trans* identities to my own. It is through joining with others in struggle, hearing their pain and connecting its similarities and differences to my own, that living is bearable, and in fact full of joy."

In the passage above, the student asserts his reasons for being in the class. The study of transracialism in the novels represents a point of entry for personal connection—not only with fictional mixed-race characters but with students in the course. Employing black feminists' critiques of the novels, I provided a discursive space for students to interrogate not only the politics of racial passing but also the complexities of gender, class, and sexuality within them. For this student, a multianalytic approach to the novel enabled him to feel comfortable locating his personal narrative within a "trans"-validated classroom space.

What makes this student's desire for "comrades, people to nurture [his] struggle" so powerful is the depth of its (self-)interrogation and the necessity for connection to a larger social context—across race, gender, and class difference(s)—to confront the racial blindness that often accompanies white privilege:

> [W]hiteness has given me privilege but simultaneously kept me from real engagement with life and happiness, has kept me blind through a form of racial myopia. By remaining invisible, whiteness tells me to look only at the ways I've been hurt, only at my experience being raised as female, being Jewish, queer, and transgender, to individuate myself instead of seeing myself in relation to others, especially those that have suffered because of their racialization. I don't mean to trivialize or become stone to [i.e., try to ignore] the real[ity] of the [multiple identities I occupy], but only by placing my pain in a larger context can it become bearable and take on more meaning. Only by seeing my whiteness, my class privilege, my U.S. citizenship, and how the marginalized identities [I inhabit] are always interacting with and being filtered [through multiple personal privilege] can I truly see myself and the world, truly begin a healing of myself and others. And only by doing this can [I] try to nurture a world where possibilities extend beyond our racialization, our gendered oppression, our class struggle.

During the semester as I read, dialogued with, and heard this student share autobiographical writings in class that would ultimately become a part of his final memoir, I came to admire greatly his will to make critical connections between the life experiences of the transracial characters in the novels and his own life as a young, transgender-identified white male. The one theme that remained constant in his memoir was the idea that his struggle for personal social justice had to be placed within a larger social framework linked to struggles against racism, (hetero)sexism, and classism. Like the white female student in the first section of this chapter, this student understands the necessity of a politics of shared struggle—across the differences of identity categories we occupy (like race, gender, and sexuality), made to appear immutable in a culture of white supremacy and (hetero)sexism.

White Males Who Pass (out of Whiteness): Not the Right Kind of White Man

Over the years, for every white male who enrolled in my classes and remained to the end of the semester, there was one who dropped them after the first or second class session. Why? Any number of reasons. But what I know, based upon my experience with white males I have taught, is that many feel they are the targets of my critique of white supremacist capitalist patriarchy. No matter how much I have attempted to prove them wrong, many of them refuse to see themselves as anything but *victims* as "straight white middle- (and upper-)class males." Considering the feminist critique of the paradigm of power signified in the image of an elite, white heterosexual male identity, is there any wonder that a backlash against feminism (of any color) would manifest itself in the antiracist pro-feminist classroom? In my classes, many straight white males who have internalized a victim mentality buckle under the pressure of suddenly being seen and engaged (often for the first time) as "white" males.

There have, however, been those rare white male students (straight and gay) who remained in my classes, not only bearing the weight of racial visibility but also discovering in memoir writing that critical self-examination in the context of feminist antiracist pedagogy can en(gender) feelings of liberation for white men in terms of class *and* sexuality. Many white males, while bearing the signifiers of race and gender power (and the privileges of heterosexuality if straight), fear race talk (perhaps, even more so than white females, given the fact that white male heterosexual power is being interrogated). Yet some white males in my classes over the years have been openly willing to call into question their identity and to admit to possessing a fractured sense of who they are.

In a popular course with students of color and white students I teach on bell hooks as a black feminist educator, students must respond in writing to an in-class exercise (conceived by a student) in which they each choose one crayon from a box of colored crayons. The assignment calls for students to write autobiographically about the symbolic meaning of the color to them—on any level they choose. At the next class session, each student would read her or his response to the class. A white male student (without identifying himself sexually) responding to the exercise (in spring 2001) wrote about self-imposed silence on race and personal and social ways of being in general. Acknowledging his fear of having to choose a crayon, he chose the color "red," hoping to remove himself from direct racial association with it. Yet he finds himself entangled in a discussion of race:

> I panicked and chose red thinking it to be more neutral than a darker or lighter color. . . . Immediately, I thought of New Mexico. Red [on the state] flag, the color of the ground. The color of the many forms of silence represented in my life. Red is the color I felt in class today and most days. Not only this class, but any class where I feel the need to speak on something subjectively, personally. My nervousness makes itself apparent on my face. It always has. . . . It manifests itself in white silence . . . It is gendered, classed, and sexualized. I never learned to speak. Silence has dominated and destroyed too many of my relationships. I never learned to speak personally. In a way that speaks not only from experience but from weakness. Self-consciously questioning my motives or my authority to the point of knotting my stomach and reddening my face but not coming out in words. . . . Red is the antithesis of the way I grew up looking at my culture. . . . My roots were "green." I identified with Ireland. I studied the plight of the Irish in North Ireland and the IRA. There my blood was running. My blood is composed of the color "green" . . . Scotland and Ireland are where I can trace myself back [to]. I use "green" to identify myself as nonwhite. . . . [In the color green], I am not white. I am Irish.

Silences in this white male student's life, whether personally or socially connected to race (or any other uncomfortable situation in which he finds himself), registers in the "red" color change on his face. But this color signifies much more to him symbolically. In addition to reminding him of his home state of New Mexico—the earth itself—it also represents the "color of blood that white colonialism built its empire upon, an empire fashioned out of silence. In New Mexico, red are the tongues that are daily bitten black in order for all to speak English."

The student above equates red with the predominance of poor people of color in the neighborhood where he grew up. Like males of all colors in a culture of male supremacy, we are taught to be silent about our feelings—even if it threatens to destroy relationships we long to maintain. Many white students, coming to consciousness about the history of white supremacist colonization globally, in the memoir-writing process begin to dissociate themselves from whiteness—not as a racial cop-out but as a bold statement of antiracism. When I have taught The Novel of Passing course, there have been gay white males who have written deeply moving narratives of race, gender, and sexual outsiderness. One white gay male student writes about the complexity of his ethnic background as the son of a father with German ancestry and a mother of Italian descent. He maintains that his ethnic background is "not an attempt to de-emphasize the systemic privilege or ideological advantage provides me by my skin color and gender; I am saying that I was not raised in the cultural absence typified by the American conception of whiteness. . . . I am part of my family's first generation of potential college graduates. I refuse to negate the cultural influence of my experience in how I interpret my life." He had a mother with "dark olive" skin, which he coveted as a child. He states that he has always been color conscious (of his own color, in particular). "I can remember in recent years how I've fought to darken myself, figuratively, literally. I know my distaste of seeing my own winter pallor." Where he lives in New York City as a college student challenges his identity as a "white" man and also his identification as an openly "gay" male:

[I]n my neighborhood in the East Village I feel like an outsider, like I'm living in the great plantation house (my building is nearly all white) surrounded by looming public housing towers. I know that when I open my door the first thing I see is "kill whitey" covered by a thin layer of off-white primer. . . . I am not offended but unsure exactly what I feel and think sometimes. . . . I know that I shave my head and grow a beard because it alters my racial appearance, at certain times allowing me to pass for Puerto Rican, and I feel just for a second before I step outside less of an outsider—until I walk by Raul's candy store and an old woman implores me in Spanish. I can only shrug and move forward. I know that when the Dominican and Puerto Rican boys who get out of school in the afternoon, hanging around the corners and in front of the bodegas, call at me "maricone," I always think it is less because of my tight pants and eyeliner and more because of my white skin.

Unlike the straight white male responding to the crayon exercise, whose "redness" betrays the whiteness of his racial silence, this student's ability to "alter [his] racial appearance" by passing for Puerto Rican becomes a way to blend into the ethnic makeup around him, making him less of an outsider. Even when accosted by a homophobic epithet, he attributes it not to being stereotyped as gay, but as white. For him, the experiences of race and sexuality are like two sides of the same coin: "[W]hen I think of myself in racialized terms, I always think of myself in sexualized terms." As a white gay male, this student underscores ways that "passing" racially and sexually are performative acts. His "nonwhite"-looking skin color accessorized with a bald head and facial hair allows him to cross an *other* ethnic line.

Of the white males I taught during my years at the college, one stands out among them. As a straight, middle-class student, he defied the stereotype in many ways both inside and outside the classroom. I conclude this section with an excerpt from the memoir of race he wrote in 1999 in the course I called "Skinwalking: Reading and Writing across the Color-line II," inspired by Scales-Trent's book. So many passages in it capture the spirit of what the most courageous of my students sought to reveal in the autobiographical narratives they wrote.

Though white, from a middle-class background, and many years younger than I, this student writes about the evolution of his racial identity in some ways that mirror mine. He writes about being an outsider, a position he came to embrace as he understood more and more how race, gender, class, and heterosexual privileges left him feeling alone— "homeless." Becoming racially consciousness, he writes, signified a journey of painful recognition: "Over the years, I had been undergoing a process of becoming more and more aware of myself as a racialized being in the U.S., interrogating my multiple privileges, and moving to understand the world from beyond the parameters of my normalized, white, Northern, middle-class, male, heterosexual framework. It has been a painful process, and one that has often dislodged me from the comfortable perspectives of my childhood. . . . Before I was actually old enough to go the boarding school, I was educated within the public school system."

In the public school system, he found himself an "outcast" from the two "classes" of white students at his school—the "athletes and the burnouts." Stratified along class lines in the nearly all-white town of his New England state, neither group was a comfortable fit. In his eyes, his middle-class standing made him unsuited to the downward spiral of the working-class group ("the ones with little hope, the ones who were on drugs or pregnant before their eighteenth birthday"). He says, "I tried harder to fit into the 'jock' camp, [but] I was never quite 'pretty' enough or athletic." It was his not-so-"pretty" looks that not only positioned him as outsider in the jock camp but also figured ways that "othered" him racially. He internalized his facial features as Negroid in appearance:

> I thought of myself as quite ugly; I considered myself to have enormously hideous lips, a big nose, big teeth. . . . I hated the fact that I didn't look like any of the other "normal"-looking white kids that I went to school with. I would stare into the mirror and ask myself "Why . . . why me?" Although I didn't have the language for this phenomenon at the time, my self-perceived "ugliness" was completely invented through a racial lens. As I was to learn later, my broad features were those commonly associated with African Americans, and the ugliness that I felt was a part of a historical force of colonial relations that imagined universal beauty through the form of the "fine-featured" European. . . . Here was Eurocentrism at work, inside of me, silent and inconspicuous in my ignorance of the racialized history of beauty, crippling my mind and self-image without a name. It was the legacy of white supremacist thought that made me feel this way. I had racialized myself by accepting a definition of myself as "ugly" and feeling ashamed of my broad features.

The racial contradiction of looking black with white skin was a conundrum that played against the white middle-class "class" politics that *whitened* him above the working-class "burnouts" of his school, and it remained a source of inner shame. Yet the realization of his class privilege coupled with feelings of marginalization in whiteness would prove a compelling force toward self-acceptance connected to an antiracist identity: "The combination of not quite feeling [racially] accepted yet not quite being totally unaccepted is something that I have carried my entire life. . . . In many ways, this sense of at once belonging and not-belonging has enabled me to integrate an antiracist politics into my lived experience that has touched the core of my being. It enabled me to challenge and transgress the rigidities of whiteness while not living in denial of my history, my privilege, my baggage." His perception about the importance of antiracism in the classroom comes through his acknowledgment of the weight Scales-Trent affords it in her own work as a law professor. It is precisely her focus on the politics of progressive transracial identity that enabled him to accept "that which has been constructed as 'other' in [our] lives." But the more he has embraced an antiracist feminist outlook on life, the more it has positioned him on the margin of "normalized whiteness"—"I [have begun] the painful process of exiling myself from the comfortable, the expected, the places that once welcomed me as 'family.'" Feminist antiracism allows this white male student to reimagine the familial and beyond: "Especially [for] white people beginning to challenge [racial] privileges giving voice to the unspoken silences of whiteness. As our interests shift, so do our alliances and with this comes a realignment and redefinition of community, family, and self."

The Crayon Test:
For Colored Girls . . . *Too* Black to Pass

sing a black girl's song
Lady in brown
& this is for colored girls who have considered suicide
but are movin to the ends of their own rainbows.

—Ntozake Shange

We learn about color with crayons. We learn to tell the difference between white and pink and a color they call Flesh. The flesh-colored crayon amuses us. Like white it never shows up on the thick Manila paper they give us to draw on, or on the brown paper sacks we draw on at home. Flesh we know has no relationship to our skin, for we are brown . . .

—bell hooks

As students quoted in the previous sections reveal, the drama/trauma of being transracial and transgender in a culture of white supremacy and hetero(sexism) embodies complexities specific to the myths and stereotypes that "other" them. For black female students too dark to pass for white, the struggle against racial and sexual dehumanization is just as traumatic. In the 2001 spring semester in which students responded to the crayon exercise in the Teaching to Transgress course, there were two responses from black women students illustrating the ways "color" remained on the minds of black females in particular. One black woman student wrote about the color brown:

I am a *brown*-skinned lady. The kind that has always known about the beauty in my skin, but I know that is a lie. My grandma just celebrated her 94th birthday this weekend. She is a beautiful woman; her skin is soft and caramel. For as long as I can remember my grandma has sported a platinum blond hairdo. In my early years, it caused me quite a bit of inner confusion. I thought, perhaps, just like those girls in junior high school, I had "Indian in my family." Having "red" blood was some how better than having white. I learned how young brown-skinned girls longed for Indian ancestry, not because they wanted to tap into that earthly spiritual side but because they, we, I simply wanted long wavy hair. Few brown-skinned girls I grew up with ever claimed to love their skin [color] or their hair or themselves, for that matter. . . . Brown-skinned ladies look at me with sharp eyes that cut me like daggers. I am their mirror. And I know that I look just as mean as they do some days. I want them to smile at me. Sometimes white men lust after my brown skin. I see them at hip-hop shows, and I want to hide because it seems their stares are powerful enough to steal my brown skin. I want to simply tell them that I am not for sale. Not your brown-skinned plaything on a sunny afternoon. . . . With my darker-brown-skinned friend, we shop—do that brown diva thing, spend and splurge. . . . Brothers walk up on us. Over us, over her. They ogle my friend's body like it belongs to them. Their comments come out in brown dirty words that anger me. My friend rolls her eyes and keeps on walking. She doesn't care it seems but I know she does . . . and if I had a crayon to color myself, it would be purple.

While the "the lady in brown" above writes about her revulsion toward white male objectification of the black female body, she is equally repulsed and angered by its objectification by black men. That incident (and, perhaps, the many others she has endured), coupled with the unacknowledged pain of her brown friend, prompts the desire to "color" herself a nonhuman hue.

For the other two heterosexual, black female students responding to the exercise, the colors they chose signified the idea for them of being *too* "black" (as dark-skinned black women). The one chose burgundy, the other pink. The young woman who chose the darker color, writes about wearing predominately dark clothes as a child: navy blue, black, hunter green, and burgundy:

[T]hose used to be my colors. When I was in sixth grade, I would wear the darkest colors possible. Everything was deep and dark, like me. I do not even think that I had white in my wardrobe. . . . I think the sixth grade was the first time I understood that I was [racially] different. I had always known that I was dark, but I never knew that I was black. I grew up with white kids. Their parents were all white parents. . . . [T]hey would look at me and say, "That

little brown girl isn't like those black people [on television];
she must not be one of them." I was just my rich white parents'
daughter, my siblings' [black] sister. I was colorless, raceless [until
I took my sixth-grade class picture]. That year the dorky white
photo guy was ordered to switch the picture backdrop from blue
to brown. I had worn my favorite green sweater, not thinking anything of it. . . . When the pictures came back a month later, I
heard [one of the white boys say in a group of white boys]: "What
is this *black* spot in the middle of the class picture . . . Oh, it's ——
[me]." I had thought the picture was a bit dark, but it was fine.
Fine until I became the f——king black spot in the middle of the
class picture. . . . In sixth grade, I did not want to admit that I was
[racially] different than my classmates. . . . [After the incident with
the class picture] I thought I was ugly. That was why I wore such
dark colors all the time. I wanted to erase my skin and all that
it meant.

I am quite familiar with the racial pain of a dark-skinned, black female
child. My second child took the color of my father, who was a dark-
skinned man. On more than one occasion, she has come home from
school upset about negative comments from students about her skin
color. Mostly, it has come from black students, which has made it all the
more painful for her (and us, her parents). In the final chapter, I write
about a (seemingly innocent) racial incident that occurred with one of
my daughter's white female friends that reminded me how cruel internalized racism can be in the mouths of children. What is clear to me in
the black female student's response above is that *colorism*, a manifestation
of white supremacist deification of white skin color, can undermine the
racial identity development of black children and children of color in
general. As I have written in part 1, growing up as a gender outsider was
as much about internalized self-hatred because of my "dark" skin color as
it was about issues of masculinity.

In fall 1999, in the course I taught called "Memoirs of Race," a black
woman student wrote about how the color "pink" conjured up memories
of deeply ingrained feelings of internalized racism. In her memoir she remembers the color related to the "pink" bedroom she created in her
home as a teenager. Associating it with the traditional color stereotypically
representing the feminine (as in "it was what every girl wanted"), it was
not her favorite. Her choice of it for the walls, curtains, "and a big full-
sized bed covered in pink sheets and a doll wearing a pink dress" was
more about possessing something that belonged to her: "The room was to
be my safe space, my getaway, my hideaway. . . . No matter where I went or

how long I was gone, my pink bedroom was there when I came back." However, for whatever reason (which she does not disclose), she was not in the space for three years. Upon her return, however, everything in the room had been changed, including the presence of the color pink:

> When I returned the bedroom seemed to violate my feelings. My pink walls, sheets, and curtains had become "white" and nothing was left the way I once had it. With things missing and painted and switched around, memories of hidden silence began to come back to me. Memories of rushing to put the bleaching cream on my face and then having my sister ask me: "What's that funny smell?" . . . There was a time in my life when I'd hide bleaching cream in my room and put it on my face every night hoping I would wake up with the light skin that was "in" the next morning. After years and years of trying and waking up to be greeted in the mirror by disappointment, I quit bleaching my skin. . . . Memories of laying the pink, blue, and white quilt my grandmother made me on the floor and holding my Cabbage Patch in my hands and crying myself to sleep. These were the points in my life when I wasn't being "black enough" to my friends whom I'd grown up with all my life . . .

In the passage above, the student's feelings of loss with the color change of her room to "white" and the removal and "switch[ing] around" of things in it cause her painfully to recall self-denigrating ideas of blackness related her skin color. Years of failed attempts to "bleach" away dark skin pigmentation only reinforced feelings of self-hatred. In white supremacist culture from slavery to the contemporary period, dark-skinned black children and adults have encountered colorism among black people. As media, the entertainment industry, and popular culture continue to glorify "light"/white skin color, dark-skinned black people— particularly black females—continue to confront internalized racism in white and black heterosexual and gay communities (as the black gay male student writes in the earlier section). For the black female student above, reentering her bedroom (once functioning as a safe space, a hiding place, a room of her own), changed from pink to white, brought back memories of the "sin of silence" about internalized feelings of "black" self-hatred. For her, being black was not only equated with racism but with poverty and racial exclusion within the black community she grew up inhabiting:

> In this room, my sin of silence sent flashbacks of why I thought I was Nigger Black, the Black that white people called me on the

street when my friends and I were loud and disrespectful in public places. Ghetto Black, the Black that I was when I didn't have enough money to bring my clothes to the dryer, so I hung them out my window (which was in the front of the building on the sixth floor). Project Black when I was with my Black friends and I used improper English. The Nigger Black that never changed. I've moved away from the Project Black. The Ghetto Black that excludes me (for not being Black enough for the way I returned after being educated in a "white college"). . . . My friends wanted to know, "How can you be so Black and act so white?" . . . I want to face this Blackness I hated, the color of my skin that I wanted to change . . . I want to face myself . . . I have wishes of being Black, bone Black, to take back what was always mine but never claimed my heart. I want to love my skin color and all that comes with it in being a Black female.

Considering the forms of blackness she experiences—being "Nigger Black," "Ghetto Black," "Project Black," and *white* Black (having assimilated into whiteness)—the student acknowledges her desire to struggle against the racist mythology of dark skin, "to face myself . . . being Black, bone Black," and to reclaim her racial identity as a black female and "all that comes with it." In *Bone Black: Memories of Girlhood*, bell hooks writes poignantly about internalized racism in black communities and in her family regarding the onus of possessing "black" black skin: "They tell me that I am lucky to be lighter skinned, not black black, not dark brown . . ." (hooks 1996, 9). Like the black female student writing above, she encountered the hurtful ways colonized black people reflect white supremacy in their attitudes about color. She writes about her grandmother's contradictory disdain for dark skin, even as she embraces the affirming image of black womanhood her mother instills:

They [she and her siblings] have a grandmother who looks white who lives on a street where all the other people are white. She tells them things like a Black nigger is a no-good nigger, that her Papa looked like a white man but was a nigger. She never explains to them why she has married a man whose skin is the color of soot and other wonderous black things, things they love—shoe polish, coal, women in black slips. She [hooks] cannot wait to grow up and be a woman who can wear black slips, black dresses. *Black is a woman's color—that's what her mamma tells her. You have to earn the right to wear the color black.* (hooks 1996, 32)

I like what hooks's mother told her as a black female child about black being a "woman's color" and that she has "to earn the right to wear the color black." Having a dark-skinned black female child, my wife and I have surrounded and infused our daughter's life with images of "black" black females to embody the idea(l) of black beauty in a feminine form. For us, it is a daily struggle against racist ignorance—most of it found in young black girls and boys her age. Her bedroom and our home are clearly black-identified culturally and spiritually. In these spaces, she sees herself in colors that reaffirm the complexity of the black color spectrum, and she knows that she is beautiful—inside and out. While there have been students of color taking my classes whose struggle for racial autonomy has not led them to overcome deeply internalized wounds of white supremacy (as if racial healing could be accomplished in a single antiracist course), students of color in classes I teach have found memoir writing a powerful, cathartic strategy to confront, contest, and resist the gendered, classist, and sexualized ways whiteness operates to dehumanize them. Teaching memoir writing in classes where all or the majority of the students are white, I have often wondered how many more students of color could benefit from the healing potential of memoir writing about race.

Becoming a pro-feminist black man means that I must not only understand the *anti*heterosexist premise of progressive black feminists, but also practice its progressive stance in the classroom. Over the years, many students of color and white students have come wounded to classes I teach; they have been wounded because of their race, gender, *and* sexual difference. In a majority-white, sexually liberated college environment, where progressive politics on sexuality would appear to benefit white GLBTQ students, there are those white students who experience otherness on multiple levels—levels related to race, gender, and class (inside and outside the classroom). Black feminist, antiracist pedagogy (precisely because of its connection to the history of struggle against heterosexism within black communities) offers students a strategic location to form new alliances across our differences. As Audre Lorde contends in *Sister Outsider*, "[I]t is not those differences between us that are separating us. It is rather our refusal to recognize those differences, and to examine the distortions which result from our misnaming them and their effects upon human behavior and expectation" (1984, 115).

When White Students Write about Being White in a Class Called "Womanist Thought"

Black feminist pedagogy embodies a philosophy that is a philosophy of liberation. Black feminism's major premise is the active engagement in the struggle to overcome the oppressions of racism, heterosexism, and classism, as well as sexism. . . . *[T]he Black feminist teacher artfully and skillfully interprets class interaction while never veering from the goals of liberation for humankind through the process of an analysis of oppressions.* . . . (Emphasis added)

—Gloria Joseph

By centering education about race on Black women, the Womanist Thought course has allowed me to address the social history of racial ideologies. It has kept me focused on actual oppression, not within a theoretical framework, but in the lived experiences of Black women. . . . Theory without application is useless, and I fear that the danger in white people learning about race is that it will become just that . . . mastery of the theory. . . .

—Nathaniel Meysenburg

My spirit has swelled with the scholarship of so many vital, explosive women.

—Andrew Daul

The words of the black women we have been reading have been exactly what I need. . . . They have offered me a vision of hope, healing and radical transformation. These qualities I need to keep close to my ear always—but especially now, during this time of imminent war [against Iraq]. . . .

—Eleanor Whitney

151

Black Women at the Pedagogical Center

Can a single course on black feminism initiate a radical transformation in the racial/social consciousness of white students? The answer is an emphatic "No!" Yet this is an ongoing question I have asked myself over the last ten years as a black male professor teaching feminist antiracism at the college. Year after year, I had to confront this question, since there was a real possibility that from one semester to the next there might be no students of color in any of my classes. I argue that "[t]he classroom can be a critical location of resistance to advance the struggle against racial injustice—most strategically waged at the intersection of sexism, classism, and homophobia" (Lemons 2001a, 1).

What happens in a course on black feminism where all the students are white (except for one woman whose skin color affords her the privilege of passing as white) and the professor is black and male? The answer to this question is the subject of this chapter. My aim is to show that black feminist thought, as a social theory of liberation and pedagogical agent of social change, can be a powerful tool toward the development of critical race consciousness in white students. Those who embrace the notion that "[b]lack feminism's major premise is," in the words of Gloria Joseph, "the active engagement in the struggle to overcome the oppressions of racism, heterosexism, and classism, as well as sexism" (Joseph 1995, 465) may intellectually come to understand multiple oppressions as a distinct feature of black women's history in the United States, but on a deeper self-reflective level can also experience a liberatory understanding of it from within. Since first reading Joseph's essay some years ago entitled "Black Feminist Pedagogy," her soulful proclamation that the feminist teacher's vigilance about teaching is for the liberation of "humankind" has stayed with me.

I teach a course called "Womanist Thought," its title inspired by Alice Walker's vision of a black feminist (Walker 1983, xi). While the course focuses on the intellectual history of black women in the United States—from Maria Stewart's 1831 call for them to "[p]ossess the spirit of independence" (1995, 29) to the diversity of thought among contemporary black feminist voices—it aims to emphasize its multidimensionality. Patricia Hill Collins has said, "[D]oing intellectual work of the sort envisioned within Black feminism requires a process of self-conscious struggle on behalf of Black women. . . . Reclaiming Black feminist intellectual traditions involves much more than developing Black feminist analyses using standard epistemological criteria. It also involves challenging the very terms of intellectual discourse itself" (Hill Collins 2000, 15). White students studying the intellectual tradition of black feminists as a catalyst for self-examination must empty out their "invisible knapsack[s]" (to borrow a phrase from Peggy McIntosh). In the process, they begin "challenging the very terms of intellectual discourse itself"—particularly that which reinforces a mind/body split. Writing about the kind of intellectual work my students at the college did in Womanist Thought makes me reflect upon the power of black feminist pedagogy as a critical launch site for antiracist education. When feminist antiracist teaching is linked to a pedagogy of composition that privileges autobiographical writing as a strategy for enabling students to connect social theory with personal empowerment, intellectual labor becomes a catalyst for *self*-liberation.

This chapter is not meant to offer a detailed study of black women's intellectual tradition. Rather its aim, as stated above, is to show the overall impact that teaching black feminism can have in a college classroom where almost all the students are white. Privileging their voices in the discussion that follows, I foreground their thoughts about the course (at the beginning and end of the semester) to formulate my own assessment of its effectiveness in combating racism and white supremacy. I simultaneously engage the questions of how sexism, classism, and homophobia interconnect to the students. Womanist Thought compels students to confront these issues through personal self-examination, a key element in the writing strategy employed as they critically analyze black women's writings in the course. It not only challenges *whiteness* as a racial signifier of power, privilege, superiority, and the complex web of social relations it enacts, but also requires that students personally take on their own internalized racism. Teaching black feminism to white students pushes them to recognize what it means to be *white* in a culture of racism and patriarchy.

As a backdrop for my discussion, let me describe certain details about the course. The course title and "rationale" statement emerged from my desire to conceptualize a course on the feminist thought of black women linked to the political vision of Alice Walker. To summarize the course objectives, it aims

> [t]o survey the major works of womanist thought primarily to understand the standpoint and theoretical foundation on which the feminisms of Black/women of color represent themselves; to understand the problematics of feminist thinking produced by Black women in relation to the struggle against patriarchy, sexism, and homophobia within communities of color; *to think through the transformative implications of womanist thought not only for Black/people of color but for all people who struggle against domination, whether it be rooted in sexism, racism, classism, or any other force which aims to dehumanize.* (Emphasis added)

In addition to students writing rigorous critical analyses of texts read in the course, students include a personal response to all of the readings (in the form of short, structured response papers, usually two each week). Readings for the course come from two primary texts: *Words of Fire: An Anthology of African-American Feminist Thought*, edited by Beverly Guy-Sheftall, and *Black Feminist Thought*, by Patricia Hill Collins. An indispensable text in black feminist studies, *Words of Fire* provides conceptual clarity and substance in my attempt to offer a historical survey of black women's nonfiction writings. It affords students an amazingly visceral experience of and engagement in the dynamic evolution of black feminist thought and shows the diverse standpoints represented in the women's ideas that characterize it. Noting this point as one of the book's main features, Guy-Sheftall writes in the preface: "The women included here are also not a monolithic band with similar world views or the same conceptions of 'feminism.' . . . Sometimes their feminist discourse is autobiographical, controversial, visionary, understated and subtle, but more often it is hard-hitting and strident. Some authors are passionate and angry, others more cautious and indirect. . . . They share a collective history of oppression and a commitment to improving the lives of black women, especially, and the world in which we live" (Guy-Sheftall 1995, xv). The fact that the women in this stunning volume "share a collective history of oppression and a commitment to improving the lives of black women, especially, and the world in which [they] live" is what makes it such a powerful text to teach and such a catalyst for the development of students' feminist consciousness.

The humanist vision set forth in the readings from *Words of Fire* is echoed by Hill Collins's sense of her task in the second edition of *Black Feminist Thought*. As a complementary secondary source for the course, it offers students interpretive insight into the texts from the anthology while giving them an incisive critical context for understanding black feminism as social theory. Hill Collins states, "For African-American women, critical social theory encompasses bodies of knowledge and sets of institutional practices that actively grapple with the central questions facing U.S. black women as a collectivity. The need for such thought arises because African-American women as a *group* remain oppressed within a U.S. context characterized by injustice. . . . Black feminist thought's identity as a 'critical' social theory lies in its commitment to justice, both for U.S. Black women as a collectivity and for that of other similarly oppressed groups" (2000, 9). Immersing white students in black women's intellectual tradition through the works of Guy-Sheftall and Hill Collins keep the course focused on the social contexts of black women's thought, while foregrounding their strategies of liberation. What remained clear in the course readings during the fall 2002 term in which I taught the class was the notion that black female liberation is inextricably linked to the struggle for human rights. For white students in this session of Womanist Thought, many of whom were active in campus organizing against the war with Iraq during the term, the history of black feminist movement served as a source of inspiration.

Looking at the World through a Black Feminist Lens

As a white woman, I can attest, firsthand, to the clarity that comes from looking at the world through a black feminist lens. I've discovered that there is an uneasy balance between being completely ignorant of, or simply refusing to acknowledge, one's own privilege, and being guilt-ridden for the injustice that is out of your hands. Now I am comfortable owning up to the privileges that I have. I am accountable for them, but I do not think they are deserved, and so I will pool the resources that I have access to and use them against this [oppressive] system. . . .

—Tyler St. Jean

Antiracist teaching linked to pedagogy for social justice promotes a more radical agenda for the feminist classroom. While the fall 2002 Womanist Thought course was not racially diverse, white students enrolled in the course as an elective for a variety of different reasons, all connected to a desire to study race. Through the firsthand accounts of students that follow, I provide a critical framework to reflect upon the effectiveness of black feminist pedagogy in a white classroom. It enables white students to confront whiteness at a deep, heartfelt level.

Students wrote a lot in Womanist Thought—two analytical papers every week during the term (maintained in a portfolio format). Of the writing requirements, two were pivotally important not only for mapping the development of critical thinking but also for charting the evolution of racial consciousness. At the beginning of the term, each student wrote a "rationale statement"—a short paper in which they stated the reasons they chose to take this course. During the following class, they read them aloud, sharing the differences (and similarities) that brought them together. As the last writing requirement for the course, students completed a take-home "final (self-)examination." The exam consisted of one question: "What does it mean to be 'white' just having completed a course on black feminism?" Considering my insistence that critical self-interrogation drive class discussions all semester long around issues of white privilege, I had gained a certain measure of faith in the students' ability to respond with astute candor. I not only knew this would be an appropriate question for the end of the semester, but also believed that the students would produce some amazing responses.

Revisiting the students' rationale statement, I discovered that on one level they were keenly aware of themselves as white people. This awareness figured significantly in their reason(s) for taking a course on black feminism. Generally speaking, in the first writing assignment most of the students acknowledged little familiarity with writings by black feminists. And, while many of them were conscious of themselves as white people, they all claimed a need to push beyond the boundaries of their existing racial comfort zone and knowledge about black women's intellectual tradition. Interestingly, some overtly expressed the idea that studying black feminism would help them gain a deeper racial understanding of themselves. Darragh, for example, a white woman student, wrote of a desire for a "safe place" to talk about race. She said, "[W]hen I have discussed race in the past I've been criticized by both black and white friends. . . . I have selected Womanist Thought because I hope it will allow me to ask the questions I've been told I shouldn't ask and maybe even those I've been afraid to ask. . . . I ask myself why is my 'safe place' to talk about race a room filled with white students?" Darragh's question about the lack of racial diversity in the class speaks to a previous question she posed about her choice to attend a majority-white college. Over the course of a decade and more, I rarely had more than two or three students of color in my classes.

Classes I taught at the college on black feminism were popularly known as "race" classes. For white students (with or without racial consciousness) who desired to study race, my classes provided the opportunity to do so. I never promise that my classes will provide a "safe" place to talk about race. Most students enrolling in my courses already knew this through word of mouth. I have no illusions about teaching race as a black man at a white school. Challenging white students to question white privilege and their relation to white supremacy and racism (from a black feminist standpoint) will not, in most cases, place a professor of color (or white professor, for that matter) in the running for a "teacher of the year" award. Having students share their rationale statement in class allows space for their desires to be acknowledged publicly. Students sharing personally at the beginning of the term tells me where they are (intellectually and emotionally) in relation to the course topic and where they want to go with it. One of my initial tasks is to help them open up more about what they want to learn, with the hope that they will feel compelled to embrace the liberatory ideology that characterizes black feminist thought.

Having students revisit their first writing assignment of the course at the end of it provides them with an autobiographical context in which to reflect upon the personal, social, and political implications of their initial decision as white people to enroll in the course. As students think back upon it, the process (taking into consideration all the writing they have done during the term) allows them to chart their own individual intellectual, critical, and emotional development through the course. Throughout the semester while teaching this course, I tried to imagine how the presence of students of color might have altered it. I continually drew attention to my presence as the only acknowledged "black" person in the classroom (who also happened to be the teacher). I worked to affirm white students' desire to engage black feminist thought, while challenging them to interrogate white privilege and the lack of racial diversity in the college. No one can say for sure what difference the presence of students of color might have made in our classroom, but I do know with some certainty that these white students opened themselves up to the transformative possibilities in studying black feminist thought. In the space of this chapter, it is impossible, however, to capture with fine detail all that students wrote in either the rationale statement or the final (self-)examination.

In the past, when writing about my work as a feminist antiracist in the classroom, it has been important to me to include student voices for two reasons: (1) to illustrate the effectiveness of teaching autobiographical writing focused on self-reflection linked to composition for critical social consciousness; and (2) to demonstrate the viability of antiracist teaching founded upon black feminist thinking. Having students write about themselves in relation to the course at the end of the semester is critically necessary to understand its impact upon them. Having white students write about being white after a semester of studying black feminist thought makes perfect sense to me. Nearly all of the responses (fourteen papers) had to do with the students' arriving at a deeper level of race consciousness where *whiteness* represented a signifier of power, privilege, and the myth of racial superiority. While every student in some way spoke about being white in a black class, there were certain ones whose perspectives stood apart from the others. Rather than expressing guilt for being racially privileged because of their skin color, these students looked within to question how the self-critical knowledge of being white had come through the study of black feminists' interrogation of white supremacy. Commenting on the reality of an all-white class and the impact of womanist thought on it, Kate said,

This has been a unique class. Unique first of all because it is a class on Black feminism wherein all the students are white. But it is also unique because many of us came to the class, if not knowing anything about Black feminists, at least having had some experience with thinking "that way" ("thinking black," as Gloria Joseph put it). In fact, I felt that one of the most important things I've learned this semester is that thinking "that way," or having a womanist-centered philosophy, is beneficial not just to people of color, but to white people too; not just to women, but also to men.

About his relation to being white, male, straight, and the questioning of such privileges, among others, Seamus declares:

I cannot return to an academic, ideological, philosophical, spiritual, political, and . . . educational system that is centered around young, rich, straight, white, Christian males. . . . The questions that I found throughout the course far outweigh the answers (so goes great education). But some of the critical questions that I will never again need to hesitate or shy from when answering are these: What right do I have as a white male to study feminism, black studies, or identify as a feminist antiracist? Why study black women? And what can I ever know about their experiences?

Having studied black feminism in an academic setting that empowered him to engage this knowledge, Seamus gained a new sense of confidence as a white male—not only challenging his racial privilege but also the normalized power of his gender and sexuality.

Another white male wrote candidly about his need to connect theory with practice, eschewing the notion that race could be studied as social theory without a student having to grapple with its implications in one's everyday life. He makes a powerful case for an approach to studying race that merges the social, political, and personal. Having read some writings by black feminists, bell hooks among others, Nathaniel (a white male who attended a majority-black high school in Pittsburgh) says:

I began the course in womanist thought stating that it is interesting to question why a white male would want to even begin thinking about Black feminism and the struggle of Black women. Through the course of the semester this question has been answered many times over, and in many ways. [Before this course] I had yet to discover that centering Black women at the place where ideas around race, gender, and class intersect would change my perspective on the world. . . . I cannot confront my own whiteness in a theory-based way. Doing this would negate the existence of racism that I myself have internalized. When I read the works of Patricia Hill Collins, Audre Lorde, Ida B. Wells Barnett, Anna Julia Cooper, and many other Black Feminist writers, I learned not only about experiences within this system. As a middle-class white male, I live with the ability to at any instant step into everything that the classist, racist patriarchy has to offer me. . . . But it is the writing of these women that keeps reminding me that the costs of my ignoring the [existing] power structures are too high. It is these women who encourage me to reject whiteness. *It is also these women who have engaged me in a deeper understanding of what my being white is in relationship to their being Black.* (Emphasis added)

Nathaniel (he preferred "Nat") acknowledges the transformative power of black feminist social consciousness illustrated in the women's texts he studied in class. Simultaneously, he (like Seamus) becomes more socially aware of the power of whiteness he possesses in relation to black women's experience of sexism and racism.

    Black feminist thought compelled some white students to look within, where the complexities of racial identity had remained hidden from external view. They spoke about a deep process of self-reclamation through an intense interaction with and inner reaction to the writings of black feminist women. Sharon (a white-looking Jewish woman who was a visiting student from Sarah Lawrence) wrote about moving from a theoretical understanding of race to one connected to the painful process of questioning white skin privilege, "passing," and reclaiming her racialized Jewish identity in this course as a means of fostering a deeper commitment to antiracist activism:

> I [had] never thought of race because I was White. Wasn't I? This is where I was wrong . . . I wasn't. And I never have been. It wasn't until Womanist Thought that I began to deconstruct what [my] identity as a Jewish woman meant to me. . . . I had never contemplated why I didn't wear my Star of David to school, why I hated my dark hair and dark eyes, why I insisted that they were hazel and not brown. . . . The politics of passing have been with me since I sprouted pigtails, from the day I learned that it was ugly to be a Jew, that it was about being Blonde (because all good Christians, all good Aryans, are Blonde. . . . I wanted to assimilate; I wanted

society to consider me beautiful. . . . In reading the [works] of these women [black feminists], in reading about their struggle and their strength on the path to self-love, I found myself compelled to follow. These women have taught me to love myself, despite what I thought I knew, despite what I was taught. Anti-Semitism, just like racism, teaches self-hate. I have come to realize that while I "passed" for white—I am not white. That I have denied much of my culture and heritage, coming from a place of shame . . . of my history and have in essence denied who I am. And it is in reading these women that I have learned . . . to begin the loving of myself—all parts of myself. . . . I am learning to live up to these incredible women who have taught me more about myself than any white woman, any middle-class woman, any Jewish woman, any queer woman, any woman, period, has ever attempted [to do], let alone succeeded [in doing].

Another "white"-looking woman in class, Bianca, publicly claimed that she too had been passing but that the primary texts we studied in *Words of Fire,* of so many black feminists and their struggles to speak out in spite of multiple oppressions facing them, had inspired her to awaken from a deep sleep and to question critically the ways she had racially assimilated and the "lies" such practice perpetuated in her daily life. Suggesting that after reading their essays she is "haunted" by the presence of black feminists, she now "keep[s] [her] eyes open at all times," by which she means she is more vigilant of the ways oppression operates in the lives of women of color:

I came to Gary's class a little confused. I'm neither white nor black, but have changed my hair color and dressed to pass as white. . . . How could I call myself critically conscious while I sat quiet [in the past] when a woman or person of color was disrespected? I feel as if I [have been] let out of a box of lies and I have been awoken. The essays written by women of color [we read] have honored me with their lessons and ideas. They have helped me to keep my eyes open at all times. Sometimes I feel a bit haunted by their presence, as if I just want to forget it and just live in a fake reality where everything is fine and equal. They are always there, though, with their words reminding me that the struggle for women, especially women of color, is far from over. I used to feel sorry for women of color but now I feel sorry for the people who do not care to understand the struggle of women of color. The book *Words of Fire* should be a required

text. It taught me more about American history than any other
book ever has. This was a book of heroes, a book that gave me inspiration for living my life. This was a book that engaged my
spirit, my mind, and my heart.

For some white students in class, as the two women above profess, "whiteness," race privilege, and white supremacy had not entered their consciousness in a visceral way. They were blind to the idea of racialization,
a common characteristic of whiteness in which white people are oblivious to how it feels to be "raced."

A second thematic pattern surfaced in the final (self-)examination, a
pattern that pointed to the emotional and spiritual transformation students experienced. They not only tapped into the emotional current of
their racial anxieties connected to a fear of dialogue on race, but also
into the internal upheaval such conversation might cause. In the writings
of black feminists, they found the courage to speak about inner revela-
tions. Amy, for example (a rather quiet and soft-spoken white woman),
wrote about coming to consciousness about white identity through black
feminism as similar to a spiritual awakening. Reflecting upon the shift in
her racial consciousness from the beginning of the semester to its end,
she states, "I came as a white girl, the 'whitest white girl I know' [from her
rationale statement], but I am certainly not leaving as such. Throughout
my journey, the beautiful and [painstaking] words of many women of
color [we read] such as Elise Johnson McDougald, Maria Stewart, Barbara Smith, Beth E. Richie, Sojourner Truth, and Margaret Alexander
have lingered with me, especially in my heart, well after I finished reading their texts." Amy speaks about how painful the process of understanding racial privilege as a white woman can be. On the one hand,
reflecting upon feelings about the internal upheaval the course was causing her, she laments not having known earlier in the semester how
deeply black feminists were affecting her everyday life. On the other, getting in touch with the empowering effects of their writings, she could acknowledge the "linger[ing]" experience of them. Among her peers,
Amy's experience was not unique. One of my aims for the course was to
create a classroom space conducive to students' desire to come to terms
(in one's own way) with the challenges of race, gender, class, and sexuality that black feminism posed. Writing afterward about an apparently difficult class session, Amy states:

I went home that night beyond confused, beyond lost, disgusted
with myself and humiliated. My once simplistic life of a sheltered
and oblivious suburban white girl was being obliterated, and as

painful as it was, it was also incredibly liberating. I didn't realize it then, but I was breaking the mold of the society which I was raised in, and ultimately raised me [with regard to] "white privilege." . . . This class [Womanist Thought] was more than a textbook-lecture kind of class; it tapped into spirituality, deep into my spirituality. I felt like a snake that was shedding her outer layer of skin . . . I learned more about myself in this class than I have on my own in the past twenty-one years. Spiritual awareness cannot be acquired through a textbook or a lecture, but rather in a safe haven that embodies a warm and open roundtable discussion.

Amy was not the only white woman to talk about the impact of black feminism and the emergence of critical race consciousness as having the force of spiritual revelation. One of several student leaders/activists in class who had spent the semester organizing on campus against the war with Iraq, Darragh passionately wrote about the inspiration of many of the black feminists named above but also added the names of bell hooks, June Jordan, and Michele Wallace. She said that they

and many others have left an everlasting impression on [my] soul and heart. Reading about and understanding the intersecting struggles and oppressions that black women have faced and continue to encounter, and their many acts of resistance in response, has encouraged me to continue down my own personal path of struggle. Their bravery and strength push me onward. They tell me to continue my resistance and fight. Their words test me to push my boundaries of "safety." Their resilience and determination in the face of oppression . . . provide a precedent for me. I am no longer the person I was before I heard the words of these inspiring women. Before their words were unleashed onto my soul, I was afraid to talk about race because I was fearful of who I was or who I might be. I'm not ashamed to say that I actually cried before the first day of class because I knew it was going to be challenging for me. The challenge has proved to be the most important one in my life. These women have unfastened my spirit and allowed me to search within. I have come to terms with the fact that I am on the margins as well.

While Darragh, like many of the other white students, found a political connection with the black women feminists they read in the course that enlivened them spiritually, others gained strength from womanist thinking to act courageously in the face of personal adversity. Another woman,

Jennifer, found personal strength in Audre Lorde's words on the necessity of voice and breaking silence about oppression. In her final self-exam, Jennifer discussed her decision to enroll in Womanist Thought in spite of having to "justify to others why [she] chose to study Black feminism" and confronting the question, "Who do I think I am [as a white woman taking such a course]?" It is, however, her thoughts about the pivotal importance of studying the work of black feminist women and its impact upon her personal life that move me most. Determining to leave an abusive relationship, Jennifer writes:

> Personally I have gone through a very trying time, overcoming an emotionally abusive relationship with a partner of a different culture [who] left me feeling riddled with guilt and confusion because I wouldn't shut up and give [in to his] control. . . . To be stultified and stifled and passive and submissive, when I have so much to say and do. Reading the work of these many brave and incredible women, I found empowerment and voice enough to walk away with my head held high, removing the guilt from my mind, and to leave without a doubt in my heart. . . . Audre Lorde changed my life [through her words in such writings as] "Transforming Silence into Language and Action" and "Uses of the Erotic." Lorde spoke differently to me than any other writer, poet, woman, warrior ever had before.

Reading statements like the one above was profoundly humbling for me. Throughout the semester, it was generally clear in the students' responses to the readings that there was a deep respect for the endeavor we had undertaken. Having taught this course two times prior with *Words of Fire* and *Black Feminist Thought* as the core texts, I already knew the writings they contained possessed the power to transform student consciousness. In one of the previous times when the course was offered, there were a few students of color (including one black male), along with two white males. Another had only six students and was composed of all white women (the few women of color who enrolled dropped the course after the first session with the complaint that the class was "too white"). That class never recovered from the absence of those women of color. Frankly, I think the white women students were angry that they left, feeling as if they had been summarily dismissed. Those feelings infected the work we did for the remainder of the term. One white woman student continually resisted the idea that she should have to feel some emotional connection with the women or the ideas she was studying. In retrospect, I believe her response arose from a complex inner struggle around several issues: my being a black man teaching the course, her own paralyzing guilt around her race and class privilege as an elite white woman, her desire to collapse critical differences between the ideas of white feminist women she had studied in the past, and the critique black feminist women in the course posed against racist practices in the history of feminism in the United States. I have come to expect that white students, as well as students of color (female and male), will challenge my position as a pro-feminist black male professor. Writing elsewhere about the problematics of my identity in the classroom, I state: "When I teach, students come to know that—regardless of the particular subject matter—my pedagogical strategies are linked to the idea of education as a holistic practice where mind, body, and spirit come together to project a vision of social change. Self-actualization as a key piece in the feminist positionality I construct in the classroom means that feminism enables me to move radically against the grain of patriarchal manhood and masculinity . . ." (Lemons 1996b, 264).

Throughout the semester, to no avail, I challenged her and the other white women to become more personally engaged in their response to the texts and to make a critical link between the "personal" and the "political," but the level of resistance was so intense that the course became a battleground between gender (represented by white women) and race (me and the "attack" black feminist women had launched against them). Needless to say, the course ended up being (for the white women and myself) uninspired, overly academic/"objective," and emotionally, intellectually, and spiritually sterile—one of the worst classes I have taught.

How would a black woman feminist have dealt with the situation? I have talked about this with some feminist black women professors who have encountered white female resistance in the classroom, and they have suggested that an intersectional approach to feminist critique of gender oppression is an inherently volatile subject, especially for individuals who possess unearned privilege—whether they are white, male, middle-class, and/or heterosexual. Even if the students have intellectually accepted the challenge of the feminist methodology I employ, the reality of its pedagogical performance is always potentially fraught with the complex interrelating dynamics of race, gender, class, and sexuality in the actual context of the classroom. Given that the majority of the students I taught, from one semester to the next, at the college were white females, race and gender issues tended to be more contentious than issues of class and sexuality, mainly because of similar backgrounds and progressive attitudes. Teaching in classrooms consisting almost exclusively of white females over the years, I have come to know that the white female classroom where black feminism is the subject will always be charged with racial tension. It cannot be avoided.

Having white students engage the issue of racism in feminism from an autobiographical standpoint, for example, moves the discussion from the theoretical to the personal. More often than not, the students discover that much of their anxiety in studying black feminism is predicated upon a fear of being politically incorrect—that they may be accused of being racist for holding certain stereotypical beliefs about black women. Creating a classroom environment that promotes honest dialogue about white myths of black womanhood is the single most difficult step in teaching black feminism in a white classroom. When white students begin to comprehend that they play a strategic role in advancing the vision of black feminist liberation, they come to know that black feminism is a humanist project for all people's liberation.

White Students Writing in Solidarity with Black Feminists

The idea that white people have a place in black feminist thought and that it can be a critical source of political empowerment for white students is a theme echoed in most of the final (self-)examinations. The articulation of this represents a profound moment of clarity in the students' understanding about the impact that studying the writings of black feminists had had on them during the semester. "Black feminism is for everyone," declared Anna (a white woman in class who maintained that her knowledge of black women's historical struggle against often insurmountable hardship helped her overcome great personal adversity during the semester). The willingness of white students in this class to embrace black feminist thought in their personal lives is not only a testament to its liberatory power but to its capacity to function as an agent of inner healing.

What made the writing in this class different from its predecessors had to do with the fact every student from the beginning of the semester openly expressed an intense desire to study black feminist thought, and throughout the term they remained open to the possibilities of such study as a transformative personal, social, political, and spiritual project. It was clear to me after hearing students read their rationale statements when we began the course that what they were expressing emanated from the same source—a deep yearning to learn from black feminists something unknown about themselves as white people in relation to ideas of social justice. The willingness of these white students to write with such candor, honesty, and emotional vulnerability about their initial desire prepared them to (help me) create a course in black feminist thought that would challenge (in varying ways) the mind, body, and spirit of every one of them. From this writing it quickly becomes apparent that the kind of intellectual, spiritual, and ongoing self-critical work they hoped to do in the course had come about.

One of the most poignant rationales came from Andrew, one of the white men in class, who rarely spoke during the semester. He wrote with searing passion about his feelings of dispossession as a gay man, the problems of dealing with the death of family members, and his desire "to learn from African American women" with the hope that "their stories . . . may in the end lead [him] to understand [his] own." Boldly he proclaimed,

> I am compelled because I am Queer, and because of that may taste at times the bitter distillation of the dispossessed, the cast aside and the thrown away. I am compelled as well to come to grips with the complexity and at times the guilt I hold in my privilege, born of European blood, male, my ability to pass unquestioned. I yearn to understand fully, if possible, the duty, right, pain, and possibility of my skin that is heavy with connotations. I am as well compelled spiritually; I feel guided to know of such things, as though those who have fallen around me [a reference to the deaths of his mother, an uncle, and close personal friends] are tugging me toward some destination I can't see and perhaps yet shouldn't. . . . I am taking this class because it seemed like a class I naturally should take. . . . What I hope to learn from African American women above all, I guess, are their stories, ones that may in the end lead me to actually understand my own.

Reading these words again reminds me how courageous Andrew was. The power of his candor shared in the first days of the term is mirrored in the unrelenting frankness of Anna's disclosure in her final (self-)exam, which helped me to understand how deeply she had internalized the spirit of the black women studied in Womanist Thought. The blistering reality of her words penetrate my consciousness, as they bear witness to the universality of suffering eased by the hope in the healing words of another. Anna writes about how the words of black feminist writers in the course gave her (as a victim of sexual violation) "the strength, the tools, and the vocabulary" to fight sexual violence against women:

> In the beginning of the course I was very interested in the subject matter . . . but I don't think the actual concept of black fem-

inism resonated so deeply within me until I experienced the ultimate practice of patriarchy—rape, about a month into the course. I now understand the dehumanization that many black women have faced before me, and their stories have shown me that I still have hope. This [should] not have to happen again to any women, and will never happen again to me. [Historically], rape was [potentially] an everyday experience for black women, and still is for some. . . . This class, and these remarkable women [black feminists read in class] have given me the strength, the tools, and the vocabulary to recognize why there are so many oppressions that all women face, what others are doing to fight against these oppressions, and what I can and must do.

Anna's will to go forward in the face of great personal adversity experienced during the course was catalyzed in her personal application of black feminist thought. For me, as a teacher committed to pedagogy of liberation, this is precisely where the viability of black feminism lies in the classroom. Anna, like the other white women and men in Womanist Thought, came to understand that its value as a course did not rest solely upon intellectual competence in reciting the words of black feminists but rather lay in a fundamental willingness to embrace intellectually and *personally* the theoretical and political framework of their work. Comprehending her individual experience of oppression as a white woman within a larger system of domination in which racism and sexism is an ongoing feature of black women's daily lives, as well as in the lives of other women of color, is something that Anna had not fully understood when the course began. Possessing the knowledge that her struggle as a white woman must be politically linked to that of black women and other women of color, she becomes a strong advocate for a key tenant of black feminism: a belief in coalition politics.

In the preface to the second edition to *Black Feminist Thought*, Hill Collins reasserts the centrality of the experiential (i.e., everyday lived experience) as a crucial location not only for understanding black women's oppression and their response to it but also for the very existence of a critical connection between individual and group political consciousness. In this edition, she has articulated these ideas within a larger transnational vision rooted in coalition politics. She notes,

> I initially wrote *Black Feminist Thought* in order to help empower African-American women. I knew that when an individual Black woman's consciousness concerning how she understands her

everyday life undergoes change, she can become empowered. Such consciousness may stimulate her to embark on a path of personal freedom, even if it exists initially primarily in her own mind. If she is lucky enough to meet others who are undergoing similar journeys, she and they can change the world around them. . . . *Reading Black women's intellectual work, I have come to see how it is possible to be both centered in one's own experiences and engaged in coalitions with others. In this sense Black feminist thought works on behalf of Black women, but does so in conjunction with other similar social justice projects.* (Hill Collins 2000, x; emphasis added)

Upon a deeper insight into black women's intellectual tradition, Hill Collins comes to realize that coalition strategizing must be a central feature of its political project. As Guy-Sheftall authoritatively demonstrates in *Words of Fire*—through the more than fifty black feminist voices represented (including members of the Combahee River Collective, who coauthored the groundbreaking and often anthologized essay "the Combahee River Collective Statement")—black women's struggle against multiple forms of oppression has always been rooted in an inclusive vision of liberation. Indeed, this was the ideological foundation upon which white students in the course were able to build a framework of solidarity between their individual struggles (whether personal, political, social, or spiritual).

White students' writing about the transformative power of black feminist thought in their lives underscores the universality of its appeal as a liberatory theory for social change. Reading their writings during the semester, I came to believe that we shared a common desire: that in black feminist thought we would find a place to ground our beliefs in social justice. Like many of the white students in Womanist Thought, I had longed to connect my commitment to antiracism with feminist movement for the equality of women, as well as with the struggles to end heterosexism and homophobia. Black feminism is inherently liberatory for all who suffer injustice. Theorizing an end to the multiple forms of oppression of black women, it lays the groundwork for a social movement that includes everyone. Black feminist thought has a universal appeal. In powerful yet poignant words, this is precisely what white students wrote about at the end of the semester. Like Anna, I too found in the stories of the black feminist women we studied and those of her peers the "strength, tools, and vocabulary" to defend my right to teach "for the liberation of humankind," as Gloria Joseph so eloquently proclaimed the pedagogical mission of black feminism to be.

Mapping White Desire,
Students Writing from the Heart

From the first day of the semester to the end, I continually drew attention to two things: (1) that I was the only self-acknowledged person of color in the classroom and (2) that I was a "black" male teacher. None of the students (mostly middle-class and upper-class, and some who did not identify as heterosexual) took issue with me (as a male) teaching a course on black feminism. While I thought white female students in the class (ten of the fourteen students) might take issue with my being a man (since being a black woman feminist would have been more politically correct), none of them (including the four white males) posed it as an issue (I am not suggesting, however, that it shouldn't have been).

During the term, we consistently addressed the class's racial makeup—why were there no students of color in the room? Given the fact that college has very few students of color, on that level alone (and considering the divergent curricular interests of students of color), we could justify their absence in the room. Nevertheless, it was always clear to us that this was a white class with a black male professor. In light of these always potentially troubling race and gender realities, we moved forward. I am almost certain that, as white students in a "black" course (feminist or not), they experienced some degree of relief that there were no students of color in the class—particularly black women. Except for the various times I might interrogate things said in class, there was no ongoing "racialized" pressure in the room to inhibit white students from speaking freely.

My experience teaching courses on race in a majority-white classroom has been that when students of color are in the room, white students are generally more inhibited, less talkative, and often resistant to engaging in discussions about race. Clearly, student-to-student dynamics in the white classroom is far less charged with issues of voice and silence when race is the subject and students of color are not in the room, although I must honestly say that the classroom space lacks a kind of racial kineticism. Yet my experience teaching antiracism through black feminism leaves no doubt in my mind that such a pedagogy possesses the power to transform the racial consciousness of white students.

When white students embrace the idea(l)s of black feminism, they come to experience an alteration of mind, body, and spirit. I know this from witnessing how (self-)critically conscious the students in this course became in a single semester. I am not suggesting for one moment that a single course in black feminism is the racial cure for the white student yearning for critical race consciousness. I am, however, maintaining that for some white students who have never really explored white identity, white supremacy, and white privilege, black feminism opens the possibility for radical self-transformation.

At the college, students were required by the administration to evaluate professors' performance at the end of the semester. The intention was to ascertain our pedagogical competence, not to judge my performance related to the racial pitfalls of teaching that calls into question white privilege. I believe that in a majority-white university the study of whiteness linked to antiracism is essential. I also know that teaching antiracism in such an environment is inherently difficult, particularly because the topic of racism in a liberal white institution is not generally engaged with candor. I say this from my standpoint as one of a few teachers at the college who overtly teach antiracist studies. The official "teacher evaluation" form afforded me little qualitative information to determine how effective my pedagogy was in promoting the need for antiracist consciousness in the classroom. This is why having all students write a final (self-)examination works as a strategic tool for teaching assessment beyond the standard institutional form.

At the end of the fall 2002 course session, every student came to understand the history of feminism for black women in the United States has never been about gender alone; and it would not be an unfair generalization to assert that each came to a deeper, more intimate self-knowledge. But importantly, what most, if not all, discovered was the power of writing that speaks "from the head and to the heart." They came to identify with the same yearning for freedom and justice they found in the intellectual tradition of black feminism. That yearning functioned as a catalyst for the production of an impassioned statement of personal desire about the need for white people to confront the privileges of whiteness, while being inspired by the feminist struggle of black women to live public lives committed to social justice and equality for all people.

➤ **8** ◄

Screening Race and the Fear of Blackness in a (Majority-)White Classroom

Theorizing black experience in the United States is a difficult task. Socialized within white supremacist educational systems and by a racist mass media, many black people are convinced that our lives are not complex, and are therefore unworthy of sophisticated critical analysis and reflection. . . . Without a way to name our pain, we are also without the words to articulate our pleasure. Indeed, a fundamental task of black critical thinkers has been the struggle to break with the hegemonic modes of seeing, thinking, and being that block our capacity to see ourselves oppositionally, to imagine, describe, and invent ourselves in ways that are liberatory. Without this, how can we challenge and invite non-black allies and friends to dare to look at us differently, to dare to break their colonizing gaze?

—bell hooks

Most folks in this society do not want to openly admit that "blackness" as sign primarily evokes in the public imagination of whites (and all the other groups who learn that one of the quickest ways to demonstrate one's kinship within a white supremacist order is by sharing racist assumptions) hatred and fear. *In a white supremacist context "loving blackness" is rarely a political stance that is reflected in everyday life. When present it is deemed suspect, dangerous, and threatening.* (Emphasis added]

—bell hooks

. . . [P]ublic conversations about race frequently invoke the language of healing. . . . [T]he underlying idea seems to be the importance of pulling together and putting the past behind us. Too often the language of

171

healing is used to squelch frank talk about race. Such talk is divisive, we are told, and likely to produce ill will and discord. . . . If engagement is the first step toward healing, then the second is pure unadulterated struggle.

—Harlon Dalton

Why Should *All* Students Study the Struggle(s) of Black People?

Teaching race over the years has led me to confront students (of all colors) in my classes who believe, in the words of black law professor Harlon Dalton, that talk about race is "divisive . . . and likely to produce ill will and discord." In a nation where the very social fabric of its history is interwoven with racism and white supremacist dogma, is there any wonder why the field of antiracist studies exists on the margins of the (white) academy? In light of this, is it surprising that race is a particularly loaded subject in classes on majority-white college and university campuses across the nation? Is there any doubt that in these same institutions, students of color (often hyperaware of their *minority* status in them) stand in as "native informants" (i.e., experts on race and ethnicity)?

Students in classes on race must come to understand that a liberal, color-blind notion of racial consciousness rooted in political correctness whitens diversity. When liberal white people say they do not see color, it reinforces racial consciousness that disassociates the term "diversity" from ongoing initiatives to increase the number of students, faculty, and administrators of color in white institutions of higher learning. Today, "diversity" has come to mean democratic pluralism and is associated with the movement for multiculturalism—not antiracism. The biggest problem with diversity of this sort is that concept stands in for the real bodies of people of color. Students need to challenge cosmetic approaches to racial diversity. Building a sound foundation for antiracist education to end white supremacy must be informed by the presence of progressive white faculty and faculty of color committed to ending racial oppression linked to sexism, heterosexism, classism, and homophobia.

Teaching critiques of racism through the history of black resistance struggle (the signifying text for creating a pedagogical framework for racial healing) means that progressive antiracist politics must defy white supremacist myths and stereotypes of blacks, must contest monolithic notions of black identity, must denounce sexism both inside and outside black communities, and must resist homophobic initiatives aimed to exclude gay and lesbian members of our communities. The history of black movement against white supremacy in the United States represents a profound illustration of a people's ability to survive the dehumanization of racism. For this reason alone its illustrative power demands critical examination by anyone doing antiracist work. However, as a long-standing advocate of pro-feminist black studies as critical tool to combat racism and (hetero)sexism, do I possess the power to absolve my liberal white students of their guilt complex or to relieve my students of color of their overly self-conscious, internalized, defensive posture? The answer is no.

This chapter unfolds through personal journal entries I wrote to my students in the spring 1999 session of a course I teach called "Screening Race." Initially composed to defend my syllabus in response to a disgruntled student in the class, the journal entries evolved into a pedagogical defense of my approach to antiracism in the classroom. Above all, they openly illustrate how progressive notions of blackness function in my teaching practice. Addressing the students' anxieties about studying race, the journal entries argue that to understand race critically, they (white students as well as students of color) must commit to a process of unlearning white supremacy. Studying its relation to the myth of black inferiority enables students to understand the systemic nature of racism and its role in dehumanizing blackness as a racial signifier, even as it reinforces ideas of *whiteness* as the signifier of humanity, power, and privilege. Moreover, the journal entries maintain that liberatory blackness, shown in the course of black people's struggle to survive in the face of a long history of racism, is an absolutely necessary and primary element for healing in antiracist education.

According to Dalton, "[I]f engagement in [race talk] is the first step toward [racial] healing, then the second is unadulterated struggle." Teaching antiracism as a black man in a white institution for over a decade has been a personal struggle of enormous proportions. My courses are committed to a vision of antiracism; they are not simply about informing white students of the evils of white racism. As I have shown in the earlier classroom case studies, confronting white supremacy in a college classroom depends largely upon who occupies it. In my experience, the tenor of a classroom's racial dynamics is substantially influenced by the racial and ethnic makeup of the class—especially when race is the subject of the course. As the case studies suggest regarding classes I have taught on race, black feminism, and/or African American literature, these subjects invariably create certain racial tensions in an all-white class situation, as opposed to a classroom space where one or more students of color are present.

Whether or not a class has students of color, issues of gender, class, and sexuality can become highly charged. As a result, an air of anxiety charges the classroom space often before a course is well under way during a semester. For white students and students of color having to confront white supremacy and other forms of oppression simultaneously, my courses are often challenging on multiple levels.

Struggling to disrupt and subvert myths of black manhood and masculinity in the larger society means in the white classroom that I must mount a personal and pedagogical campaign to represent myself both as a group member and as an individual. In contrast, white male professors benefit from a level of unearned racial privilege simply because they are white men. At the same time, my position as a *male* professor grants me gender privilege over female students in a male supremacist culture. I am always acutely aware of students using me as a scapegoat for their racial fears, anger, and anxieties. In my experience, teaching antiracism and black feminism has become increasingly more difficult. In classroom spaces of all-white or majority-white students who have little experience dialoguing on race (with each other and/or people of color)—especially in the context of talk about myths of white supremacy and black inferiority—learning becomes an exercise in the expression of pain. This is not necessarily a bad thing, particularly when many students who study with me have experienced the pain of white supremacy and racism whether they are gay or straight, materially privileged or not, people of color or white. I have found that while white students experience white privilege, white supremacy, and racism very differently from students of color, they often express pain about being perpetrators of race oppression. Memoir writing against racism from a black feminist standpoint represents a strategic means toward getting students to engage in complex dialogue on race that leads to serious self-reflection about the impact of domination in their daily lives.

Over time, white students and students of color have increasingly begun to challenge my approach to antiracism. While both groups have been less resistant to the idea that race is a social construct, some have been far more overtly contentious about having to examine race in relation to black feminist critique of racism and white supremacy. As I have mentioned, many white students (female students in particular) who take my classes have studied feminism previously in varying degrees, but have little academic experience in race or black studies. Many believe that feminism is only about gender. On the other hand, those students of color (primarily female) who study with me have often read writings by bell hooks and Audre Lorde, and they offer an incisive perspective on the simultaneity of oppression. They are also vocal about being female and "colored" in majority-white institutions of higher learning and in daily life. On rare occasions, over the years, there have been white students who have studied with me who not only have studied the struggles of peoples of color (both in the United States and transnationally) but also possess a nuanced understanding of the feminist liberation politics of women of color. They have taken great risks in the classroom as antiracist allies.

However, enabling white students and students of color to talk and write openly about race autobiographically remains a challenge. The history of black feminism serves as an illustrative model for progressive antiracist study. It is precisely the long-standing history of black resistance to racial oppression in the United States that offers students a very specific case study of a people's sustained battle against racism, while at the same time embodying for them lessons of universal appeal that relate to every individual's struggle for personal freedom.

Why Is *Black* the Color of Your Struggle?

Having formulated memoir writing against racism as a strategy that places black feminist liberation struggle at the center of the critical pedagogy I employ, it does not necessarily follow that every student will appreciate its personal and social value. As mentioned, the introductory course I teach on race in the media (designed for first-year college students) came under attack from a student in the class, causing a serious turn in its pedagogical direction. One afternoon, midway through the term, before class, an Asian woman, one of the two students of color in a class of fifteen, came to my office. She said she had "questions" about the course, but rather than discuss them in my office, she preferred to pose them in class later that afternoon. Her request to address the class struck me as odd, but I agreed.

Since it was midterm (when students at the college normally receive reviews from professors), the thought that students should also have an opportunity to evaluate the course seemed appropriate to me. For a student in class who had said little during the term before this point (unless called upon), she did not mince words. Not only did she lambaste the goals of the course and its foundation, she charged me with having willfully misled students through my allegedly biased approach to the class (my being black and the fact that most of the material in it focused on black culture). The student claimed, despite what the syllabus said, that she thought the course would be (1) "multicultural" (celebrating cultural diversity, rather than a critique of white supremacy), (2) would enhance race relations between white students and students of color (herself and the other woman of color), and (3) would make the process of "racial healing" painless.

Given the racially tense atmosphere that the subject of race had already produced in the class, it was in my best interest not to interrupt her or take issue with what she said; I feared that white students would turn on me as well. With her last words, she began to weep. Trying not to show it, I felt she had underhandedly manipulated the situation. However, what happened next completely caught me off guard. As she sat weeping, most of the white students (all female with the exception of two males) immediately leaped from their seats and rushed to embrace her. They applauded her courage (whether justified or not) for speaking. After students returned to their seats and she had calmed down, I asked if she had any "questions" for me—since that had been the reason she had requested time during the office visit earlier that day. There was no response. With that the class resumed, the air remaining thick with ill will.

At the time, the student's complaints seemed retaliatory and vindictive, especially since she had been performing poorly in the class up to midterm. In retrospect, the accusation that there had been no evidence of racial healing in the class and that my approach had hampered her attempts to "make friends" with white students in class was one version of a general complaint I had, in fact, heard before from students over the years in other classes. In the past, however, it did not occur to me that my approach to teaching race had to be justified. While the Asian student's criticisms reminded me in some respects of ones other students had lodged in the past, in other respects hers was different. It did not feel liberatory at the time because it was so tinged with invective, but behind her attack there was a crucial question, one that continually points to the challenges of antiracist pedagogy based in black studies. Why does it have to be so hard? She helped me to formulate an answer—a justification, as it would become—for my method.

To say that the criticism of one dissatisfied student could act as a catalyst for me to admit my fear of teaching antiracism at a white institution and for me finally to think out my claims about the healing power of blackness may sound overly dramatic, but it really was such a catalyst. Perhaps over the years, I had been just as afraid as my students were. To talk about race in a way that exposed my level of discomfort with the subject would make me vulnerable to student criticism. After all, it is only reasonable for them to expect that the teacher should be comfortable with what she or he teaches. Coming to know that the same fear of race talk was also holding me hostage (even as I called for students to liberate their voices) and being engaged in the process of eradicating the fear of talking about race mean doing what my students must do—coming clean about the personal fear racial dialogue creates. Not only did the anxiety of being vulnerable before my students keep me from really opening up about my feelings, but the possibility of white students and students of color challenging my decidedly black-identified approach to antiracism filled me with trepidation.

Allowing students to experience me as vulnerable in the classroom touched upon issues related to stereotypes of the emasculated black man—weak, intellectually inferior. Ultimately, fear that students would reject the work of racial healing often had posed a barrier to my full engagement. Freeing myself from the angst of rejection and failure would mean that my personal stuff had to be put on the line. The challenge for me was to relate the personal to the pedagogical. But the truth was that the Asian student's disruptive behavior had left me feeling the struggle to engage the class in open dialogue on race was over, the trust we were building was severely compromised, and my credibility was lost. Would we go through the eight remaining weeks of the course bitter and disillusioned?

Writing a Pedagogical Defense: When the Teacher Moves from Silence to Voice

I was seriously in doubt about how to return to class after such a difficult session with any hope of reestablishing its momentum, but I had to respond to what had happened. The goals of the course were at stake. Over the weekend after the infamous class, I feverishly wrote a response. Writing out everything that came to mind related to the course, the process yielded thirteen single-spaced pages of free writing. As raw as they were, the passion and conviction displayed within them renewed my faith in the aims of the course. Without fear, reserve, or apology, I claimed the right to teach racial healing from a black standpoint. This seemingly simple articulation represented a personal triumph. It was the student's specific complaint that everything we studied had to do with black people that ultimately fueled my unrelenting passion to engage students about the fundamental role black studies must have in antiracist studies. From that weekend of free writing emerged the journal entries that follow. Writing them for my students *and for myself* proved immensely self-healing.

Entry 1—*Racism is a Thing of the Past . . . Can't We All Just Get Along?*

To begin, when most well-intentioned white students enroll in my courses on race, more often than not they enter with ideas about race steeped in politically correct dogma and clichés—like "Racism is a thing of the past," "Can't we all just get along?" "One of my best friends is black" and "It doesn't matter if you're black or white." These statements reflect a type of postintegrationist mentality suggesting that the playing field of race has been leveled. Not only do many whites believe that race is a thing of the past, but they also believe that affirmative action should be as well. In light of the increasing challenge to affirmation action on college and university campuses across the nation, it has become clear that "diversity" is no longer associated with race but with a multicultural curriculum and democratic pluralism. Diversity is always an issue in my race classes, particularly with regard to the presence or absence of students of color. Truthfully, they simply are not present in sufficient numbers at the college for there to be a racially diverse student body.

When the college is overwhelmingly white, when students of color (sometimes one, other times two, rarely three, most recently none) enroll in my classes on race, students of color automatically become racial ambassadors—black students especially. In white supremacist culture, blacks bear/wear the "badge of race" (as it is called in Stuart Hall's film, *Race, the Floating Signifier*). Whites do not. While students of color may perform academically well in my classes, rarely do they hold up well under the weight of white students consciously or unconsciously performing racially inherited privilege. For example, many of the white students believe that studying race should have little to do with issues of social justice and equality. Most often students of color complain that white students in race classes are clueless about the existence of racial privilege based on whiteness. Students of color who take my classes are generally politically conscious about the mechanics of racial oppression, which obviously becomes a source of tension for white students.

In the liberal, purportedly racially friendly environment that the college represents itself to be, racial dynamics heat up between the two groups when white students and students of color alike take my classes believing they have no hang-ups about race. Many believe that their past or present involvement in interracial relationships is itself evidence of progressive racial views. There are those who come thinking that affirmative action is wrong and that racial diversity is not about addressing the underrepresentation of people of color on white college and university campuses across the country—it is only about the free exchange of ideas and culture. Before entering classes on race, seldom have many thought about cultural appropriation. Seldom are they conscious of the subtle ways white privilege, white power, and white supremacy coalesce to normalize whiteness as the signifier of "American" culture and identity in everyday life.

Few of these students come prepared to grapple with the reality of U.S. pop media production and perpetuation of white supremacy—from the advertisement of clothing we buy and food we eat to the evening news, sitcoms, and dramas we watch on television, to films we watch at movie theaters. These same students tend to resent my call for their being socially responsible and personally accountable for ending white supremacy. They accuse me of overpoliticizing the subject of race and say that it need not be linked to antiracist work. Unquestionably, the first challenge for students taking my courses is for them to move beyond the fear of talking about race; they need to move beyond correct jargon and white liberal romanticization of diversity reminiscent of that represented in the Bennetton ads, for example, where people of all colors unite under the banner of a high-profile, trendy fashion label. The fashion industry, keyed to the commercial success of diversity, has exploited the cross-cultural, racialized popularity of hip-hop and has packaged blackness as a wearable, high-priced commodity. If you have a black look, you can be black (whatever that means to the wearer). The second challenge that is the most difficult for students in my classes is to confront issues of racism in their personal lives as perpetrators or victims of white supremacy.

Entry 2—*Toward the End of "Liberal" Political Correctness on Race*

If, from the foundation of this nation, it took four hundred years for the institution of slavery to end, how could one four-month course accomplish what took several centuries to even begin to eradicate?

Nevertheless, well-intentioned, liberal-minded white students and students of color have come in the past and continue to come to my race classes with the idea that I will work some magic whereby everyone (1) will be relieved of racial guilt, or be allowed to mask it in politically correct posturing, (2) will become "friends" with someone of a different ethnic or racial identity in the class, (3) will be confirmed in her or his belief that racism does not really exist, or (4) will be assured that a focus on our similarities, not our differences, is the key to solving our racial problems. When students discover that my race courses are not multicultural in the sense that they do not collapse ethnic differences into a smorgasbord of cultural consumption, they are (more often than not) disappointed, angry, and frustrated; they resist the idea that racial healing is about a life's work rather than a quick fix, and feel exposed, embarrassed, and silenced. White students and students of color accuse me of not making them feel good—about themselves, each other, and the course content.

I am not a spin doctor of racial healing. Sure, I will admit that I am the source of pain for many white and nonwhite students who unwittingly enroll in my classes. Many feel initially that, by having bravely decided to take one of my classes, they should be rewarded with a race-friendly environment, a guarantee of safety, and an unspoken promise that I and other students in class will accept each other for who we are— well-meaning human beings. They believe I should take them at face value as having brought no racist baggage into the classroom because, after all, they did register for the class. Isn't that proof enough of their good intentions?

What does it mean for a black man to self-identify as a feminist antiracist teacher? In the minds of many white students and students of color who take my classes, there is something inherently fearful about a black man who is dark-skinned, six feet four, and bald, and has a commanding voice, teaching antiracist studies—especially when he is challenging students to examine their own internalized racist notions of blacks and other people of color. The truth is that racial profiling does not just happen to black men driving on an interstate highway. Even holding a doctorate in English from New York University cannot compete with the racist myths and sexualized stereotypes from centuries ago my body bears as a black man. Race, color, and the perception of the body is precisely where my course begins to deconstruct the stereotypes that inform how many of my students view people of color in a culture of white supremacy, based on blackness as the sign of racial inferiority.

At the beginning of the semester students had to respond to a quote from Kalpana Seshadri-Crooks's *Desiring Whiteness* that reads: "Racial practice is ultimately an aesthetic practice and must be understood above all as a regime of looking" (2000, 19). I ask students to begin to think about its meaning within the racist, ideological framework of *white superiority* and *black inferiority*. A "regime of looking" is where we must begin in the course analyzing the representation of race in U.S. media construction of racial identity. It is, however, not where we should end up. As stated, the underlying premise of Screening Race is that through an analysis of the ideologies of *whiteness* and *blackness,* we can begin to comprehend the systemic and institutionalized representation of race in popular visual media.

In "White Negroes," Jan Pieterse concludes that in the Negroization (my term) of all nonwhites "[t]here emerges the top-dog position, whose profile is approximately as follows[:] white, western, civilized, male, adult, urban, middle-class, heterosexual, and so on. It is this profile that has monopolized the definition of humanity in mainstream western imagery. It is a programme of fear for the rest of the world populations" (1995, 26–27). The "profile" Pieterse identifies is particularly helpful in my argument for a critique of race in the United States. Just as the representation of the "straight, white, middle-class male" operates to determine the humanity of all "world populations," this image network produces, reconstructs, and perpetuates a universal fear of the Other predicated upon the fear of all that it is not this image. Systematically and institutionally in the history of race in the United States, race fear is generated through ideas of black inferiority most viscerally represented through the mythification of the *black* body, whether that body is of African, Asian, Latin, or of indigenous extraction.

Entry 3—*In the Equation of White Supremacy Black (Always) = Less Than*

Whether black people and other people of color ever come to grips with the depth of pain our colonization under white supremacy has wrought—in all of the varied and multiple ways these ideologies continue to inform how blackness remains the sign of the objectified Other—the truth of the matter is that we all (white and nonwhite) have been colonized to believe that anything associated with blackness is less credible, less productive, less intelligent, less trustworthy, less sensitive, less deserving of respect (in terms of social and civil rights), less culturally accomplished, less likely to succeed, less civilized, less human, just all-around *less.* I have come to know that when race is the subject in the classroom, I am just as likely to be confronted by critically unconscious students of color as by whites when I am putting forth an aggressive critique of racism. In general, for every student of color who accuses white students of being critically unconscious about the unearned privileges that come with white skin, there is a student of color who is critically unaware, insensitive, painfully resistant, and in gross denial about the insidious ways white supremacy shapes, distorts, commodifies, objectifies, and dehumanizes him or her.

Entry 4—*Race Talk and the Silence It Speaks*

For many white students, "race talk" engenders the fear that students of color will perceive them as racist if they cannot speak in politically correct terms or that their privilege as white people will be exposed, mainly through association with their class privilege (if they are of the middle class or above). Class status was often well masked through trendy fashion statements such as punk or grunge or by wearing secondhand, worn-out clothing, but many white students at the college were middle class and above. Because many of the white students I teach at the college possess little or no consciousness (critical or otherwise) about their relationship to whiteness, race talk is a painful discourse. It forces students to deal with race and class privileges (for the first time for many). Race talk exposes the enormous power whiteness wields in the classroom as racial blindness—that is, the privilege of not having to see oneself as "raced." Race talk of this sort inherently produces emotional fallout; for white students.

White student racial blindness and silence in the classroom when race is the subject is always counterproductive to honest dialogue about white privilege and its role in the lives of people of color. More often than not, people of color dislike having to teach white students about race. White students take but give little in return. As a result, the more vocal students of color opt to be silent in response to a lack of engagement from their white peers. On many occasions when students of color have stopped talking about race in the classroom, there is a deadening silence in the space. When this happens, I have learned to incorporate *racial silence* as an effective pedagogical strategy. What does the silence say? Often in liberal, majority-white institutions of higher learning, the pressure exists for "non-whiteness" to perform color: (1) to validate the white, liberal, "I'm not a racist" attitude; (2) to show the white administration's commitment to diversity; (3) generally to spice up the dull dish of the white classroom, particularly in classes that deal with race. I know this pressure in the classroom is enormous. I feel it in every class on race I teach or have taught at majority-white institutions or in classrooms where I first began my college teaching career as teaching assistant many years ago.

To begin to call out (to "out" whiteness as an empty signifier of power without blackness) creates an enormous rupture in the white classroom. The celebratory line from the spiritual "Amazing Grace" "I once was blind, but now I see!" is not the line that most often comes from white students (and students of color) in a class where race is the subject and critically interrogated from an anti-white-supremacist standpoint. This standpoint works to remove the encrusted scales that render the

eyes of white students and students of color blind to the systemic opera-
tion and institutionalized function of racism rooted in white supremacy.
Students (white and of color) resist having to analyze racism in this way;
more often than not, they think misguidedly that studies of race ought to
be less explosive and more about the varied contributions that Other cultures have made to "American" culture; they say my course intentionally
omits a variety of cultural (benign) perspectives. They accusingly ask,
What about Latina(o), Asian, West Indian, and indigenous cultures? Why
aren't they being represented? My answer is that they are always being
presented and *re*presented in the *black* and *white* color-line politics that
are the ideological hallmark of race in the United States. The nation's
history of racial binarism effectively erases the influence of ethnicity on
race, enforcing black/white colorism that de-emphasizes transracial, interracial, and intraracial difference. The institutionalization of racial
binary thinking continually reinscribes the ideology of white supremacy,
making the hegemony of whiteness invisible while reinforcing myths of
black inferiority (for anyone whose skin color cannot pass as white).

I argue that this is what makes white supremacist colonization of the
Other so painful to have to examine—whether the examiner is white or a
person of color. All who enter the examination room (in this case the classroom) are being shown something they would rather not have to experience. The white students want to remain blind to the privileges of having
white skin; and many students of color feel that I or white students will put
them on the spot through having to represent their entire race.

I cannot expect (nor have ever expected) that white or students of
color can simply begin talking about race and the implications of racism.
Even when students come to my classes with intellectual and critical sophistication about these subjects, I cannot assume that they have a clear
handle on the emotional fallout race talk may provoke. In other words, I
cannot take for granted that even my most critically astute students of
color and white students of race have reached an emotional place where
they are no longer carrying emotional baggage about the subject.

Many of my brightest and most critically conscious students of race
are individuals who have experienced enormous dehumanization because of the way(s) they are racialized in terms of gender, class, sexuality,
religious practice, and all other forms connected to how the process
of racialization has (de)formed and (mis)shaped who they are. It is an
intensely personal, visceral understanding of racism through critical
analysis that transforms the trauma of being "raced" into a source of empowered resistance and liberation. But this work can only come through
a struggle against denial, resistance to silence, and a conviction that

racial healing in the United States can only come about when we begin to acknowledge the force, the power, and will of whiteness to make us all invisible—voiceless (willingly and unwillingly) and powerless (willingly and unwillingly), and complicit (willingly and unwillingly) in our worship at the throne of white supremacy.

To break the cycle of silence in the classroom when race is the subject, I am compelled to push boundaries of (racial) safety for white students and students of color, challenging internalized racist myths and stereotypes (of people of color and whites as well). Under these terms, the classroom is always charged with an air of discomfort for students and me. In this way, Screening Race could never have been a course conceived around notions of simplistic, consumerist ideas of multiculturalism as the pathway to racial healing. Multiculturalism rooted in the performance of diversity where difference is shown as inviting, non-threatening, and depoliticized through *exotic* customs, foods, and ethnic dress suggests that our racial/cultural differences really make no difference, that they are not connected to issues of equality and social justice. This brand of multiculturalism is not a sustaining foundation for an antiracist pedagogy aimed at achieving racial healing.

In my classes on race, I do not pass out tickets into blackness or validate assimilationist moves into whiteness. I will not end class early. I will not award an "A" to anyone simply for having endured a semester of discomfort. I cannot allow any student to disregard issues of personal responsibility and accountability for the work this class requires, which means beginning to come to terms with the blind spots that can cloud one's racial vision.

The fact is—if we are to be truthful—race talk has made them and me sick; they and I are *dis*eased because of it. And I have allowed it to happen, have given space for it to circulate and engulf the room, have willfully infected each of them. The students and I never sat at the table and held hands; we never stood shoulder to shoulder for a chic, all-colors-welcomed fashion spread; we never proclaimed that we should ignore our race, gender, class, and sexual identities; we never did anything to make the study of race fun, exciting, interesting, or user-friendly. How could we sustain a process of healing under such conditions?

Entry 5—Talking B(l)ack to White Power

As I have said, when the subject of the class is race, one of my ongoing struggles in the white classroom is to get white students to talk. I remember conducting one Screening Race class session early in the term when racial tensions really flared as I confronted the issue of ongoing white silence in the room. Basically, white students simply would not engage in discussion; they were fearful that one of the two women of color or I would judge them racist. Having grown accustomed to white silence as a stage in the process of race consciousness white students must pass through, I am reminded how the issue was addressed in one of my other courses on education, which featured the writings of bell hooks and Paulo Freire. An outspoken black woman student passionately expressed her need to talk about race as matter of "life or death." She spoke about the urgent necessity for white students to not hold back in the classroom when race is the subject—to not be silent about the fear, pain, frustration, or anger that racial dialogue may invoke. For this black woman, coming to voice about the personal effects of white supremacy and its relation to her education inside and outside the college was not a luxury. Even the risk of being stereotyped as the "angry black woman" was not enough to silence her in a classroom where white students often sat voiceless, paralyzed with fear. For her, that silence was death. Without women of color (one black, the other three Latina; there were no males of color) speaking about race in this class, white silence would have killed it, rendered it empty, hollow, spiritually and emotionally anesthetized.

As stated, students of color in majority-white college classrooms continue to be hypervisible precisely because their numbers are often so low. No matter how unobtrusive, apologetic, or liberal-minded about race white students may be toward students of color, students of color bear the onus of racial visibility in ways white students can never fully comprehend in a white school. The fact is that in the racially blind imagination of whites, *color* is the badge of race. Therefore, students of color (whether comfortable or not while doing so) must speak the speech of race. Through angry rejection and reverse silent treatment from students of color, white students often learn the hard way that being a "minority" in a white environment creates an enormous amount of pain, anguish, anger, and frustration for always having to represent race. In my classes, however, where race is always the subject, both groups learn that no one has the right to stay silent. Commitment to dialogue is a course requirement.

In theory, a requirement is a requirement. In practice (considering the enormous racial baggage many white students and students of color bring to the classroom), race talk inherently produces silence. Requiring my students to commit to race talk is risky business. The more candid students learn to become, the more tension escalates in ways that none of them can ever fully anticipate, control, or contain. In fact, one of my goals is to push white students, students of color, and myself out of the zone of safety of political correctness—to a place where paralyzing self-consciousness falls away and courage to break the silence begins to take hold. As stated, teaching feminist antiracist pedagogy where liberatory representations of blackness serve as the "screen" for critical race consciousness necessitates that students be open, honest, and emotionally invested in dialogue. Teaching students to become critically conscious about race through popular culture enables them *to see* that race is not only an ideology of power rooted in white supremacy, but that it is constantly reinscribing a pernicious mythology of blackness on the bodies of black people. Teaching the history of U.S. racist attitudes and behaviors toward black people through film enhances students' ability to develop analytical tools to deconstruct representations of race at the intersection of gender, sexuality, and class. This kind of critical looking is difficult to hone. It demands that students screen race through a multilens approach that continually exposes the power of white supremacy operating within a complex web of social and personal relations in which we are all implicated.

Posing blackness as a complex constellation of shifting signifiers in films by radical black filmmakers prompts students to examine critically why black resistance to white supremacy stands as emblematic of antiracist struggle inside and outside this country. Kathe Sandler (*A Question of Color*), Marlon Riggs (*Tongues Untied, Ethnic Notion*, and *Black Is . . . Black Ain't*), Cheryl Dunye (*Watermelon Woman*), Isaac Julien (*Looking for Langston*), and Spike Lee (*Bamboozled*) employ race to break silences of gender, class, and sexuality and to provocatively engage viewers in soul-searching journeys into blackness. They give rise to heartfelt dialogue that opens the way for racial healing—not only for black people but for anyone who has experienced racial oppression or desired to be in solidarity with the oppressed.

Of the films shown, *Black Is . . . Black Ain't* is the most powerful representation of autobiographical material placed in the service of racial healing. Any student who has faced seemingly insurmountable odds is sure to feel empathy with Riggs in his journey/struggle to live in the face of AIDS and certain death. To refuse to come into an engaged, intimate understanding of Riggs's work in this film is to miss (avoid) its transformative effect(s), its power to effect racial, gender, and sexual healing across cultural, ethnic, and class differences. On the one hand, I did want students to come to appreciate the history of African American struggle for humanity that Riggs metaphorically represented and to show his life as a life-and-death battle for survival. On this level alone, the film is brilliant. On the other hand, I wanted students to hear and to understand its strategic call for us all to think critically and self-reflectively about our own mortality (within and outside of racial-identity politics) and the crucial urgency to end racism and white supremacy. At this very deep, human level of consideration, no work we encountered during that term asked us to relate so viscerally to the import and power of critical race consciousness. If students could empathetically align themselves with the representation of black humanity in the film (through the intimate portrait of Riggs's life), perhaps they could envision the possibility of celebrating (race/ethnic) difference—not as a vulgarized form of superficial multicultural celebration, but as journey toward liberatory ideas of racial consciousness modeled through the loving embrace of blackness.

To further the idea of liberatory blackness as healing text and critical centerpiece for my vision of racial healing, students study antiracist work by two of today's leading black theorists on race: bell hooks and Stuart Hall. hooks has become a major voice in popular film criticism with several books to her credit—*Black Looks: Race and Representation, Outlaw Culture: Resisting Representation,* and *Reel to Real: Race, Sex, and Class at the Movies.* Along with the two-part video *Cultural Criticism and Transformation,* in which she offers a compelling feminist critique of race, gender, and sexuality in recent U.S. popular film, at the beginning of the term students read Hall's writings on race and view his video *Race, the Floating Signifier,* which provides an excellent historical overview of the subject. It informs the analysis of white supremacy Riggs historicizes in *Ethnic Notions,* which lays the historical foundation for Lee's exploration of such themes as blackface and minstrelsy dramatized in *Bamboozled.* Students also view several films by or about white women in which the cultural appropriation of blackness by whites is the subject. Madonna (*Blonde Ambition*), Sandra Bernhard (*Without You I'm Nothing*), and Jennie Livingston (*Paris Is Burning*) serve as provocative case studies on the issue. Because bell hooks has written on all three, students are able to compare their readings of these women's work, while studying how black feminist critique can be a strategic tool in antiracist criticism.

Entry 6—*To Live Again*

Metaphorically, I view Screening Race as a passage from death (of the colonized mind) to life (synonymous with the birth of critical consciousness). I understand the urgency of the black woman student's employment of the phrase "life and death" to invoke the seriousness with which she spoke about her desire to be racially vocal; it was related to the ill effects of racial silence in the classroom and the need for critical race consciousness. Contemplating Screening Race as a course about life, death, and the possibility of rebirth through blackness, I think about Alain Locke, one of the architects of the Black Arts Movement of the Harlem Renaissance. He codified the idea of a "New Negro" emerging from the 1920s. This "New Negro" would be more radically expressive, break tradition, and be more revolutionary in self-identity, an identity predicated upon self-determination, exemplified in black art (mainly, literature, music, painting, and sculpture).

In sum, this "New Negro" would exist in stark contrast to the "old Negro" born out of American slavery. No longer would the "Negro" be "looked upon" in images of the mammy, Uncle Tom, coon, buck, or Sambo (Locke 1968, 14), but the truth of the (racial) matter is that, as Stuart Hall has said, traces of the "old Negro" live on (Hall 1995, 39). In pedagogy of decolonization, students of color and white students oppositionally interrogate traces of the "old Negro." Investigating contemporary pop cultural representations of the black body, they critically root out vestiges of white supremacist ideology fixed on perpetuating and reinventing blackness as the supreme signifier of otherness—as something to be desired, fetishized, and simultaneously dehumanized.

Students studying gender-progressive representations of the black body in Screening Race work against narrow, heteromasculinist notions of black subjectivity. Feminist pedagogy of decolonization advances a vision of gender justice free from xenophobic, patriarchal, nationalist, and homophobic imperatives. In this vision, blackness cannot be consumed as a dish or flavor of the month, or reduced to a fad, trend, or style of clothing, or absorbed through gangsta images, rhymes, or profile. It is this gender-progressive vision of blackness that drives my approach to antiracist pedagogy.

Entry 7—Breaking Silences, Healing Racial Wounds

As a single course on antiracism, Screening Race cannot guarantee that every student who enrolls in it will experience a racial transformation that could be identified as racial healing. It is about a process that cannot be measured in terms of courses and classrooms. It may be more fruitful, instead, to think of racial healing as taking place in developmental stages over the "course" of a lifetime commitment to antiracist struggle. My hope is that white students and students of color embrace the goals of Screening Race and that by the end the semester, they come to understand that critical race consciousness comes with the death of silence.

Having to defend my teaching approach in Screening Race, a course on race that focused on black people's struggle against white supremacy, marked an important shift in my work as an antiracist teacher. Before this course, the idea that a class on race ought to enable students to grapple with racial issues at the personal level had worked successfully.

Having students write about race from an autobiographical standpoint had served as a strategic feature in my critical writing pedagogy. The difference was that this time a student challenged the premise that black liberation struggle possesses the power of cross-cultural appeal. At no point in the course was it suggested that the resistance stories of other oppressed groups in the United States were not as meaningful as those of blacks. My aim, as stated in the opening of this chapter, was to lay claim to the therapeutic nature of studying black antiracist struggle.

In the end, my resolve was strengthened. Facing my own fear that my talking back to students' racial anxiety would only create more ill will, without having to launch a counterattack against student dissent and without compromising my beliefs I broke the silence. At the end of the semester, every student who had enrolled in the course remained. The dreaded rebellion of white students that contributed to my silence that day in class never happened. While the student who had been the catalyst for my own healing did not change her mind about the course, she too remained. Whether or not, in the end, the class had experienced some measure of racial healing none of us could tangibly determine. We had come to know one thing: that talking about race—even when it may potentially cause division, ill will, or discord—cannot be avoided and requires an honest engagement in serious dialogue that exposes the depth of pain racism has caused if the wounds of racism are to heal. Screening Race compels everyone in the class "to see" complexities of racialization embedded in relations of gender, class, and sexuality. It not only challenges student and teacher to confront internalized racial fears, but also heterosexist and homophobic anxieties connected to them. Together we struggle to deal with them honestly, seeking to get at the root cause of their origin.

On Teaching Audre Lorde and Marlon Riggs

Ten Thousand Ways of Seeing Blackness

[S]traight men want to preserve the presumption of heterosexual identity; they want to preserve this presumption not so much because of what heterosexuality signifies in a positive sense but rather because of what it signifies in the negative—*not* being homosexual. And straight Black men might be especially concerned about preserving the presumption of heterosexuality . . . it is the case that heterosexual privilege is one of the few privileges that straight Black men *know* they have—not being a "sissy, punk, faggot."

—Devon W. Carbado

An inheritance from Black Cultural Nationalism of the late sixties and Negritude before that, today's Afrocentrism, as popularly theorized, premises an historical narrative which runs thus: Before the white man came, African men were strong, noble, protectors, providers, and warriors for their families and tribes. In precolonial Africa, men were truly men. And women—were women. Nobody was lesbian. Nobody was feminist. Nobody was gay.

—Marlon Riggs

The problem, then, is not that we have this or that sexual orientation or preference, but that we are hostage to it. Courage in this regard requires only that we not be hostage to our sexual orientation, and not that we pretend that we do not have a given sexual orientation. Arguably, only in a world in which people are hostage to their sexual preference could it turn out that our sexual identity has metamorphosed into the controlling phenomenon that it is.

—Laurence Mordekhai Thomas

Teaching visionary autobiographical narratives by Audre Lorde and Marlon Riggs, among other black lesbian or gay pro-feminist writers and filmmakers, I have challenged myself to confront my own internalized heterosexist and homophobic notions of gender. As a gender-progressive teacher and preacher, I defy the condemnatory rhetoric of heterosexism that has come to define the black nationalism and homophobic religious dogma of so many black churches today. Sexual difference, like feminism, is a taboo subject in many black communities. Having painfully grown up in a culture of black homophobia and heteromasculinist ideas of blackness, I experienced ways they barred me from exploring my uniqueness as a black male who never fit the script of black machismo. Embracing black feminist critique of heteronormativity and homophobia in black communities has created in me a deep affinity and respect for the autobiographical work of Lorde and Riggs, in particular. In similar and different ways, their visions of black subjectivity bring us to a deeper understanding of the complexity of sexual difference and the humanity of *all* black people. I have been empowered by their work. I have found the freedom to be fully self-actualized—beyond the fear of heterosexism in me(n) that for years relegated me to the margin of masculinity for being a "black boy outsider." Teaching about sexual difference from a black standpoint in the visionary narratives of Lorde and Riggs, I try to empower students to embrace the whole self—mind, body, and spirit. This is the intrinsic value of teaching students of color *and* white students black lesbian and gay subjectivity that opposes a vision of black liberation mired in heterosexism and homophobia. This is education about black struggle that is truly liberatory—a vision of "blackness" as sacred, holy.

As revealed in part 1, I grew up in the Pentecostal church. One thing is for sure: homosexuality and lesbianism was outlawed. Without stereotyping or perpetuating homophobic myths about male choir members, directors, and musicians in the "Holiness" church, somebody always knows somebody in the music department that swings to a different (sexual) tune. What has amazed me over the years in the church is the unspoken rule of sexuality: "Don't ask, don't tell." Heterosexism and homophobia, twin forces in the church's dogma-bound policing of sexuality, were evident only when a "flagrant," public display of outlawed sexuality had reached the pulpit on Sunday morning in the form of a fire-and-brimstone sermon railing against it. Even then, depending upon the known (or suspected) sexual disposition of the sermon deliverer, she or he might or might not venture very deeply into the subject.

The church's dogma I have most vehemently opposed over the years, since high school through my adulthood as a member and ordained elder, has been its duplicitous attitude and hypocritical treatment of gay and lesbian persons. On the one hand, the church—while biblically opposing any form of sexuality that is not heterosexual—claims to accept all people (on biblical principle). On the other, as I have witnessed on so many occasions, there are blatant and intentionally mean-spirited acts of homophobia in the church—from the pulpit to the general congregation. As a gender-progressive minister and professor, I cannot justify being a member of any group, religious or not, that professes a love for humanity but so dishonors the human spirit. It would not be accurate to say that in the various Pentecostal churches, in which I have been a member for over thirty years, everyone was homophobic. It would be, however, fair to say that *very* few church members in my experience spoke out against it. Consistent with my beliefs in the foundation of love (upon which the Bible speaks) and the human rights values I espouse in the classroom, I cannot condone homophobic acts and attitudes in the name of the church that devalue the lives of individuals who do not identify as heterosexual—regardless of the benefit I receive from identifying as a practicing heterosexual male.

As I have also written in part 1, in defense of my position (and in opposition to its male hierarchy, political conservatism, and class pretensions), I left the church of my youth after thirty some years. Free of its intolerance, patriarchal, heterosexist dictates, I have, however, held on to the teachings on love taught to me in my childhood Sunday school classes. "Thou shalt love thy neighbor as thyself" was a commandment drilled into our class by Mother Finch. I have never forgotten the persistence of her quiet voice as she pressed it into our memory as the greatest of all the commandments. As a pro-feminist professor, when thinking about being a black male outsider (and pondering my reasons for leaving the Pentecostal church I grew up in), I take to heart the mind, body, and spirit of the many students who enter my classes wounded. Many of them (like myself) have been cast as outsiders—outside white skin privilege (students of color as well as white students without class privilege), outside sexist gender norms (female, male, and transgender students), outside the script of heterosexuality and heteronormativity (lesbian, gay, bisexual, or individuals who question its code of privileges). In a real way, I feel I owe these students my nonjudgmental support. Being a pro-feminist minister and professor means that I must teach against the grain of societal norms (religious or otherwise) that dehumanize and dishonor the mind, body, and spirit of the students I teach. Teaching holistically is a way of educating that gets us to the *heart* of our students' struggles against domination.

Resisting the Mockeries of Separations

And where the words of women are crying to be heard, we must each of us recognize our responsibility to seek those words out, to read them and share them and examine them in their pertinence to our lives. That we not hide behind the mockeries of separations that have been imposed upon us and which so often we accept as our own.

—Audre Lorde

I first taught Audre Lorde's autobiographical short story entitled "Tar Beach" in 1994, in a course I called "Redefining Womanhood." Its purpose was to deconstruct racist and heterosexist ideas of black womanhood that existed outside the boundaries of heterosexuality. The first time I taught the course at the college, it was composed of all females. However, it was also the first time the number of female students of color almost equaled that of the white students. Conceptually, the course relied on writings primarily in *Home Girls: A Black Feminist Anthology* (ed. Barbara Smith). Secondary texts included Audre Lorde's *Sister Outsider, Daughters of Africa* (ed. Margaret Busby) and *Theorizing Black Feminisms* (ed. Stanlie James and P. A. Abena Busia). Largely, the discussion of the course that follows is based on a 1996 essay I wrote about teaching it, entitled 'Young Man, Tell Our Stories of How We Made It Over': Beyond the Politics of Identity" (in *Teaching What You're Not: Identity Politics in Higher Education*). Preliminary to an examination of our work in the course, I recalled the power of Lorde's words quoted above and how they compelled me to think about the kinds of connections I desired to make between students and myself—across race, gender, and sexual differences.

I began the essay by quoting from Audre Lorde's "The Transformation of Silence into Language and Action" in *Sister Outsider*. Publicly, it was a way to position myself strategically in the classroom as a committed advocate of feminism. My aim was not to appropriate her words in a self-aggrandizing manner to speak in the place of women or for them, but to render myself an ally in the struggle against racism and heterosexism. Deeply moved by Lorde's call to action in the piece, I selected the passage above as an epigraph to open this section because the words are haunting. They conjure up ghosts from my past as a child survivor of domestic violence. I have heard "the words of women [that] are crying to be heard." I "recognize [my] responsibility to seek those words out, to read them and share them and examine them in their pertinence to [my life and the lives of the students I teach]." I will "not hide behind the mockeries of separations that have been imposed upon us and which so often we accept as our own." Long ago, my experience as a male victim of family abuse positioned me in an adversarial relationship to violent heteromasculinist manhood that I have carried into adulthood. I bear the psychic, emotional, and physical scars of my mother's abuse of years past.

Teaching against inner anguish and the fear of becoming my father of those traumatic years has given me much solace and helped me to reconcile myself to the past. In defiance of the script of heteromasculinity (that for years filled me with feelings of emasculation and self-hatred), I have accepted the "call" to pedagogical action, teaching the stories of women crying to be heard. In my heart, I cry with them. In the process of becoming a pro-feminist professor, I have come to realize that "engaged pedagogy" (as bell hooks calls self-transformational, oppositional teaching) is righteous work rooted in a sacred calling to serve. It is about teaching that connects students compassionately to the struggle for human dignity across divides of difference. Lorde resists teaching that promotes a politics of separation:

> "I can't possibly teach Black women's writing—their experience is so different from mine." Yet how many years have you spent teaching Plato and Shakespeare and Proust? Or another, "She's a white woman and what could she possibly have to say to me?" Or, "She's a lesbian, what would my husband say, or my chairman?" And all the other endless ways in which we rob ourselves of ourselves and each other. We can learn to work and speak when we are afraid in the same way we have learned to work and speak when we are tired. *For we have been socialized to respect fear more than our own needs for language and definition, and while we wait in silence for that final luxury of fearlessness, the weight of that silence will choke us.* (Lorde 1984, 43–44; emphasis added)

Lorde contests identity politics or internal fear that would bar *anyone* with a passion for social justice from teaching as a proponent of it. She advocates teaching that seeks to liberate, that cannot be policed by the limits of identity. In the passage above, I understand Lorde as saying that teaching that transforms must emerge from a deep place in the teacher, a place connected to human need. I feel her saying that human need is about a longing for connection, in a deep place in us where the soul resides— a place full of (com)passion. I feel her saying, it is the place where body and intellect are superseded by a higher calling through the spirit. I feel her saying, it is the place where the soul resides, a place of wholeness, not separation. There we long to release ourselves, to speak from a place of yearning, to express our greatest desires, to communicate a way of moving and being that surpasses the plane of the rational and corporeal.

In "Uses of the Erotic: The Erotic as Power," Audre Lorde speaks about the liberatory nature of the *non*rational in the lives of women and the threat it poses to men: "As women, we have come to distrust that power which rises from our deepest and nonrational knowledge. We have been warned against it all our lives by the male world, which values this depth of feeling enough to keep women around in order to exercise it in the service of men, but which fears this same depth too much to examine the possibilities of it within themselves" (1984, 53–54). Engaging with the problematics of "men doing feminism" (Tom Digby's phrase and the title of his edited collection), while thinking about the fear in me as a man who resists movement into the space of "nonrational knowledge," I struggle to free myself from the patriarchal power of the "male world." Feminist pedagogy for males (whether teachers or students) is necessarily rooted in risk-taking. Feminist critique of patriarchy necessarily means that our manhood and masculinity are called into question, along with our sexuality. Men challenging men on this ground is like walking into a minefield. Michael Awkward sounds a cautionary note on the function of black male feminism. On the one hand, he maintains, it should be "rigorous" in its critical engagement. On the other, it must be "self-reflexive" and vigilantly aware of its own patriarchal traps, no matter how seemingly well-meaning:

> [A] rigorous, conscientious black male feminism need not give in to traditional patriarchal desires for control and erasure of the female. To be of any sustained value to the feminist project, a discourse must provide illuminating and persuasive readings of gender as it is constituted for blacks in America and sophisticated, informed, contentious critiques of phallocentric practices in an effort to redefine our notions of black male and female sexuality and subjectivity. And in its differences from black feminist texts that are produced by individual Afro-American women, a black male feminism must be both rigorous in engaging these texts and self-reflective enough to avoid, at all costs, the types of patronizing, marginalizing gestures that have traditionally characterized Afro-American male intellectuals' response to black womanhood. (2001, 190–91)

Liberatory pedagogy conceived by pro-feminist black men in resistance to sexist and heteronormative practices requires teaching strategies that defy the "safe" space of professorial authority, moving us to rethink our academic training as "field experts." These strategies may call for us to transgress the script of masculinity and identity politics that would have us teach only what we "appear" to be. In *Teaching to Transgress*, bell hooks maintains that a liberatory pedagogy is freeing for student and teacher: "Progressive professors working to transform the curriculum so that it does not reflect biases or reinforce systems of domination are most often individuals willing to take risks that engaged pedagogy requires and to make their teaching practices sites of resistance" (1994, 21). No matter how progressive I may claim my gender and sexual politics to be, teaching a course on black lesbian subjectivity from a "male feminist" standpoint still requires a radical departure from ideas of the classroom as a "safe" space for me(n).

Redefining Womanhood, the Course: From *Home Girls* to *Sister Outsider*

Home Girls and *Sister Outsider: Essays and Speeches by Audre Lorde* (1984) not only challenge heterosexist notions of the (black) feminine, but also put forth critical agendas that promote efforts to rethink definitions of womanhood. Moreover, they neutralize the myth that real blackness obtains in the framework of heterosexuality. For students critically engaged in deconstructing myths and stereotypes that racially and sexually "other" black women, these texts are enabling tools, empowering students to construct serious feminist critiques of universalized white womanhood. Contemplating my reason for teaching a course dealing with black lesbian subjectivity, I began the course with Jewelle Gomez's essay "A Cultural Legacy Denied and Discovered: Black Lesbians in Fiction by Women." Reclaiming the invisible lives of black lesbians in black women's fiction, Gomez provided students in the class with a literary history and tradition from which to begin theorizing new notions of womanhood: "The shadow of repression has concealed the Black Lesbian in literature in direct proportion to her invisibility in American society. . . . Not surprisingly, we are the least visible group not only in the fine arts, but also in popular media, where the message conveyed about the Lesbian of color is that she does not even *exist,* let alone use soap, drive cars, drink Coke, go on vacations, or do much of anything else" (Gomez 1983, 110). Employing the black lesbian literary text to critique heterosexist/racist ideas of womanhood, I found in *Sister Outsider* an invaluable resource. I had to resist the fear that my reading and representation of it would smack of appropriation or exploitation of black women's discursive practice for the sake of my own "male-conceived" ideas of progressive *anti*(hetero)sexist pedagogy.

Lorde's essays on the transformation of silence and the erotic offered me the precise theoretical model to teach black lesbian fiction. What did I need to bring to the table to teach this work? As stated in the beginning of the chapter, my commitment to progressive feminist movement to end sexism means that I must also be actively committed to the eradication of heterosexism. When I first conceptualized the course on black lesbian subjectivity, it was not about prurient voyeurism. Rather, my goal was consistent with Jewelle Gomez's assessment of the invisibility of black lesbians in a culture of white supremacist, capitalist, homophobic patriarchy. Teaching in a college where lesbian-identified students (white and of color) are a visible and vocal presence, I desired to offer courses on black feminism that reflected its divergent streams.

Audre Lorde's "Uses of the Erotic" critically clarifies how the personal, spiritual, and political dimensions of female power as erotic expression work in Lorde's "Tar Beach." "Tar Beach" was the first piece of fiction we chose to read in the anthology. This short story represented a powerful space in which to critique, through a study of the narrative's politics of gender and sexual freedom, heteronormative ideas of the feminine while radically reformulating it. "Tar Beach" is a story about the love and sexual intimacy that evolve between the narrator and a black woman singer named Afrekete (whom we come to know as "Kitty" as the narrative develops). I linked its thematic representation of eroticism to Lorde's belief in the transgressive power of black lesbian women crossing the boundary of heterosexuality. A critical reading of the narrative necessarily acknowledges its celebratory response to the erotic, which Lorde reclaims as a crucial element in the survival of women: "As women we need to examine the ways in which our world can be truly different. I am speaking here of the necessity for reassessing the quality of all the aspects of our lives and of our work, and of how we move toward and through them. . . . When I speak of the erotic, then, I speak of it as an assertion of the lifeforce of women; of that creative energy empowered, the knowledge and use of which we are now reclaiming in our language, our history, our dancing, our loving, our work, our lives" (Lorde 1983, 55).

Situated in the *Home Girls* section titled "Black Lesbians: Who Will Fight for Our lives But Us?" "Tar Beach" narratively unfolds through several thematic strands anchoring its "uses of the erotic" in the language, history, dance, loving, work, and lives of black lesbians. Set in Greenwich Village and Harlem in the late 1950s, the narrative autobiographically unfolds a woman-identified cultural landscape where Lorde describes/celebrates butch/femme fashion, nature, the goddess myth, the black female body, and the erotic—all functioning together and symbiotically converging in "fluid" images of water, sea, tide, and juices. Lorde's sensual representation emerges from a location of deep feeling within the self, a feeling connected to a union of the spiritual and the political. The narrative description of lesbian fashion codes signals the intense interest of the author in projecting a "style" of clothing, music, and body performance that enhances an aesthetic/sensual appreciation for lesbian space.

As Lorde shows in the quotation above, the power of the erotic in the lives of the story's main characters has resonance in the political realm as well as in the sexual one, and it is its power in the political realm that can empower all women with the capacity to effect change. "Recognizing the power of the erotic within our lives can give us the energy to pursue genuine change within our world" (1984, 59). Lorde does not exclude men from its liberatory power, but she speaks of men's fear of "examin[ing] the possibilities of it within themselves" (54). It is men's fear of the power of the erotic that causes them to devalue it and reduce it to the pornographic. Focusing attention on the political dimensions of eroticism, Lorde notes, "There are frequent attempts to equate pornography and eroticism, *two diametrically opposed uses of the sexual* [emphasis added]. Because of these attempts, it has become fashionable to separate the spiritual (psychic and emotional) from the political, to see them as contradictory or antithetical" (55–56).

As a text written as a fictional autobiography, first-person telling steers the narrative movement of "Tar Beach." The voice we hear most often is Audre Lorde's, pointedly recalling conversations with Afrekete: "We talked sometimes about what it meant to love women. . . . Once we talked about how Black women had been committed without choice to waging our campaigns in the enemies' strongholds, too much and too often, and how our psychic landscapes had been plundered and wearied by those repeated battles and campaigns" (1983, 154–55). And Afrekete, responding to the experience of black lesbians in the political struggle of women loving women that Audre describes, testifies to its pain but also the resiliency born of it: "And don't I have the scars to prove it. . . . Makes you tough though, babe, if you don't go under. And that's what I like about you; you're like me. We're both going to make it because we're both too tough and crazy not to!" (155). That the women are both "too tough and crazy" not to survive signifies the notion of living against the grain, transgressing the boundaries of heterosexism, "do[ing] that which is female and self-affirming in the face of a racist, patriarchal, and anti-erotic society" (Lorde 1984, 59). Lorde, interpreting her relationship to Afrekete in political terms, articulates the price "paid for that toughness"—knowing that living in a space of black lesbian subjectivity necessarily means continual struggle and negotiation of the idea "that soft and tough had to be one and the same for either to work at all" (Lorde 1983, 155).

Reflecting on the breadth, depth, and "lifeforce" of the love Audre and Afrekete shared, appropriately Lorde (as author) registers its chemistry figuratively in a trope on nature: she says it was "like elements erupting into an electric storm exchanging energy, sharing charge" (157). Acknowledging the depth of the relationship and the deeply felt presence of "Kitty" in her life, Audre declares the core of its meaning: "[Afrekete's] print remains upon [her] life with the resonance and power of an emotional tattoo" (157–58).

Letting Go of Heterosexual Privilege

Personally, teaching "Tar Beach" was a liberatory process, where I let go of the fear that being a man could only mean necessarily misrepresenting the author, her text, and its meaning. I summoned up courage to transgress internalized (hetero)sexist ideas that men (straight or gay) have no business teaching feminism or writing feminist criticism—whether about the feminine, womanhood, or women's sexuality. Teaching this fictionalized memoir, I sought to contest, undermine, and subvert the phallic power men represent by putting my own heterosexist insecurities about teaching feminism out for class discussion early in the term. Just as my students learned to cross borders in Redefining Womanhood, so I came to understand the power of Audre Lorde provoking me toward a redefinition of (black) manhood. Straight as well as gay black men must not only interrogate the destructive power of heterosexism and homophobia, which have dominated and impaired visionary black liberation struggle; we must also denounce it in all sectors of our public and private lives.

In class sessions in the course where the all-female class and I talked about my identity as a feminist teaching the course, its race, gender, and sexual dynamics revealed the complexities of our (identity) differences and our ability to navigate them. Commenting on the impact of reading *Home Girls* on her, one woman in the course remarked,

> Black feminist consciousness pushes your own boundaries and provides you with the material necessary to push those of others. The short stories in *Home Girls* forced me to redefine my conception of womanhood by giving me greater knowledge and a better understanding of black lesbian identity. They made me realize that though well intentioned in my condemnation of homophobia, my ignorance had led me to hold beliefs that were just as unenlightened as those of the people whom I was opposing. I was

defending lesbian identity without knowing exactly what it was. Before reading stories by black lesbians, my only contact with fiction centering around lesbian subjectivity written by a lesbian had been through a white lesbian writer. I now feel my personal/ political views of lesbianism are more firmly grounded. I have works to refer to when discussing black lesbian identity and I no longer have to make uneducated assumptions.

In this course, as well as in other courses on feminism I teach, at several points during the semester (the first day of class, midterm, and at the end of the course) I ask students to respond in writing to the syllabus and the fact that the course is being taught by a black male professor. What difference does it make for a man to teach feminism to a group of women or men (or to transgender students)? What does it mean for a *black* man to teach feminism to a class in which all the students are white or in which white women predominate?

Thinking about these questions specifically in relation to Redefining Womanhood, I had to consider what it meant for me to teach feminism to a group of all women in which there were diverse racial, sexual, and class politics. Responding to my location in this mix, one woman student (from a multiracial background) wrote,

> The different racial, sexual, social, economic and political identities of those in the seminar were highlighted by the Black male professored situation. [His] race meant that some of us could identify with [him] on racial grounds, but most could not. The ties between the group were established through a common identification with and appreciation of black feminist thought and the common desire to redefine womanhood. At times I forgot the existence of those ties and felt alienated from the class because of my own multinational and multiracial standpoint. However, reading the works of international women proved to be what was necessary for me to become refocused on the ties within the group while at the same time taking into account the differences. *They helped me realize that it is possible for us to find unity through difference.* (Emphasis added)

Before midsemester we had tackled the pedagogical questions mentioned above. Contesting the rigidity of fixed identities (while calling into question the idea of men teaching feminism), on the first day of class I placed front and center the question, "Since men are not women, should we teach courses in feminism?" At the same time, I posed other related questions. Should white professors teach black, indigenous American, Asian, or Chicano/a studies, for example? Should heterosexuals teach gay or lesbian studies? What gender politics obtain in the classroom when the professor is transgender? Broaching such complex questions as a means to discussing the limits of politics of identity in the classroom means taking risks, particularly when the teacher's body/identity stands at the center of contestation. One of the women in the seminar reflected on my fear connected to teaching the course, after I had openly shared it with the class: "[He] articulated [his] initial fears related to being a black man teaching a class on feminist theory. . . . [I]t was important that [he] brought [his] problem to the table from day one. It enabled us to discuss the issue as a class, and for me, the discussions helped me to problematize and deal with my own position as a *white* [emphasis in the original] female in a class on black feminist theory." I remember distinctly one class session when some of the women students voiced their opposition to men as feminists and spoke of how much I "dominate[d] class discussion." For them, my being a man in the class brought up issues of sexism and patriarchy not only having to do with my physical presence as a "black man" (with all its myths and stereotypes in tow) but also with the privilege with which my male, professorial voice resonated. One of the students questioned the power of my voice: "What I have to stress again [as she had in her midterm evaluation] is the degree to which [he must] keep struggling with how much [he] dominate[d] class discussion. It [points to] the need to interrogate the role [male] authority plays in the classroom." She further stated that "every time someone raised their voice or disagreed with me . . . they were turning into my dad." Reading midterm course evaluations, I realized that forces far beyond my control were mediating the dynamics of gender, voice, and power in the class.

Black Feminism in a Transnational (Con)Text

During the second half of the course, we concentrated on memoir writings by black women in the "Third World," Europe, and the Caribbean. Employing selected readings from *Theorizing Black Feminisms* and *Daughters of Africa*, I aimed to introduce the students to a diasporic representation of women of color. Many of the essays, stories, poems, and memoirs were by transracial/multiethnic women—all in political struggle for women's liberation. Discussing and writing about the contested identities these women voiced, we undertook a reconsideration of the ways our privileged position in the U.S. had provided us only one view of women's lives. Reading transnational black feminist texts, we gained insight into the complex matrix of oppression that determined their lives.

At times in class discussions, however, it appeared differences among us in the course were too great to overcome. Critically foregrounding our differences, however, we accepted the fact none of us could claim safety in race, gender, class, or heterosexual privilege. Racial difference remained a hard topic in class discussions. They were complicated by the history of racism in the United States and in the feminist movement. Its long-standing effect resonates in one black woman student's comments on race and who spoke or *chose* not to speak in class:

> The strategy of using silence to gain power or control has been used continually and consistently throughout this course for the "white feminists" to gain power in terms of what has been discussed, what [would] be discussed and what [was] accomplished this semester. . . . I [did] not feel it [was] my responsibility to engage these white feminists in dialogue to produce a useful class. Everyday I have to push myself as a woman of color, poor woman, black woman, oppressed, sometimes privileged woman to speak. . . . I believe that the majority of students used silence to counteract what they were learning.

I remain conscious of the potential for racial silence to occur in a college where few white students are comfortable talking about themselves as *white* people.

Our understanding of the relationship between race, gender, class, sexuality, and *nation* took on a much deeper resonance when M. Jacqui Alexander (my colleague at the time) came to class to discuss her essay "Not Just (Any) *Body* Can Be a Citizen: The Politics of Law, Sexuality, and Postcoloniality in Trinidad and Tobago and the Bahamas" (which I had assigned). It was on the status of women's "citizenship" in the Caribbean— with particular regard to the legal criminalization there of lesbian identity. Students came to class with written responses, prepared to engage Professor Alexander on the essay's multilayered analysis. Alexander offered an incisive theoretical and critical reading that situated the *reality* of her identities as a Caribbean feminist scholar. The essay begins:

> I am an outlaw in my country of birth: a national; but not a citizen. Born in Trinidad and Tobago on the cusp of anti-colonial nationalist movements there, I was taught that once we pledged our lives to the new nation, "every creed and race [had] an equal place." . . . Subsequent governments have not only eclipsed these

promises, they have revised the very terms of citizenship to exclude. No longer equal, I can be brought up on charges of "serious indecency" under the Sexual Offences Act of 1986, and if
convicted, serve a prison term of five years. In the Bahamas, I
can be found guilty of the *crime* of lesbianism and imprisoned
for twenty years. . . . Why has the state marked these sexual in-
scriptions on my body? Why has the state focused such a repressive and regressive gaze on me and people like me? (1994, 5)

Contesting the heterosexist laws of her land that policed the sexuality of
its female citizens, and speaking with amazing clarity from an analytical
standpoint rooted in the experiential, Alexander employed the germinal
questions above to guide us through the essay's complex analysis of legal-
ized heterosexualization in the Caribbean. She says she "look[ed] back at
the state, to reverse, subvert and ultimately demystify that gaze by taking
apart these racialized legislative gestures that have naturalized heterosexuality by criminalizing lesbian and other forms of non-procreative sex"
(5). Her presentation charged the students' response with kinetic energy
I had not witnessed in class before. Alexander's personal and scholarly relationship to the imperatives she set forth in her discussion spoke clearly
about the political power of the erotic Audre Lorde had so passionately
articulated. Responding to her analysis how class, legislation, and the
criminalization of sexuality outside the boundary of heterosexuality
worked in the lives of Caribbean women, a student had this to say:

One of the most interesting and intense readings we [did] this
semester [was] M. Jacqui Alexander's piece. . . . Although I was
moved to think about many issues brought to light in this text,
this piece really challenged my way of thinking along the lines of
state and government . . . [as] expression[s] of ruling-class interests . . . adjudicat[ing] on behalf of the ruling class only. . . .
the idea of consensus is manufactured. . . . This was interesting
to me in that I had always thought these things myself, *but never
really had a name for it or could locate this way of thinking in an established body of thought.* (Emphasis added)

During that class session, observing Jacqui's self-possessed manner,
which I have come to associate with her teaching style, I experienced the
joy of learning from one's comrade.

My collegial, pedagogical, and scholarly relationship to Jacqui
Alexander affirms the cross-gender comradeship bell hooks speaks of in
Feminist Theory where women and men struggle together in feminist soli-

darity to end the sexual oppression of women. Thus, I teach the narratives of black women persecuted, sexually assaulted, and even killed because their lives do not fit into colonial, national, sexist, patriarchal, homophobic, unitary, or static ideas of womanhood, and I believe that their stories (inside or outside the United States) must be read and taught without censure. I hear the voices of these women telling me that their stories must be told, that I cannot be governed by the dictates of the politics of identity.

We have arrived at a moment of crucial urgency in the academy for those of us who educate as the practice of freedom. We know that crossing borders has been a question of life and death for the disenfranchised globally. In the stories of women of color, the voices of the oppressed tell me that I have a political obligation to teach about them—their struggle, the battles they wage for liberation. Communicating this imperative to the students in Redefining Womanhood represented a daunting task. However, I refused to allow the limits of my identity to delegitimize the willingness I possessed to transgress its borders by "teaching what I'm not." Was the course a success? Self-defensively I ask, "On what grounds?" Did students find it beneficial? In the final evaluation of the course, the expectation that every student in the class would find it valuable would have been naive. However, one white woman student asserted:

> I wonder sometimes what I [was] doing taking a course on black feminist theory. I wonder [whether] I [was] "culture surfing." . . . But then I read a text such as Jacqui Alexander's or bell hooks', and find myself thinking, "Yeah right," or "I'm so glad I'm not the only one who thought that," or "I didn't know that, but now something else makes sense to me," and I know it [was] a good choice. Black feminist theory is not all about black feminists. If it were, where would it leave Gary [Lemons], as a black man? *And why, when I can see parallels in my own experiences . . . within my own working-class white hometown, shouldn't I use those experiences to build bridges between myself and those who are like-minded? Does one have to be a black woman to be engaged with black feminist theory? Hardly not.*
> (Emphasis added)

For the student above, as a white woman studying black feminism, to "see parallels in [her] own experiences . . . within [her] own working-class white hometown" enabled her "to build bridges" and to connect to "like-minded" individuals. "Does one have to be a black woman to be engaged with black feminist theory? Hardly not," she responds. It is a bold statement as a white woman. But this student is not just any white woman. She is a student of black feminism. Studying it (even for just a semester), she found a place in it that was not simply about "culture surfing." Rather, she claimed her desire for a *lived* connection with what she was studying. I share this student's desire to make a lived connection to the narratives of feminist black women I teach, which call me to take a stand against *hetero*sexism in the classroom and in the pulpit.

Having chosen to teach a course on the racist and heterosexist social construction of womanhood, I intended in no way to hide the problematics of masculinity and manhood (in a culture of heteromasculine privilege)—as some of the students pointed out. Attuned to the politics of male hegemony, the students' antisexist vigilance never allowed the position I occupied as "male feminist professor" to become the center of class discussions. Rather, in the pedagogical spirit of Audre Lorde's antiseparatist sentiments we grappled with ways to understand that our (gender, race, class, and sexual) differences were not points of separation but rather aspects of who we are that provided compelling reasons for coalition building. Across difference, rather than in spite of it, we read black feminism as liberatory social theory grounded in the intellectual and experiential knowledge of black women.

Cooking (in Class) with Marlon Riggs: Gumbo as a Metaphor for Blackness

What lies at the heart, I believe, of black America's pervasive cultural homophobia is the desperate need for a convenient Other *within* the community, yet not truly *of* the community, an Other to which blame for the chronic identity crises afflicting the black male psyche can be readily displaced, an indispensable Other which functions as the lowest common denominator of the abject, the base line of transgression beyond which a Black Man is no longer a man, no longer black, an essential Other against which black men and boys maturing, struggling with self-doubt, anxiety, feelings of political, economic, social, and sexual inadequacy—even impotence—can always measure themselves and by comparison seem strong, adept, empowered, superior.

—Marlon Riggs

While conceptualizing a course in cultural studies on race in U.S. film and television in 1998, I searched for a liberatory representation of blackness by a pro-feminist black man. I sought to expose students to progressive black filmography illustrating the race, gender, and sexual complexities of blackness that undercut its heterosexist interpretations in popular culture. I discovered in Marlon Riggs's film work another location to press my case for the viability of black men's pro-feminist profession that complemented progressive documentary films I had selected by Kathe Sandler (*A Question of Color*), Cheryl Dunye (*Watermelon Woman*), Julie Dash (*Daughters of the Dust*), and Issaac Julien (*Looking for Langston*). From the Emmy Award–winning *Tongues Untied* to the posthumous release of *Black Is . . . Black Ain't*, Riggs brought to the screen an antiheterosexist, oppositional interpretation of blackness rooted in his life experiences as a gay black man. More than any of his other films, *Black Is . . . Black Ain't* is a tour de force on the survival of black people in the face of great adversity. Its frame of critical reference, while intensely intimate and personal, registers on a much larger historical and social level. The film is an amazing work of cinematic autocritography. I teach it as Riggs's final heroic testament to life in the face of his own struggle against adversity, but I also celebrate it as a stunning visual memoir of one black man's pro-feminist beliefs.

Marlon Riggs was a visionary filmmaker. The painstaking manner in which he made *Black Is . . . Black Ain't* is a testament to his vision of black self-liberation—not only for himself but for black people across time and space. In the April 26, 1994, issue of the *Village Voice*, Michele Wallace remembered him. In her Brooklyn apartment, Wallace recounts (upon anticipating the shooting of her film segment for *Black Is . . . Black Ain't*): "[M]y husband and I fell in love with the resiliency of Marlon's spirit, with his passion and courage" (1994, 60).

I recall the first and last time I met Marlon Riggs. It was in 1991 at the opening-night plenary session of the historic conference "Black Popular Culture" sponsored by the Dia Art Center in New York and held in the crowded ground-floor, gallery space of the Studio Museum in Harlem. We were packed into this space like sardines, with hardly enough room to breathe. Somehow managing to find a seat for my friend and me, we sat waiting for the "who's who" of black cultural studies to enter the space. Looking around the room to see who was there, I noticed a man literally lying down next to my chair; he looked up and asked me if the photograph on the cover of the magazine I was carrying was Isaac Julien. I responded by saying yes and continued to scan the room for any notables. It was only on the next morning at the first session as Michele Wallace introduced the first presenter that I recognized who he was. I sat there abashed, realizing that I was looking into the eyes of the man who, the night before, had lain next to my chair inquiring about the magazine cover shot. He was Marlon Riggs. The critically acclaimed black British filmmaker, Isaac Julien would later recall Riggs's presentation at the same conference: "Marlon was some fierce and fearless black diva. At the . . . Conference on Black Popular Culture, he gave an amazing paper, 'Unleash the Queen,' a read on the conference itself, where he demanded more realness from the participants . . ." (Julien 1994, 60). Marlon Riggs's commitment to liberatory consciousness never waned. *Black Is . . . Black Ain't* is a testament to the challenge he posed for anyone committed to antiracist education.

Marlon Riggs has had a germinal influence in how I employ autobiographical writing and black film in the classroom to effect a pedagogy of race, gender, and sexual healing. I am convinced that any interrogation of white supremacy and the mythic and stereotypical construction of "blackness" would be woefully incomplete without *Ethnic Notions* (1987) and its sequel, *Color Adjustment* (1990). Similarly, any understanding of racism and gay identity in the United States would be lacking without his landmark film *Tongues Untied* (1991). It is, however, *Black Is . . . Black Ain't* that makes his most profound statement on race and the interrelation of domination. Riggs used a documentary style to construct a complex representation of black identity that brought onto the scene a rendering of the ways African American culture is rooted in issues of race, class, gender, sexuality, and religion. The film serves as a masterpiece for my work in the classroom. *Black Is . . . Black Ain't* is a pro-feminist cinematic memoir by design, illustrating through autobiography and through critical voices of well-known feminists and social critics how systemic racism, heterosexism, and homophobia perform in the daily lives of black people in the United States.

More than any lecture, text, or prior film on the complexity of U.S. racial ideology I had presented to students in Screening Race, Marlon Riggs's vision of "blackness" in *Black Is . . . Black Ain't* simultaneously brought together powerful critiques of white supremacy, sexism, homophobia, classism, and intraracism and interspliced them with intensely autobiographical narrative. It is this method of documentary filmmaking, where personal narration is linked to a larger social critique, that makes this particular film so critically important in illustrating the writing technique I designed for this course. As I taught students a writing strategy that drew upon their personal feelings and experiences of being racialized and *sexualized* as a means to challenge internalized racism and heterosexism, Riggs's use of autobiography functioned as a critical vehicle to expose prevailing myths and stereotypes of African Americans who are black and gay. Through the cinematic lens of a black man fighting to live with the ravaging effects of AIDS, viewers watch and listen as Riggs takes us on an intimate journey into his/story.

As we travel back to his Southern roots, we come to know his family, as well as other African American women and men he interviews to craft a complex vision of African American cultural, intellectual, social, generational, and economic diversity. At the same time that we gain knowledge of Riggs's journey toward self-determination in his search for personal freedom, we begin to grasp how his narrative of survival metaphorically represents the African American struggle to live courageously in the face of a history of dehumanization. Through *Black Is . . . Black Ain't*, students in this course not only came to understand that the personal is political, but also realized that it can be a life-or-death matter. At a profound level, invoking a central tenant of feminist thinking, the film's narratorial technique worked pedagogically as visual exemplum of my writing strategy. If I could get my students to approach writing about the personal effects of being racialized and sexualized as openly as Riggs addressed the impact of AIDS on his life, I knew their narratives would be infused with transforming power. With unbridled candor (as he lies on a hospital bed during one of the film segments), he tells us that his is a struggle to live "against the odds." It is this strong will to live in the face of despair that fuels his passionate desire to speak earnestly about the lives of black people in the United States. My hope in teaching *Black Is . . . Black Ain't* was that students would find within themselves the strength to write with conviction about the need for education against racism and heterosexism.

This film not only proved to be a strategic tool for the visualization of autocritography, but also dealt with African American cultural politics in a critically sophisticated but lucid fashion. Its incisive critique of the interrelation of heterosexism and homophobia lent credibility to my approach to teaching memoir writing. Students had read critiques of racial oppression and white supremacy by leading experts in the fields of race and feminist studies in the course before viewing the film, but their readings were enhanced by seeing and hearing several of the authors on film. As icons of black feminist thought, Angela Davis, Barbara Smith, bell hooks, and Michele Wallace provide Riggs with a critical foundation for the film's decidedly progressive attitudes about blackness that defy monolithic notions of gender and sexuality in black communities. Essex Hemphill and Cornel West masterfully deconstruct heterosexist notions of black manhood and masculinity.

Riggs does not employ only "experts" to aid him in the struggle to de-essentialize blackness. He foregrounds the cultural practices, narratives, and voices of black people across a large patchwork of diverse experiences. One of the most important signifiers of black diversity Riggs constructs and places at the metaphorical center of the film is the image of gumbo. Thematically, this eclectic dish—composed of varied spices, chicken, sausage, and seafood (among numerous other ingredients) symbolically represents the "grand narrative" of African American experience(s). Throughout *Black Is . . . Black Ain't,* Riggs's mother is shown in the family kitchen making gumbo. As the filmmaker enlarges his catalog of images, voices, and scenes from his past and present, the myriad ingredients of black culture and its multiple manifestations are mixed and blended like the disparate flavors in the gumbo his mother prepares. Riggs represents blackness as a performative constellation of moving images; it is illustrated by the motion of dance from be-bop to the postmodern interpretative expressions of Bill T. Jones and to the varied musical forms that have defined "black" music, including jazz, the spiritual, and hip-hop, for example.

In *Black Is . . . Black Ain't,* Riggs moves against the grain of black history with light speed, as the end of his journey draws ever nearer. We watch him physically decline before our very eyes. Yet, his purpose remains clear—blackness is a multilayered representation of cultural performativity. Simply speaking, it is most like the "roux" in gumbo—that indefinable ingredient that is distinctive in and of itself but cannot be so clearly distinguished from all the other spices of which it has become a part. As the film closes, we see Marlon Riggs—as we first saw him in the opening scene of it—naked, appearing to wander aimlessly through a thickly wooded forest. He is on a journey. He is in search of a place. Perhaps a home? As this scene fades, another image replaces it. It is a scene of an expanse of water. We are told in the voice-over by the filmmaker that it is a river. He has seen it in a dream where he and Harriet Tubman (the great conductor of the underground railroad) cross the river together. In his crossing over, he tells us that his spirit remains in the work of this film—that he has lived to pass it on for people to use in their own lives and that we must have faith in one another, in a belief that "against all odds" we will come through. As the film ends, the image of the river fades into an upbeat, historical clip of young black women and men joyously be-bop dancing.

We have traveled with Riggs into his personal history, one that leads us into a critical reconsideration of our own, not just for African Americans but for all who struggle to transgress the boundaries of racial myth; it leads us to a place where we too can dance in a moment of ecstatic joy, vitality, motion, and remembrance. *Black Is . . . Black Ain't* is a hard film to watch. For young college students who may never have seen anyone suffer the ravages of AIDS, it touches every emotional pressure point. In classes where I have shown the film, students have expressed their reactions in provocative ways when asked to respond in writing. One white woman student wrote after viewing the film, "Marlon Riggs gives us his own identity throughout the film through what he says and how he shows himself. He is dying. This is something that bridges every gap; we are all going to die. . . . Marlon Riggs gives himself personhood by showing us his family, telling us his stories, and speaking of his struggles and dreams. . . . The sharing of the struggle to be black and free, to be black and joyous amid oppression, seems to be what makes up the 'roux' (of Blackness)."

Another student, a Jewish white male, had this to say about the ingredient of blackness that is key to defining its cultural diversity: "[T]he 'roux' is the undiluted runoff of what was originally soaking in the pot so it would be the most concentrated part of the gumbo." Among the various comments students wrote in response to the film, meditating on what defines blackness related to a specific cultural seasoning, was that of a Latina woman, who asserted," [F]ood embodies cultural, political, religious, class and gender qualities that make [it] more meaningful . . . from [the moment] of cultivation . . . and ending with the consumption of it. A process that manifests community, survival, spirit, life. In my culture food is a metaphor for differences [even as] each ingredient [is needed to make a certain dish]. . . . [I]t does not at all mean these ingredients . . . are the same, and that is precisely what Riggs wants us to see." In the program notes that accompany the film, Patricia A. Turner and Herman Grey address the varied ways *Black Is . . . Black Ain't* clarifies our vision of blackness: "Riggs' film thus constructs a cinematic space for ten thousand ways of seeing and understanding blackness in America" (Turner and Grey n.d., 2).

It is precisely the film's power to evoke multiple ways of looking at black identity that provides its distinctive flavor. Rather than "spice for the dull dish of whiteness," as bell hooks would insist, Riggs offers us a critical vantage point to see ways *intra*-racism and heterosexism work in tandem to flatten out blackness by reinscribing the myth of it as monolithic, masculinist, and homophobic. He challenges the ideological foundation of black identity ("no one is racially pure around here," according to an elderly black woman in the film). Like Audre Lorde, however, he compels us to perceive our sexual differences not as a "threat" to black solidarity but as a fact of our existence that is the essence of its savory roux.

Committed to progressive feminist critiques of blackness that defy (hetero)sexism and homophobia, I teach visionary autobiographical narratives by Audre Lorde and Marlon Riggs to oppose the script of black machismo and religious dogma inculcated into me as a child. The "profession" of feminism in the classroom enabled me to craft pedagogy in defiance of its heteropatriarchal rhetoric, a rhetoric void of compassion that demonizes, discriminates against, and dehumanizes all individuals in our communities who are not heterosexual. Challenging the strictures of my religious upbringing that outlawed gay and lesbian identity, I put my profession of feminism to the test in the classroom *and* in the pulpit.

What Is the Color of Liberation?

Visionary, progressive teachers committed to struggle against racism must impart to our students hope that a coalition movement for racial equality and social justice is possible. It means, however, that white people must divest themselves of the power of institutionalized whiteness and that people of color must transgress the color line and be willing to forge multiracial alliance with antiracist whites. Students must come to know that the struggle against white supremacy will never be waged successfully by people of color alone. "Colorism" itself—the internalized, racist notion that light (white) skin is better than dark skin—remains a central issue in communities of color, a self-deprecating effect of racist colonization. The increasing *multi*racialization and *multi*ethnic *re*composition of communities of color suggests that African Americans, Latino(a)s, Asians, indigenous Americans, and other U.S. people of color can no longer construct a litmus test of color to determine who is authentic and who is not. People of color loving people of color must know that our political allies may not always look like us. At the same time, white people can no longer claim to be purely "white."

Visionary people of color and progressive, antiracist whites must be committed to taking risks across the color line. We must move to contest a politics of white supremacy that reinforces the myth that our social, political, and spiritual destinies are separate, for the clear reality is that our futures are inextricably tied. Political alliance to end racism will come about when the nation comes to grip with its past of miscegenation born of the history of slavery. In understanding the "whiteness of blackness" and the "blackness of whiteness," we begin the hard process of erasing the color line. To find the racial Other in oneself will surely lead to a (racial) identity crisis, particularly for those whose skin color has afforded them centuries of undeserved privileges because of it. But it is precisely this risk that must be taken for the nation to heal itself of the holocaust that American slavery represents to black Americans.

People of color need visionary, antiracist white people at the front line of the struggle against white supremacy, fighting for their own humanity. I believe it is a vision of progressive, antiracist whites fighting at the front line with like-minded people of color in the struggle for racial equality that will initiate a revolutionary coalition movement predicated upon a love of justice and a love of human rights. If, as progressive teachers, we can believe that men can be feminists, standing against sexism and the power of patriarchy, that heterosexuals can be outspoken advocates for equal rights for gays and lesbians, and that folks with economic privilege and institutional resources can employ them to eradicate poverty, we must also believe that whites and people of color can cross the color line to affect a radical coalition for a nonracist society.

In 1994, I founded the Memoirs of Race Project to promote the practice of critical race consciousness beyond the classroom. For the first time, in March 2000, six students in the project presented their work in a historic conference called "Poets on Location," convened by Jacqui Alexander (then chair of women's studies at Connecticut College) to honor the twenty-fifth anniversary publication of *This Bridge Called My Back*. Since then, project members have continued to make presentations in high schools and universities inside and outside New York City. Sharing their memoirs in these varied locations, my students become practitioners of racial healing. Their work is inspiring. Impassioned and deeply moving, it critically transgresses the color line. It articulates a new, liberatory line of antiracist communication that defies simplistic notions of race and the myths and stereotypes that inform its inherently flawed representation. Students promoting racial healing outside the classroom constitute the final step in a layered process whereby antiracist theory leads to transformative social practice. Students publicly reading the memoir of race challenge their listeners to step imaginatively inside the skin of an*other*. More often than not, those who hear their work respond as if awakened from the dulling slumber of racial blindness.

A Pro-Wo(man)ist Postscript

Return to the Margin of Masculinity
Teaching and Loving outside the Boundary

I am persuaded that the men and feminism debate should be about political vision *and* action. . . . *A fundamental goal of male feminism should be
to facilitate the process of men unbecoming men, the process of men unlearning the
patriarchal ways in which they have learned to become men.* (Emphasis added).

—Devon W. Carbado

Realizing that the full potential and empowerment of the Black community depends . . . on integrating feminism into our politics, I believe
we must come to terms with feminism and learn to see it as a fundamental aspect of our politics. . . . A feminist perspective affords us the
opportunity to identify and take into account the ways in which race,
class, gender, and sexual orientation intersect to shape the problems
and interests of our entire community.

—Luke Charles Harris

In "Sexism: An American Disease in Black Face," Audre Lorde critically opposes the diatribe of the black sociologist Robert Staples against black feminism. He had attacked Michele Wallace and Ntozake Shange, and his essay
"The Myth of Black Macho: A Response to Angry Black Feminists" spawned
what became known as the "black sexism debate," a series of responses to
Staples' piece that appeared in the *Black Scholar* (March–April 1979).
Highly critical of the anti*black* feminist rhetoric Staples spews out (conceived in his belief that black feminism is a white-inspired conspiracy to
emasculate black men), Lorde writes to defend the feminist standpoint of

215

black women on the grounds of their own concerns as black females. "BLACK FEMINISM is not white feminism in blackface. Black women have particular and legitimate issues which affect our lives as Black women, and addressing those issues does not make us any less Black" (Lorde 1984, 60). Lorde argues in her response to Staples that, while racism is a pervasive issue that all black people face, black women cannot be the scapegoat for black male disempowerment in a culture of white male power. Instead, she (and hooks and other progressive black female and male feminists) calls for our political partnership, connected to the necessity of black male gender-consciousness-raising:

> As a people, we most certainly must work together. It would be shortsighted to believe that Black men alone are to blame for . . . situations in a society dominated by white male privilege. But the Black male consciousness must be raised to the realization that sexism and woman-hating are critically dysfunctional to his liberation as a Black man because they arise out of the same constellation that engenders racism and homophobia. Until that consciousness is developed, Black men will view sexism and the destruction of Black women as tangential to Black liberation rather than as central to that struggle. So long as this occurs, we will never be able to embark upon that dialogue between Black women and Black men that is so essential to our survival as a people. This continued blindness between us can only serve the oppressive system within which we live. (64)

One thing I have learned from Audre Lorde is that becoming a profeminist black man has not made me any less black. Perhaps, in the eyes of many heteropatriarchal men it has made me less of a man. But I no longer seek legitimation of manhood and masculinity from men who believe themselves superior to women; who sexually exploit, objectify, or abuse them to make themselves feel more "manly"; who emasculate (violently or otherwise) any man outside "male" heterosexist notions of masculinity or gender. I am a pro-feminist black man because of my belief in the right of all people to be free from oppression with respect to gender and transgender identity, sexual difference, race, or class.

Teaching black feminism at a majority-white college for more than a decade, exposed many of my racial and gender anxieties; it made me feel even more vulnerable than when I first began there. While I have taught in and have been educated in majority-white schools for the greater part of my life, I have never gotten over the feeling of *otherness* associated with being a "minority" in them. In some ways the feeling of racial otherness is similar to the feeling of gender outsiderness I feel as a black male who has never fit the mold of heteronormative masculinity. The experience of race and gender outsiderness is a strategic location from which to practice memoir-writing pedagogy founded on black feminist thinking. For years, shame and low self-esteem kept me believing that I would always be on the margin of blackness and maleness. Ironically, teaching white students black feminist antiracism enabled me to understand that being black and male cannot be reduced to a set of myths and stereotypes of black manhood and masculinity. I did not learn this from white students. I learned it from the theory and political practice of black women feminists. Many of them, precisely because they occupy the position of "outsider" in terms of gender, sexuality, and race simultaneously, necessarily envision an inclusive politics of liberation.

I have chosen to work outside the systems of patriarchy and white supremacy. Neither has shown me a way to be mentally, socially, and spiritually healthy, whole within myself. This is why I have chosen to remain on the margin of masculinist ideas of blackness and heteronormative notions of black masculinity. At the core of this memoir is my personal struggle for survival. I am fighting for my own self-liberation—not from a place of selfish desire, as parts 1 and 2 of this memoir hopefully have shown. Rather, I fight *for* myself and *for* the human rights of students who enter classrooms where I teach, many of them in search of ways to feel whole. I met many of them at the margin of their feelings of outsiderness—as students of color outside white privilege, as whites outside the standards of white superiority, as women outside the privilege(s) of male superiority, as transgender individuals outside the social construction of gender binarism and biological determinism, as GLBTQ persons outside heterosexual privilege(s), and as students outside the privilege(s) of economic elitism.

After years of silence about the wounding effects of patriarchy and white supremacy, I determined to write my own narrative confession. bell hooks writing confessionally about her struggle to move from "object to subject," to speak in "the liberated voice," led me to a way of writing and teaching that turned me inside out. Memoir writing forged in black feminist thought forced me to confront the patriarchal and white supremacist demons of my past. It compelled me to do what I had done and pushed my students to do in the classroom over the years: to talk back to racism and sexism. Confessing publicly enabled me to let go of years of internalized silence(s)—about the childhood trauma of domesticviolence, the wounds of patriarchal fatherhood, the pain of boyhood outsiderness, the feelings of racial inferiority associated with white supremacist education, and the spiritual hurt related to leaving the church of my youth after more than thirty years. Teaching confessional writing through black feminist thinking has been personally and pedagogically healing. As this memoir has sought to represent, as a vehicle of self-recovery it helped move me from a place of personal self-doubt about the power of feminism to transform men's lives to a place of *professor*ial empowerment.

bell hooks served as a mentoring figure to me years ago and continues to inspire me with her unrelenting critique of patriarchy, particularly as it relates to black men. Her voice speaks for liberatory consciousness—not just for women alone, but for all people yearning to be free from domination. My hope is that my "profession" of feminism in this memoir will inspire more "brothers" to defect from the ranks of patriarchal manhood and masculinity. Under the law of patriarchy, as long as ideas of manhood and masculinity are linked to the subjugation of women in a culture of white supremacy, black men caught up in the myth of black machismo will forever be bound by it, seduced by its power to dehumanize. In the patriarchal father's house, we are not men, but willful agents of our own demise.

hooks asserts that the margin can be a strategic site for struggle. Masculinity at the margin of black machismo (once a site of shame and failure for me) has become a site of self-recovery. Outside the bounds of patriarchy and white supremacist and black nationalist ideas of masculinity, I teach to promote liberatory consciousness for all who long to break silence about the wounds of outsiderness patriarchal thinking exacts on the mind, body, and spirit. As a black man on the margin of heteronormative notions of black manhood, teaching black feminist antiracism at the college for more than a decade, I came to identify with white students and students of color who contested their position on the margin of heteronormativity, those struggling against it as racial, gender, class, or sexual outsiders. Never attempting to erase our differences, I challenged them to analyze systemic domination and institutional oppression interrelationally, and to critically think and write about the political impositions of white supremacy on the *personal*. Black feminist thought provided us a place to meet, interrogate, and sometimes embrace our differences rather than always viewing them as intractable boundaries separating us. Gender and sexuality are sites of great conflict and pain between black men. When we dismantle barriers between us that have emerged from them, we confront the racist, heterosexist, and homophobic myths attached to them. Black men in critical dialogue about our differences, no longer allow them to separate us into what has become basically two opposing classes among us: those with male and those with nonmale identity. We are killing ourselves—and those we claim to love. Black men coming to voice, ending silence about the ways patriarchy undermines our humanity, initiate radical dialogue toward our collective healing.

"Passing as the Black Girl . . .": A Final Classroom Case Study

I have been passing as the black girl that is okay with privilege, that has gotten over, matter of fact has never really been entangled in the idea of being oppressed. I am living out my dreams, in a predominantly white college, among minds . . . there is no evidence of my inferiority, right? *A dream of mine was to be in a majority-white school. Looking at where my dreams come from show me how much I digested the acceptance of my racialization. I wanted to be in a school of mostly whites because I thought it would make me look smarter.* This class has turned me inside out. I never thought I would have to look at my desire to confront my own self-oppression. I would have never thought this would have been the place to interrogate my dreams. I guess it makes sense, my dreams being my home of delusion. (Emphasis added)

The passage above, written by a black woman student, is taken from her memoir writing project completed in the 2003 session of the Novel of (Racial) Passing course I taught at the college. I required all students in the class to write a "memoir of *trans*raciality" based on the novels we read as a "final reexamination" of the course. I have chosen to comment on passages from her memoir as the *final classroom case study*. Of the autobiographical narratives produced in the class, this black female student's memoir is poignant and particularly moving because it reflects her struggle to break silence about her feelings about being black and female in a culture of whiteness and male supremacy. The emphasis she places on her identity as a black female in a majority-white classroom is especially touching for me, precisely because it reminds me of my own struggle to overcome years of silence about internalized wounds of patriarchy and white supremacy.

Many times during the semester in the course, I wanted to talk to her about her feelings as the only student of color in the class. I did not want to make her any more racially self-conscious than she often appeared to be. Moreover, I also sensed early on that she did not want to be the spokeswoman for "black" female identity—given the fact that of the five novels of passing we read, four had *trans*racial female protagonists whose stories were complicated by racist ideas of blackness. What must it be like to be a student of color in a course on racial passing where all the other students are white? I must have asked myself this question a thousand times during that semester. At the beginning of the term, I directly addressed its race and gender makeup (five white females, six white males, one white transgendered student, and the one black female). While the course required that students remained critically attuned to the power of whiteness in the novels related to the representation of blackness, one of my pedagogical aims was to make them aware of the race/gender dynamics of the class itself, though, as I say, I had no intention of making being black and female a burden for the only black female in the room (nor of making the room a site where she would stand in as the native informant). The class agreed that it would be unfair to cast the only student of color in the room in such a role, yet for the remainder of the term the room's air was heavy with the weight of color represented on the body of the black female student.

That this student would be placed in the position of native informant seemed a constant source of anxiety for all of us, however, and her countenance often reflected it. Was she attempting to make herself invisible by her silence, speaking most of the time only when prompted to respond to someone? I remember that once she and I talked outside of class about the stress related to being black in a majority-white class and school. More than anything, my desire was to communicate to her my concern for how she was experiencing the class. Given the history of my education in majority-white institutions of higher learning, I felt personally comfortable engaging with this student's feelings. From my undergraduate years as an English/art student through a decade of graduate training in English departments in the South and at New York University, I remember feelings of intense performance anxiety as the only student of color in nearly all my classes; I had never really gotten over the debilitating pressure of being the racial icon. The weight of race representation in the classroom as the only student of color is a feeling, then, with which I am all too familiar. As a college student, I was highly conscious of this, and in order not to draw attention to my race I simply never mentioned it—never addressed race unless it was overtly necessary (and it usually was not). Race was hardly ever discussed in my classes with white students or by our white professors.

In thirteen years of undergraduate and graduate schools combined, only one of my professors was of color (a black woman with whom I had one course in my senior year of undergraduate school). Moreover, I never took an English course dealing with black writers (or other writers of color, for that matter). I bought into the racist notion that writers of color were not worthy of formal study, since they were not in *the* canon at the school where I studied. It really didn't matter. I had no desire to study black writers. Studying white writers and being the only student of color in English classes made me feel smart, superior, a part of an elite circle of white English majors (overwhelmingly female). The disavowal of one's culture is critical to racist colonization. Like my black woman student I, too, wrapped my feelings of racial insecurity in the belief (read: dream) that "in a predominantly white college, among smart minds . . . there [was] not evidence of my inferiority, right?" In both cases, however, it is the approval of whites that is sought. To speak in the white classroom as a person of color might invariably signal inferiority. Not only that, to speak as a black *female* in a classroom where white males out number female students (rarely the case in my classes) may add to feelings of inadequacy. She recounted two experiences involving white males outside class where issues of race and gender combined to make her feel particularly vulnerable, so it is clear that they figured prominently in her "passing as the black girl that is okay with white privilege." In the first instance, a job-related incident involving a white male with whom she worked became a defining moment of racial consciousness. On one occasion, perceiving that he had accused her of stealing from the store where they worked, she tried not to give a direct retort:

> . . . I did not challenge him on that. I made a very high-pitched voice, constructing it so that I sounded slightly offended, but mostly playful and harmless. The latter sound I forced in my throat so that I would not upset him. . . . I recall him saying something like, "Yeah, I know how you people are." I stood outside of the door frozen from the shoulders down. I shifted my head a little to act like I was looking for my ride, even though I was taking the bus . . . I didn't want him to see me sinking. . . . Just in case he was watching, I kept my head up as I stood there thinking, *was that my first racist comment?* I was seventeen.

Trying to downplay the racial overtones of white male stereotyping illustrated in the scene above, the student writes about the "sinking" feeling his words have on her. Not allowing him to detect the painfulness of his words, "I kept my head up," she says—as if they made no difference. The white male's obliviousness to the wounding nature of his words point to the systemic blindness of white privilege. What recourse did she have?

> If I made this a big deal, where would it lead to, who would support me, and most of all how would it disrupt the everyday flow of

things. . . . I did not turn back and ask him what he meant by his comment because I didn't want any confrontation. I sacrificed holding him accountable to keep the peace in my daily routine as a non-threatening young black woman. This was not the first time I had acted out this role; it was just the first time I had felt so embarrassed. And my embarrassment had come from feeling like I was being exposed. I had done nothing, yet was being stripped.

Clearly, from her reflection above, one can surmise that his words were psychologically devastating. She acknowledges that the fear of being a confrontational black woman lies at the core of her silence; she did not want to "disrupt the everyday flow of things." From the beginning, the student believed she had no recourse—no channel for complaint, no one in place to hear it, and (more than anything) complaining would make trouble. In the end, her role as a "non-threatening young black woman" resulted in two things happening: (1) she "sacrificed holding [a white male] accountable *to keep the peace* [emphasis added]" and (2) she was left feeling "embarrassed . . . exposed . . . stripped."

Coming to consciousness about the wounding effects of racism often means remembering painful moments in one's life. Writing about her childhood ten years before the event she recounted above, the student recalls the profound effect ideas of white superiority had in shaping her values, friendships, and self-image—even at the age of seven. The image of a little white girl would come to signify beauty, order, and cleanliness in her life. For her this little white girl was "magical":

We were seven years old. She lived in a blue and white house on the corner of Judson Street. She owned two guinea pigs and had her own room on the top floor. Sharon and I were best friends. I thought she wasn't like my black friends who wanted me to dance real nasty, prove I could fight, and tongue kiss a boy in front of them. We played with Cabbage Patch dolls in her pink and white room and fed the guinea pigs. I always thought of her as the one that was clean and smart. She always came to school matching: a purple shirt with purple socks, every day all her colors magically complementing her sandy blonde hair and blue eyes. *I thought she was magical.* (Emphasis added)

Sharon is the epitome of everything her black female friends are not. Her black friends call her to a world that is far from innocent for a seven-year-old. For her, it is sexually charged and violent. In contrast, Sharon's world is filled with innocence. Guinea pigs, Cabbage Patch dolls, matching clothes ("complementing her sandy blonde hair and blue eyes"), and a bedroom of pink and white all contribute to the magic that Sharon is. Moreover, she is "clean and smart." For a seven-year-old black girl from a lower-class background, the attributes above not only are personified in the material reality of the white friend's higher class standing, but also are emblematic of all that the black woman student did not possess as a child. The girls' friendship unfolds in a series of race, gender, and class contrasts. Bereft of innocence, young black female identity, by implication, can neither be characterized as clean nor smart. While the writer notes that her black girlfriends focused on "nasty" dancing, fighting, and "tongue kissing a boy," she points out that her "best [white] friend" not only played with dolls (in addition to being clean and smart), but also "always came to school *matching*" (emphasis added).

This statement provides critical insight into the race and class dynamics that govern the relationship. Put on a pedestal by the young, impressionable black girl (as shown in the text above), Sharon, her friend, possesses privileges of innocence, intelligence, cleanliness, upper-class standing, and matching-*color* clothing. Symbolically, however, "all her colors magically complement[ed] her blonde hair and blue eyes," including her "blue and white" house, her "pink and white room," and "a purple shirt with purple socks." Thus, color not only enhances the little girl's (life)style and image, it represents her *white* body as the idea(l) of (black) girlhood. This black woman's remembrance of her girlhood, steeped in the myth of white perfection, is vividly described in her recollection of the very painful meaning a pair of Sharon's purple socks had for her:

> I was jealous and amazed at her purple socks. I looked at them thinking she comes from a home where her socks match. One is not tinted lighter than the other nor missing the pink elephant on the ankle part that the other one has. She didn't have to rummage through black plastic trash bags in the basement of her grandma's house, digging for a match amongst her mother's, sister's, and brother's clothing in the same bags. She didn't have to worry about hoping that she would find one so that she would look more put together, cleaner, so that maybe Mrs. Wagner would stop asking her about her ringworms. She never dealt with only finding an imposter at the bottom of the bag, riddled with the smell of the dog mess that hung thick in the air of the basement where she slept, with the three dogs, her brother, her sister, and her mother. She must have had each pair folded into each other,

neatly balled with all the other matching socks in the top drawer
of her own dresser in her own pink and white room on the top
floor. *I thought about her life in this way, all properly put away and easy
to find. I even made myself fight for Sharon.* (Emphasis added)

Reading the passage above, I am struck with the clarity of contrast—
how the lives of two little girls can be so very different. The writer describes the class differences that separate them with little emotion. For
her, searching for matching socks is a bag filled with other family members' clothing is about revealing the awfulness of the environment where
she lived as a child. A space where few signs of economic privilege exist,
the basement is everything that Sharon's home is not. It is far from clean.
It is rodent infested, cramped, a space with virtually no privacy for any
family member—or pet, for that matter. It is a place where searching for
matching socks is about an ever-present danger lurking at the bottom
of "black plastic trash bags" (makeshift clothes hampers). Images of
inhumanity as experienced by a seven-year-old black girl underscore the
reality of life lived in abject poverty. For a poor little black girl, owning matching socks takes on huge symbolic meaning. Against images of
squalor that define her home life, she fantasizes about Sharon's *matching socks* and the meticulous care she gives them: "She must have had
each pair folded into each other, neatly balled with all the other matching socks in the top drawer of her own dresser in her own pink and white
room. . . . *I thought about her life in this way, all properly put away and easy to
find. I even made myself fight for Sharon*" (emphasis added).

Not only does this little black girl believe that the quality of her white
friend's life is personified by the imagined orderliness of her socks in a
drawer, she is willing to "fight" for a place in it. She remembers physically
competing with another black girl in a race "for the privilege to play in
[Sharon's] pink and white room with guinea pigs." "Now," looking back
at the incident, she says, "I feel like we were the guinea pigs, the only
ones left racing against each other, fighting against darker and lighter
skin tones, me accepting yet fighting against the acceptance of the position my darker tone placed me in." Recognizing the dehumanizing effects of racism rooted in the inferiority of dark-skinned black people is a
key point in uprooting racial self-hatred. Coming to an awareness of the
deeply wounding ways class and race intersect to reinforce the negative
image of herself sharpens its analysis. But in the mind of a poor young
black girl, the light-skinned black girl (who rode to school each day in a
black Mercedes Benz) "fit together better" with the race and class privilege of the white girl, whom both girls desired to be:

I thought they were both prettier and cleaner and smarter than I was. I accepted that . . . her brighter skin, the black Benz every morning, and the matching socks she wore too meant she was *made* [emphasis in the original]. At seven years old this was not a social construction in my mind; it was the natural order of things, as I understood them. . . . As I look back, my image is of us trying to run each other into the ground, trading in our integrity for the privilege to play in a pink and white room with guinea pigs.

Perhaps, in revisiting images from her early childhood and late teenage years, this black woman student illustrates clearly in the memoir how deeply the lack of gender, race, and class privilege directly influenced her behavior as a black female in a majority-white classroom. In a final reflection, she recalls a feeling of powerlessness when at an entrance to an automatic teller machine two well-meaning white males showed her how to use her ATM card correctly to open the door. Without seeming overtly paranoid about their impression of her, she wondered whether they stereotypically judged her as technically incompetent because she was black and female: ". . . I felt defeated . . . I grappled with power and defeat. Strange how things get soft and fade away, the way battles aren't as piercing and obvious *once I get into a place of comfort, how all that matters then is that I'm comfortable, all is forgotten*" (emphasis added). Her account of growing up without the power to resist the idea of whiteness as higher intelligence, pure beauty, and ordered cleanliness provides an insightful look into her classroom behavior, particularly as it related to white privilege: "My compliance has been the problem. Not that I have complied because I wanted to have white people like me, so that I could get nice things and nice titles, but even worse, I have done it to get approval. I have wanted praise that says I have been doing it right, 'it' meaning being the minority in the right way: hard-working, expressive but not leading discussions, acquiescent but carving out a place where only I can stand, alone, not anxious, calm and approachable."

Consistent with the passage I quoted in the beginning of this student's narrative, she has passed "as the black girl who is okay with white privilege." However, it is her *compliance* "as a non-threatening young black woman" that is the ideological foundation for approval (from whites)—"I have wanted praise that says I have been doing it right, 'it' meaning being the minority in the right way." In truth, *being the minority in the right way* has left her masking a feeling of loneliness, of being (mis)read by whites as even-tempered and "approachable." To continually have to betray one's true feelings (as a person of color) is a high price to pay for white approval. As quoted earlier, for this black woman student living out her *dream* of attending a majority-white college means being "in a school of mostly whites because it [will] make [her] look smarter." In a culture of white supremacy, the myth that quality in education remains coded within a system of white privilege continues to inform colonized ideas of *higher* education—for example, that students of color simply by being in majority-white schools appear to "look smarter" (than who does? students of color without such access?). As an impressionable fourteen-year-old black youth, such thinking only reinforced my internalized, media-driven belief in white superiority.

Based on some of the autobiographical passages included in papers she wrote before midterm, I knew she had a take on the experiences of black females in the texts that would further enrich the already intense class discussions white students were generating. Without making her the spokesperson for black female identity, I required everyone in class to write critically about the presence (or absence) of race in their own daily lives in the context of how it intersected with gender, race, class, and sexual oppression in the lives of black females crossing the color line as white women. Most of the time, unless she voluntarily spoke, I suppressed my urge to call on her to participate in class discussions. On more than one occasion, I could feel by the way this student intently listened to others speak that she was holding back. And she was. In the first month of the course, she wrote: "[I]n this class I listen and soothe the quaking emotions in my heart to speak by telling myself to be quiet and shut down, feel and listen because when your little black voice speaks it will not be with the diction and intuitiveness that is needed to qualify your ideas."

The Difference *One* Student of Color Makes in a White Classroom

I have already spoken of how race talk itself generally engendered tremendous fear in students (of color and not), especially those unaccustomed to a rigorous analysis of racism. Nevertheless, the statement above is particularly telling. On the one hand, it expresses the reticence its writer feels speaking as a young black woman. On the other, her words speak to the struggle of students in my classes as they have attempted to find the right words to express their insecurities and anxieties about race. Yet the passage above unmistakably emerges from the sensibility of a student not only in touch with being the racial "minority" in a class of white students but also with having grown up hyperconscious of her desire for white acceptance.

This black woman student's racial feelings are not unique. Students of color who have taken my courses have complained to me about the lack of racial diversity in their classes. Like the black female student in this class, many feel overwhelmingly self-conscious about being in white or nearly all-white classes. Whether they want to be or not in such cases, they automatically become native informants on race. Often when white students in my courses have complained about feeling unsafe in class discussions, few express concern for the feelings of students of color. Since becoming more consciously aware of the antiracist implications of my teaching, and as I have become more rigorous in challenging all my students to examine self-critically how race functions in their daily lives, I am even more acutely aware of the isolation, alienation, and sheer loneliness students of color feel in majority-white classrooms. More often than not, there have been those students of color whose presence and voice in my classes have had an enormous impact by enlivening class discussion, transforming white students' thinking about race, reinforcing the need for more racial diversity at the college, and reaffirming my belief in the value of antiracist education.

While she may not have spoken in every class discussion, the student in her memoir passionately engages how deeply rooted the myth of white superiority can be in an impressionable young black girl's mind and how debilitating its residual effects can be in the adult life of people of color. At the end of her memoir, she expresses her feelings about the course: "This is the place that I am in as I end this class: frightened and feeling moved by something powerful." As mentioned, she writes about the impact of the class in another place in the memoir: "This class . . . has turned me inside out. I never thought I would have to look at my desires . . . I would never have thought this would have been the place for such interrogation. I guess it makes sense, my dreams being my home of delusion." As recounted in part 1, like this student, I grew up creating my own dream of white approval/acceptance through identification with white middle-class suburban life depicted on television sitcoms in the 1960s. While race mixing was never a subject any of them represented, my predisposition to the idea of white superiority had already taken shape long before my education with whites in high school began. Having internalized the belief that schooling with whites brought with it the promise of a better education, I longed to be in a majority-white school. "Better" meant that a quality education was inherently linked to white teachers and students. Like the black woman student, I really thought being educated with whites would validate my intelligence.

In so many ways I feel personally attached to this young woman's story. My education in white schools (from high school through graduate

school) was about being the model black male student, the one who had
little trouble passing for white (by denying my blackness). I was "passing
as the black [boy] that [was] okay with white privilege." Seeking academic approval from whites became a way to escape the painful experience
of being almost always the only student of color in classrooms where
(more often than not) I felt completely invisible. How many times in the
course did the presence of this student remind me of myself when I was
the only student of color in more white college classrooms than I care to
remember. With every novel we read, I was always consciously aware of
her presence, wondering how she felt about the class.

On *Passing* the Final Reexamination

I have always taught novels of racial passing as if the characters in them
were real. By the end of the semester, we had examined ideas of *passing*
in the context of race and whiteness. In the course's "final reexamination" that the students' memoirs represented, we understood the concept of *passing* more broadly as having to do with one's crossing over into
or out of of seemingly fixed identities (for complex reasons we may or
may not fully comprehend). At the end of the course, we had become
more willing to question the fit of our individual identities. For most of
the students in the fall 2003 session of the Novel of Passing, if not for all,
writing a "memoir of *trans*raciality" represented an opportunity to examine critically the formation of our racial identities and the politics that
keep us bound to them. We began to see correspondences between our
struggles against racism, (hetero)sexism, and homophobia. Sharing our
critical autobiographical responses over the course of that semester, we
listened and we grew as we gave way to the emotional tide of the texts we
read and wrote. In so many class sessions, we read our responses filled
with feelings. Sometimes we released them, and we were washed clean by
our tears. In the process, according to one student, our classroom had
become "a sacred refuge, an intimate circle."

Teaching on the Margin and Loving It

As black men understanding our differences—outside the mythology of
black machismo—we can embrace our complicities and move toward
reconceptualizing the idea of a "strong black man." In antiheteronorma-
tive notions of black manhood lies our greatest strength. In them we are
free to be black and male in multiple ways that do not compromise our

sense of allegiance either to self or to community. We are no longer bound by "either/or" binary thinking. Teaching black feminist thought against white supremacy over the last decade in all-white and or majority-white classrooms, I came to understand the value of embracing difference. Despite all of the complex and complicated differences we faced in the classroom, black feminist thought proved self-transforming in life-sustaining ways for everyone in it who remained receptive to its healing dimension. I hope *Black Male Outsider* will also serve as a testament to the power of voice against silence. It promotes black feminist memoir-writing pedagogy that opposes all forms of domination, and it promotes the critical necessity of one's movement from silence to voice about the effects of its dehumanization—personally and politically.

Black feminist pedagogy sustains, renews, and transforms projects of decolonization. In a white supremacist culture, where the commodification of blackness renders the black body an object of fetishization and demonization simultaneously, black feminist thinking speaks to the necessity of antiracist struggle inextricably tied to a gender-progressive vision. For me, becoming a "professor" of feminism has been about a personal life-sustaining journey toward self-love. I have learned to love myself again as a black male who has *chosen* to remain on the margin of heteronormative ideas of masculinity. I have broken silence about my past. In doing so, I have determined to free myself from the bounds of patriarchy—as well as gender-conservative, heterosexist, and homophobic notions of blackness. I have returned to the margin—changed.

NOTES

Chapter 1.
Toward a *Profession* of Feminism

1. Here White cites several sources to argue her point (Kimmel and Mosmiller 1992; Terborg-Penn 1978; Lemons 1998a; Byrd and Guy-Sheftall 2001).

2. I can remember vividly the phone conversation in which Aaronette White spoke these words. Right before I had to teach a class one morning several years ago, she called my office. These words have remained with me.

Chapter 3.
Learning to Love the Little Black Boy in Me:
Breaking Family Silences, Ending Shame

1. Richie (1995, 398) makes a significant contribution to contemporary literature on black women/women of color experience of domestic violence.

WORKS CITED

Alexander, M. Jacqui. 1994. "Not Just (Any) Body Can Be a Citizen: The Politics of Law, Sexuality and Postcoloniality in Trinidad and Tobago and the Bahamas." *Feminist Review* 48:5–23.

———. 2005. *Pedagogies of Crossing: Meditations on Feminism, Sexual Politics, Memory, and the Sacred.* Durham, NC: Duke University Press.

Awkward, Michael. 1999. *Scenes of Instruction: A Memoir.* Durham, NC: Duke University Press.

———. 2001. "A Black Man's Place in Black Feminist Criticism." In Byrd and Guy-Sheftall 2001, 177–73.

Baldwin, James. 1955. *Notes of a Native Son.* Boston: Beacon Press.

Black Men for the Eradication of Sexism of Morehouse College. [1994] 2001. "Mission Statement." In Byrd and Guy-Sheftall 2001, 200–04.

Byrd, Rudolph P. 2001. "Prologue. The Tradition of John: A Mode of Black Masculinity." In Byrd and Guy-Sheftall 2001, 1–24.

Byrd, Rudolph P., and Beverly Guy-Sheftall, eds. 2001. *Traps: African American Men on Gender and Sexuality.* Bloomington: Indiana University Press.

Carbado, Devon W., ed. 1999a. *Black Men on Race, Gender and Sexuality.* New York: New York University Press.

———. 1999a. "Epilogue: Straight Out of the Closet, Men, Feminism, and Male Heterosexual Privilege." In Carbado 1999b, 417–47.

Combahee River Collective. [1974] 1983. "The Combahee River Collective Statement." In Smith 1983, 275—76.

Cross, William E. Jr. 1991. *Shades of Black: Diversity in African-American Identity.* Philadelphia: Temple University Press.

Dalton, Harlon. 1995. *Racial Healing: Confronting the Fear Between Blacks and Whites.* New York: Doubleday.

Daniel Tatum, Beverly. 1997. *"Why Are All the Black Kids Sitting Together in the Cafeteria?" and Other Conversations About Race.* New York: Basic Books.

Digby, Tom, ed. 1998. *Men Doing Feminism.* New York: Routledge.

Dines, Gail, and Jean M. Humez, eds. 1995. *Gender, Race and Class in Media.* Thousand Oaks, CA: Sage Publications.

Du Bois, W. E. B. [1920] 1999. *Darkwater: Voices from within the Veil.* Mineola, NY: Dover.

Ellison, Ralph. [1950] 1989. *Invisible Man.* New York: Vintage Books.

Fisher, Antwone. 2003. *Who Will Cry for the Little Boy?* New York: Harper-Collins.

Freire, Paulo. [1971] 2001. *Pedagogy of the Oppressed.* New York: Continuum.

Gomez, Jewelle. 1983. "A Cultural Legacy Denied and Discovered: Black Lesbians in Fiction by Women." In Smith 1983, 110–23.

Guy-Sheftall, Beverly, ed. 1995. *Words of Fire: An Anthology of African-American Feminist Thought.* New York: New Press.

Hall, Stuart. 1995. "The Whites of Their Eyes: Racist Ideologies and the Media." In Dines and Humez, 1995, 18–22.

Harris, Luke Charles. 1999. "The Challenge and Possibility for Black Males to Embrace Feminism." In Carbado 1999a, 383–86.

Hill Collins, Patricia, 2000. *Black Feminist Thought.* 2nd ed. New York: Routledge.

———. 2001. "Womanism and Black Feminism." In *Issues in Feminism: An Introduction to Women's Studies*, ed. Sheila Ruth. Mountain View, CA: Mayfield Publishing Co.

———. 2004. *Black Sexual Politics: African Americans, Gender, and the New Racism.* New York: Routledge.

hooks, bell. 1984. *Feminist Theory: From Margin to Center.* Boston: South End Press.

———. 1992. *Black Looks: Race and Representation.* Boston: South End Press.

———. 1994. *Teaching to Transgress.* New York: Routledge.

———. 1995. *Killing Rage: Ending Racism.* New York: Henry Holt and Co.

———. 1996. *Bone Black: Memories of Girlhood.* New York: Henry Holt and Co.

———. 2000. *Feminism Is for Everybody: Passionate Politics.* Boston: South End Press.

———. 2003. *Rock My Soul: Black People and Self-Esteem.* New York: Atria Books.

———. 2000a. *We Real Cool: Black Men and Masculinity.* New York: Routledge.

———. 2000b. *The Will to Change: Men, Masculinity, and Love.* New York: Atria Books.

Hot Springs High School, *Old Gold Book,* 1971. Yearbook. Hot Springs, Arkansas.

Hughes, Langston. [1933] 1900. *The Ways of White Folks.* New York: Vintage Books.

James, Joy. 1997. *Transcending the Talented Tenth: Black Leaders and American Intellectuals.* New York: Routledge.

Joseph, Gloria. 1995. "Black Feminist Pedagogy and Schooling in Capitalist White America." In Guy-Sheftall 1995, 462–71.

Julien, Isaac. 1994. "Long Live the Queen." *Village Voice,* April 26, 60.

Kimmell, Michael, and Thomas Mosmiller, 1992. *Against the Tide: Pro-Feminist Men in the United States, 1776–1990, a Documentary History.* Boston: Beacon Press.

Lazarre, Jane. 1996. *Beyond the Whiteness of Whiteness.* Durham, NC: Duke University Press.

Lemons, Gary L. 1996a. "Teaching the Bi(Racial) Space That Has No Name: Reflections of a Black Male Feminist Teacher." In *Everyday Acts Against Racism: Raising Children in a Multiracial World,* ed. Maureen T. Reddy, 158–70. Seattle, WA: Seal Press.

———. 1996b. "'Young Man, Tell Our Stories of How We Made It Over': Beyond the Politics of Identity." In *Teaching What You're Not: Identity Politics in Higher Education,* ed. Katherine J. Mayberry, 259–84. New York: New York University Press.

———. 1998a. "A New Response to 'Angry Black (Anti)Feminists': Reclaiming Feminist Forefathers, Becoming Womanist Sons." In Digby 1998, 275–89.

———. 1998b. "To Be Black, Male, and Feminist: Making Womanist Space for Black Men on the Eve of a New Millennium." In *Feminism and Men: Reconstructing Gender Relations*, ed. Steven P. Schacht and Doris W. Ewing. New York: New York University.

———. 2001a. "Education as the Practice of Racial Healing: Teaching Writing Against Racism." *Academic Forum* 9, no. 2: 1, 48–53.

———. 2001b. "'When and Where [We] Enter': In Search of a Feminist Forefather—Reclaiming the Womanist Legacy of W. E. B. Du Bois." In Byrd and Guy Sheftall 2001, 71–89.

———. 2002. "Skinwalking and Color Linecrossing: Teaching Writing Against Racism." In *Race in the College Classroom: Pedagogy and Politics*, ed. Bonnie TuSmith and Maureen Reddy, 277–85. New Brunswick, NJ: Rutgers University Press.

———. 2004. "Challenging Whiteness in a Black Feminist Classroom." In *Identifying Race and Transforming Whiteness in the Classroom*, eds. Virginia Lee and Judy Helfand, 213–33. New York: Peter Lang.

Locke, Alain, ed. 1968. *The New Negro*. New York: Atheneum.

Lorde, Audre.1983. "Tar Beach." In Smith 1983, 145–58.

———. 1984. *Sister Outsider: Essays and Speeches*. Freedom, CA: Crossing Press.

Majors, Richard, and Janet Mancini Billson. 1992. *Cool Pose: The Dilemmas of Black Manhood in America*. New York: Lexington Books.

Marable, Manning. [1983] 2001. "Grounding with My Sisters: Patriarchy and the Exploitation of Black Women." In Byrd and Guy-Sheftall 2001, 119–52.

McIntosh, Peggy. 1988. "White Privilege: Unpacking the Invisible Knapsack." Excerpted from Working Paper 189.

Neal, Mark Anthony. 2003. "My Black Male Feminist Heroes." February 26, http://popmatters.com/features/030226-blackfeminists.shtml.

Pieterse, Jan. 1995. "White Negroes." In Dines and Humez 1995, 23–27.

Powell, Kevin. 2003. *Who's Gonna Take the Weight? Manhood, Race, and Power in America*. New York: Three Rivers Press.

Richie, Beth. 1995. "Battered Black Women: A Challenge for the Black Community." In Guy-Sheftall, 1995, 398–404.

Riggs, Marlon. 2001. "Black Macho Revisited: Reflections of a Snap! Queen." In Byrd and Guy-Sheftall 2001, 292–96.

———. 1995. *Black Is . . . Black Ain't* California Newsreel.

Roediger, David R., ed. 1998. *Black on White: Black Writers on What It Means to Be White.* New York: Schocken Books.

Scales-Trent, Judy. 1995. *Notes of a White Black Woman: Race, Color, Community.* University Park: Pennsylvania State University Press.

Seshadri-Crooks, Kalpana. 2000. *Desiring Whiteness: A Lacanian Analysis of Race.* New York: Routledge.

Shange, Ntozake. 1975. *For Colored Girls Who Have Considered Suicide When the Rainbow Is Enuf: A Choreopoem.* New York: Macmillan.

Stewart, Maria. 1995. "Religion and the Pure Principles of Morality, the Sure Foundation on Which We Must Build." In Guy-Sheftall 1995, 26–9.

Smith, Barbara, ed. 1983. *Home Girls: A Black Feminist Anthology!* New York: Kitchen Table Women of Color Press.

Stoltenberg, John. 1994. *The End of Manhood: A Book for Men of Conscience.* New York: Penguin Books.

Terborg-Penn, Rosalyn, and Sharon Harley. 1978. *The Afro-American Woman: Struggles and Images.* Baltimore, MD: Black Classics Press.

Thandeka. 2000. *Learning to Be White: Money, Race, and God in America.* New York: Continuum.

Thomas, Laurence Mordekhai. 1988. "Feminist Ambiguity in Heterosexual Lives: Reflections on Andrea Dworkin." In Digby 1998, 335–36.

Turner, Patricia A., and Herman Gray. n.d. "What Is Black? Too Black? Not Black Enough?" Program notes to the film *Black Is . . . Black Ain't*, by Marlon Riggs. California Newsreel.

Tu Smith, Bonnie, and Maureen T. Reddy. 2002. *Race in the College Classroom: Pedagogy and Politics.* New Brunswick, NJ: Rutgers University Press.

Walker, Alice. 1983. *In Search of Our Mothers' Gardens: Womanist Prose by Alice Walker.* New York: Harcourt Brace Jovanovich.

Wallace, Michelle, 1978. *Black Macho and the Myth and the Myth of the Superwoman.* New York: Dial Press.

———. 1994. "A Fierce Flame." *Village Voice*, April, 26.

West, Cornel. 1994. *Race Matters.* New York: Vintage Books.

White, Aaronette M. 2001. "John Coltrane's Style of Jazz and the Improvisational Lives of Profeminist Black Men." *Journal of African American Men* 6, no. 3 (Winter): 3–28.

———. 2001/2002. "Ain't I a Feminist?" *Womanist Theory and Research* 3, no. 2/4, no.1:28–34.

Whitman, Victor. 1998. "Langston's Lost Years." *Hot Springs Sentinel-Record*, September 3.

Woodson, Carter G. [1933] 2000. *The Mis-Education of the Negro*. Chicago: African American Images.

Index